Understanding Y
Taking Control of Your Mental Health

MINDING YOUR MIND

PROF IAN HICKIE and JAMES O'LOGHLIN

PENGUIN BOOKS

UK | USA | Canada | Ireland | Australia
India | New Zealand | South Africa | China

Penguin Books is part of the Penguin Random House group of companies
whose addresses can be found at global.penguinrandomhouse.com

Penguin
Random House
Australia

First published by Penguin Books in 2022

The information in this book is provided for general purposes only and does not take into
account your personal situation, objectives or needs. Before acting on any of this information,
you should consider its appropriateness to your own situation, objectives and needs, and if you
have underlying health problems, you should contact a qualified medical professional.

Cover design by Christabella Designs
Cover image of brain: Shutterstock
Internal design and typesetting by Midland Typesetters, Australia

Printed and bound in Australia by Griffin Press, an accredited
ISO AS/NZS 14001 Environmental Management Systems printer

A catalogue record for this
book is available from the
NATIONAL LIBRARY OF AUSTRALIA
National Library of Australia

ISBN 978 0 14377 878 3

penguin.com.au

MIX
Paper from
responsible sources
FSC® C009448

We at Penguin Random House Australia acknowledge that Aboriginal and Torres Strait Islander
peoples are the Traditional Custodians and the first storytellers of the lands on which we live
and work. We honour Aboriginal and Torres Strait Islander peoples' continuous connection to
Country, waters, skies and communities. We celebrate Aboriginal and Torres Strait Islander
stories, traditions and living cultures; and we pay our respects to Elders past and present.

As always, to the fam

– James

For Liz, the kids and the others who really matter

– Ian

Contents

Introduction

James

In the early 2000s I hosted *The Evening Show* on ABC Radio in NSW and the ACT. One evening, we had a guy called Ian Hickie on as a guest. I can't remember the exact topic, but it was something to do with mental health. It was immediately clear that Ian was what we callously call in the media 'good talent'. That is, he knew what he was talking about, and he spoke about it in an enthusiastic and engaging way. My producer and I asked him to do a regular segment on mental health, happily he agreed, and over the next decade or so, Ian and I talked about all sorts of topics connected to our mind and how it works.

When I say 'we talked', I mean I would ask him everything I could think of about various mental health topics, and he would tell me all sorts of fascinating things about the space between our ears, how it worked and what we could do to help it work better. His enthusiasm never flagged for a second, even at 9.45 on a Thursday evening.

After Christmas in 2020, I bumped into Ian on the beach up the coast and suggested we do a podcast on mental health.

'We should,' he agreed. I thought it would be one of those good ideas that never goes anywhere, but with his customary energy Ian made it happen. We began recording a few months later, and the first episode of our *Minding Your Mind* podcast was released in June 2021.

I ask the questions, and Ian answers them. I supply the curiosity, Ian the expertise. In each episode, we pick a topic that has something to do with our mind and our mental health and discuss it. At the time of writing, we have recorded over eighty episodes, and we haven't got close to running out of subjects yet.

Now, thanks to the nice people at Penguin Random House, we have turned a selection of these topics into a book, which is divided into three parts:
- How Our Minds Work,
- When Things Go Wrong, and
- Improving Our Mental Health.

We have tried to explain what goes on inside our mind, and share lots of practical strategies to help it work better.

This book isn't just for those who have a specific mental health issue, such as anxiety or depression. Our mental health is not something we should just pay attention to when we are unwell. Just as maintaining a good diet, sleep routine and exercise help keep us in good physical health, there are things we can do (or not do) that are good for our mind and help us to be mentally healthy. We wanted to outline some of the practical things we can all do to make our mind happier.

I've never been much interested with how my knee or my spleen works, but I'm fascinated by how my mind does. Why do I sometimes get nervous before I give a speech, but other times I don't? Why am I sometimes powerless to control my anxious thoughts, while other times I can distract my mind away from them, and they fade into the background? Why do I get the feeling that I can trust some people and not others? Is that feeling reliable or not?

One of the biggest things I've learned from talking to Ian is that those things that arise in our mind – thoughts, feelings, hope, anxiety, anger, depression and the rest – are not *just* about our mind. They are also about our body. Anxiety can cause our heart to race. Depression can make us feel so heavy that we can't get out of bed. We are not a separate mind and a body. We are one connected mind–body.

Another thing I've learned is that we can change. In the old days, if someone (my wife, Lucy) said, 'You're pretty impatient,' you used to be able to get away with, 'Well, that's just the way I am. Can't do nothing about it. Sorry.' Now that we know more about our mind's ability to change, that excuse doesn't cut it anymore. There are strategies we can use to become less impatient. There are others that help us become less pessimistic, or that raise our self-esteem, or help us control our temper, or even reduce our control-freak tendencies and help us learn to give up the remote control.

These sorts of changes aren't easy (rats) and they can take a while (which is a challenge for those of us who are impatient), but it can be done. Over time, we can tune up our mind and make it even better at helping us stumble through life.

Ian

In late 2000, I was fortunate enough to be appointed the inaugural CEO of Beyond Blue: the national depression initiative. Having moved to Melbourne to take up this fabulous opportunity courtesy of the Victorian and Federal Governments, and led by the mercurial ex-Premier Jeff Kennett, my principal task was to engage in a national but informed conversation about common mental health problems. To do that, you need to have at least two parties who were seriously interested. A megaphone of dull public health messages was never likely to work.

At that time I was very fortunate that people like James, with the support of the ABC, were prepared to do just that: talk seriously and openly about mental health, what it is, how to build it and how to manage common problems if they arise – but without being too serious, overly technical or just plain boring. Some were a lot better at it than others. James has a unique capacity to raise a serious or just really interesting topic, reflect on it personally and then ask the sort of questions that really matter to the wider audience.

During the COVID period, mental health concerns came screaming back into the public domain. I found myself repeating many short messages about the importance of taking care of our collective mental health, in continuing rounds of media engagements. But I was also frustrated at the lack of opportunity to have longer and more informative conversations with those outside the professional and social networks that I inhabit. So when James suggested that podcasts were now the best way to pursue those goals, I jumped at the opportunity.

The podcast has been much more successful than I could have imagined. It has managed to engage people (including members of my own family) in ways much of the rest of my public education and information efforts just don't achieve. It depends not only on James's expertise as a broadcaster and professional facilitator but on his genuine willingness to go places that others avoid.

Hopefully, this book conveys some of the joy that we experience while producing the podcast. While a book is a different thing, we've tried to still convey the engaged discourse of the live segments. We've added, however, more specific reflections on how the mind and body really work ('The Body Clock' chapter, for example); how emotions, thoughts and feelings really interact; and what works to achieve long-term changes.

Most weeks, I have some media, political or health official turn around to me and say, 'Ian, you know it's really true that our mental health is actually more important to our quality of life than our physical health'. 'Yes,' I reply. 'That's what many people have been telling me for many years.' What we really need, however, is the knowledge about what is going on 'under the hood' and what we can all really do each day to improve our own – and our collective – mental health. We hope that this book, and the podcast, contribute to that process.

PART 1

HOW OUR MINDS WORK

1

What Runs in Families and What Doesn't

Dad, you and Mum supplied my genes, and you created my environment. So either way, anything bad I do is your fault.

One of James's daughters, aged 14

What runs in families? What doesn't? We know we inherit eye colour and height, but if your father was anxious, does that mean you will be? What if your mother was optimistic? Will she pass that on?

We accept we have Dad's nose or Mum's sporting ability but are less sure where our quick temper or propensity to depression came from. To what extent do we inherit character, temperament, thinking styles and vulnerability to mental illness? It is important to say at the outset that when things run strongly in families, it's likely that both inherited (genetic) and learned (environmental) factors are both playing a role.

For example, you might have the best sporting genes in the world, but if you grow up in an environment where sport is not valued or readily available, you are unlikely to become a champion.

Conversely, you may play sport every day, and be the most dedicated trainer in your team, but if you are genetically smaller, slower, weaker and less coordinated than others, you might find it difficult to excel at the top level.

How Environmental Factors Influence Our Development

Determining the impact that various environmental factors have on our development is tricky. You might think that something bad that happened to you when you were five has affected you in a particular way. 'My parents accidentally left me behind at a petrol station, and now, in every relationship I have, I'm terrified of being abandoned.' While that narrative may make some sense, in fact, the real cause might have been something completely different that happened when you were two. We like simple explanations – 'This happened and therefore I am like that.' Often it is not that straightforward.

Environmental factors influence our emotional, cognitive and physiological development. A mother may have had an infection (like German measles) when six months' pregnant, which has life-long impacts for her baby. Birth trauma or an infection at age two can change the course of a child's brain development. A head injury at age twelve or the use of brain-damaging drugs (like methamphetamine) at age sixteen may disrupt the maturation of critical brain circuits during the teenage years.

Environmental factors, at every age, occur against the background of our genetic template. It is a bit like painting an identical picture on two different surfaces, canvas and wood. The finished product will look different, because of the different background. The big differences in our genetic backgrounds mean that similar events can affect us quite differently. Someone who has inherited an anxious temperament will probably be more affected by financial stress than someone who has inherited a more carefree outlook.

Who Do We Breed With?

We tend to be attracted to, and feel more comfortable with, those who are similar to us, emotionally and intellectually. We like people who think like us more than we like those who think differently. Those with particular temperaments, for example anxious, or optimistic, or social, often pair up with those with similar characteristics. That's why our parents are more likely to be similar than very different.

Initially, we tend to be fearful of those who are different. It is an evolutionary thing, and occurs across other animal species. We stay close to those who have reared us since childhood. We are more wary with those who look and sound different, at least until we are assured by experience that they are no real threat.

People often ask, 'If you vote Labor, could you marry someone who votes Liberal?' or vice versa. Some people do pair up with those who have different political and ideological views, but it can get awkward at election time. There is no Labor or Liberal gene, but there are emotional and cognitive (i.e. thinking) characteristics that tend to be associated with voting one way or the other, and some of those characteristics do run in families. Other good examples of things we might not think of as being inherited, and yet can be, like shared spiritual beliefs, willingness to take physical or financial risks, and concerns for the welfare of others.

Parents Do Not Maketh the Child

Many believe personality characteristics are determined by what happens in the first six months of life, but actually, many parents with two or three children realise, almost immediately after birth, that there are significant genetic, temperamental differences between their children. Right from the start, the second child might be different to the first. She might settle and sleep differently, and respond differently to human contact. The parents didn't do anything to make her that way. She just started out that way.

It is important that parents recognise temperamental differences in their children, and understand they might need to parent kids who have different temperaments quite differently.

Our temperamental (how we react emotionally) and cognitive (how we think) characteristics are strongly inherited, and vary greatly because, as a species, we have needed a whole range of different characteristics to survive and prosper. For example, we need people who are anxious to anticipate possible dangers and prepare for them. We also need risk-takers, or we would never explore, invent or innovate.

Parents often get blamed if their child has poor self-control, or is difficult or disruptive. 'It must be bad parenting.' Not necessarily. Most of the time, parents try really hard to provide love and support. There are strong, genetically determined temperamental differences between children that affect who they are, and how they behave. Most parents respond as best they can to the different challenges. The idea that parents have the ability to make children into what they want is mistaken.

The environment parents provide is important. The quality of attachment and emotional bonding within families matters, but the environment children are exposed to is much wider than just their parents. There are siblings, extended family, friends, daycare, schools, neighbours, netball team, sport coaches, music teachers and many more. In fact, the more the merrier.

Understanding our own problems isn't all about blaming Mum and Dad. They, themselves, are a product of their own genes and environment. They may have had their own difficulties – a tough upbringing, different cultural expectations or practices, difficult school experiences, war, or living in a family where there was abuse. That is not to excuse bad behaviour across generations, but rather to recognise that parents may have faced their own challenges.

Sharing the same home environment with parents and siblings can lead to us acting like them when we are young. As we get older, first as teenagers and then as adults, and move into different environments, we become more different and eventually we each become who we are.

Inheriting Temperament

If your father was shy, you are more likely to be shy. Similarly, if your parents had quick tempers, or were anxious, or optimistic, you have an increased chance of also having those traits. Importantly, although we each have two (biological) parents, we don't inherit equal amounts from each and, sadly, one good set of characteristics doesn't necessarily cancel out some bad characteristics from the other. Genetic factors are complex, with many different genes often combining in an individual to underpin their specific emotional and behavioural characteristics. Those with many brothers or sisters will have seen lots of different combinations of inherited features being evident in the one family.

If you get angry quickly and often, it may be your dad (or mum) did too, as did his dad. The question then becomes, 'How do I break the cycle?' Inheriting a quick temper does not mean you are powerless to change. You can learn strategies to deal with it (see Chapter 20, 'Anger'). In fact, understanding that you have a genetic propensity toward anger can actually spur people to try to learn how to control it.

Your genes are your architectural blueprint, but you still have agency to alter those plans, and do some renovating.

'I'm Worried I Inherited Anxiety'

Your underlying central nervous system's response to environmental stress has a strong genetic foundation, and you carry that with you through life. So, yes, we can inherit an anxious temperament and, when bad or scary things happen, be more sensitive to them than others and get more distressed. It also means we might worry more, and anticipate and plan for the worst, rather than assume everything will turn out fine. (See Chapter 9, 'Anxiety'.)

Being shy, or socially anxious, has an upside. Yes, you freak out every time you walk into a party, but you are also likely to be sensitive, thoughtful and a better life partner.

Being very sensitive has advantages and disadvantages. Those who are very insensitive are bad social animals. If you are on the sensitive side, you will pick up more emotional cues from others, and be good at helping them through tough times. However, you may get upset by lots of things that others would ignore, and that can lead to anxiety and depression.

Getting to know and understand your own temperament is important.

Know Thyself

A good place to start is to identify the characteristics you have in common with those you share genes with: parents, siblings, grandparents, uncles, aunts, cousins.

If you realise pessimism runs in your family, and that you are also pessimistic, you can allow for that when calculating risks. 'I'm scared of getting on the plane, but I know I'm pessimistic by nature, so maybe I am overestimating the risk of something bad happening.' Same for perfectionism. 'Maybe I go too far when I try to make everything exactly as I want it.'

If your parents are anxious, they might have encouraged you to avoid the things that make you nervous, rather than confront and overcome your fears. Knowing that, you can ask, 'What strategies can I use to help me overcome the fears that my temperament wants me to avoid?' If you have inherited anxiety and shyness that manifests in a fear of public speaking (something both Ian and James have experienced), you can learn to overcome it through exposure. (See chapter 9, 'Anxiety'.)

If you know that your terror of public speaking is at least partly inherited, rather than being an intrinsic part of you, it might encourage you to try to overcome it. Just because a characteristic is inherited, it doesn't mean it cannot be changed. Just look at the hair replacement industry.

Ian's family contains a lot of shy people. His father encouraged public speaking to help them overcome it at an age when, if they had had the choice, they would have avoided the anxiety associated with it.

Others who have an extroverted, risk-taking temperament are outgoing, fun-loving, don't worry about anything, and learn to parachute and rock-climb. However, they usually underestimate risks, and spend more time with plaster-covered limbs that others.

Do we inherit empathy, emotionality and connectedness with others? Or do we learn them? Again, it is a cocktail. We do know that there is wide variation between individuals in these key emotional traits, and that they too have strong genetic underpinnings. For those with a 'natural' gift for understanding the emotional world of others (high 'emotional intelligence'), social skills are easily learned. For others who struggle to anticipate how others might react, learning to do it better can be difficult.

Inheriting the Way We Think

People think in different ways. Some of us slowly, logically and dispassionately weigh the evidence before arriving at a decision, whilst others are more impulsive, and more influenced by 'the vibe'. Those different styles of thinking can also be inherited.

Some like to hear details, work their way through each step of a process, take the emotion out of their thinking and give weight only to the observed facts. They can get stuck, procrastinate and go over and over the same material without getting any closer to a conclusion. Buying a new computer will take months of investigation of all the possible permutations of brand, model, capacity, capability and cost. This type of thinking also tends to see only black or white, right or wrong. No shades of grey and little tolerance of ambiguity.

By contrast, some are more trusting of conclusions drawn by others and less perturbed by uncertainty. They are not weighed down by the search for further evidence to support their view. They are more easily shifted from their original point of view, and are more fluid and flexible in their thinking. They accept that different people draw different conclusions from the same facts and believe that all outcomes have both good and bad characteristics.

Other cognitive attributes include the capacity to move freely and quickly from one thinking task to another, and being able to see the possible links between apparently unrelated concepts, which can allow artistic, musical or scientific creativity.

There is a strong correlation between parents and their children of both IQ (a measure of intelligence) and EQ (a measure of emotional awareness). Having said that, both concepts have limited usefulness on their own.

Is Mental Illness Inherited?

We don't inherit illnesses. We inherit genetic predispositions to an illness, which means we have an increased likelihood of getting that illness at some point. If we inherit a propensity to depression, that doesn't mean we will get depression. It means that we have a greater vulnerability to it than others.

The link between the genes we inherit and mental illness is hard to study, because if your parents were anxious and you grow up to be anxious, did it happen because:

a) You inherited their propensity to anxiety?

b) You grew up with two anxious parents, and you 'learned' how to be anxious from them? Or,

c) A bit of both?

With anxiety and depression (and almost everything else), the answer is c). Studies of twins, adopted children and other family studies reveal that about thirty per cent of the risk of any adult having anxiety and depression is genetic, and seventy per cent is the impact of their environment through their life. That seventy per cent environmental impact is broken down into three areas, worth ten, forty and twenty per cent. It seems only about ten per cent is due to a person's family environment when they were young. The biggest component, forty per cent, is due to our current environment (relationships, work stressors and other ongoing life difficulties). The remaining twenty per cent is made up of things we're not certain about, including errors in measurement. Now, these are averages across the population, so between individuals the actual mix of genetic, childhood and current environment will vary.

If you have a strong genetic vulnerability to anxiety or depression, and then add an adverse childhood environment where you were exposed to terrible things, not cared for, left in danger or abused, the chances of experiencing anxiety or depression as an adult increases.

When assessing your chances of getting some of the most serious mental health problems such as bipolar disorder or schizophrenia, there is a higher genetic component than with anxiety or depression.

Ian often asks patients if they have a family history of suicide, or if there are family deaths that aren't accounted for. Often the answer is, 'I don't know.' Families often avoid discussing histories of postnatal depression, bipolar disorder, psychotic episodes and other types of mental illness. 'What happened when Uncle Jack went off to a hospital and never came back?'

It is important to know our family history, so we know what vulnerabilities we might have inherited, and can then learn strategies to lower our risk of being adversely affected. This is true for both physical and mental illness. If you know you have a family history of melanoma, you can lower your risk by being fanatical about wearing a hat and sunscreen. With a family history of breast cancer, you can get regularly screened. If you know you have a family history of depression, you can lower your risk by doing regular exercise, learning how to reduce stress, managing your sleep–wake cycle, working on improving your personal relationships and reducing your use of alcohol and other drugs. (See Chapter 10, 'Depression'.)

Over the next decade, we will learn a lot more about the genetic risks individuals face and be able to give people more information about what they are at heightened risk of, and what they can do to lower that risk. Matching new and more specific treatments to individuals is already happening with cancer patients, and Ian expects it to occur much more in mental health over the next few years.

Alcoholism and Addiction

Some of the most challenging problems in the community relate to alcohol and other drug abuse. While the patterns of use are strongly influenced by social factors, the propensity to become addicted to many substances also has a significant genetic component.

The relationship between mental health and addiction to alcohol and other substances is complicated, but at least now we are better at talking about it. Many, especially men, use alcohol to treat their depression and anxiety. While that may provide short-term relief, in the long term it adds to the problem.

Just like with other disorders, knowledge of the problems of past generations in your own family is empowering. If alcohol or other drug use has been an issue in your family, you can take a much more conservative approach to their use in your own life. The later in life you start using any of these things, the lower the risk that you'll ever have a major problem. (See chapter 15, 'Addiction'.)

CHECKLIST

- Ask yourself, 'What am I like? What is my temperament? What is my thinking style?'
- What mental health problems run in your family?
- What things have worked in your family to help those in trouble?

2

Is Decision-making Rational or Emotional?

Let's not forget that the little emotions are the great captains
of our lives, and we obey them without realising it.

Vincent van Gogh

How do we make decisions? Are we rational beings, driven by logical thought, or are we primarily emotional, driven by our feelings?

Many of us like to think we are rational, that we weigh up the pros and cons of competing choices, then pick the best option. But is that what you did when you last started a relationship?

Choosing Partners, Ice-Creams and Holidays

Did you dispassionately assess your potential partner's strengths and weaknesses, work your way down a checklist of preferred traits, and undertake a rational analysis of how compatible you would be together? Or did you *feel* something. 'I really like him/her/them.'

Sure, you may have retrospectively reverse-engineered an explanation of how your strengths perfectly complemented each other,

21

that he is the glove that perfectly fits your hand, but it was likely a decision driven by strong emotions, as rationality sat powerless in the back seat hoping it didn't end in (another) crash.

If your mother thinks you should marry the girl down the road because she has excellent parents and she's very bright, you might respond, 'But Mum, I'm not attracted to her. There's no spark, no chemistry.'

Is the decision to eat ice-cream rational? No, because we know it's not good for us. But it tastes good. It gives us momentary pleasure and makes us (emotionally) feel good. We share these basic pleasures – food, drink, sex, touch, smell – with other animals. Whether we want to believe it or not, the desire for these pleasures drives many of our decisions.

How do we choose holiday destinations? We think, 'I like Queensland, the beach, hot weather, and I can get a good deal on a place with a pool.' Those are rational factors. However, in the background as you think all this, you might have this little movie playing in your head of you and your family sitting around the pool or at the beach, laughing and having a great time. That's the emotional part.

Primarily, what most people want out of a family holiday is not sun or the beach. It's pleasure. It's for everyone to have fun. Sun and the beach might help you achieve that, but they are just a means to get to that emotional end. So you start from that emotional aim, 'I want everyone to have a good time,' and work backwards, more rationally, to figure out what will get you there.

Big Career Decisions

When we make big decisions – moving house, changing jobs – we often weigh the pros and cons in a logical way, but we also ask ourselves if it feels right. Even if a new job would be a good career move and pay us more, if it doesn't feel right, or we are emotionally drawn to something else, that can often be the deciding factor, even when the final decision seems counterintuitive or irrational.

Sometimes the best decisions combine both the emotional and rational. As James was about to embark on a career as a lawyer, he saw a night of stand-up comedy and immediately knew it was for him. It was an immediate, powerful emotional feeling of connection, but it would have been very risky for him to turn his back on a stable career before he knew if he would be any good at comedy. So (rationally) he hedged his bets, doing both jobs for several years, then going part-time as a lawyer, and eventually, when his comedy career seemed viable, giving up law completely. The emotion came first, followed by a series of logical steps.

Animals that live in groups, like dogs and apes, struggle between group cohesion and the desire to get to the top. So do we, in our corporate, organisational and political cultures. People certainly make rational, strategic and tactical decisions to help them get to the top, but why are they doing it?

The television show *Breaking Bad* tells the story of Walter White, a bored, mild-mannered high school teacher, who, after being diagnosed with cancer, gradually becomes a ruthless drug dealer. His initial justification is, 'I have a son with a disability, a wife and a baby, and I need to make sure they will have enough money after I die.' However, it slowly becomes clear his deeper motivation is his emotional need for power and excitement. In the final episode he admits his motivation was more emotional than rational: 'I did it for me. I liked it. I was good at it. And, I was really . . . I was alive.'

Justifying Emotional Decisions

Humans often downplay the extent that emotion drives their decisions. We like to think we make decisions rationally. So, when you are analysing a decision you made that turned out badly, think about why you made that decision. Not just the surface desires you were trying to fulfil, but also your emotional impulses or deeper needs. Say tasks were being allocated at your workplace; you thought it was being done unfairly and decided to argue. You thought you would be calm and composed, but when you started talking, you were upset and angry. You may have had rational points to make, but what happened had much more to do with your *feelings* of being ignored and left out.

Often the rational explanation has very little to do with it. It is just an elaborate attempt to explain what was impulsive and instinctual.

We are often drawn to certain things, even though they would predictably result in chaos. People frequently start new sexual or other intimate relationships despite the likelihood that they will wreak havoc on their existing world. Then they try to justify it in some rational way: 'Me and my partner lost our spark. I've found my soulmate.' However, their decision-making is usually much more emotional than rational.

Can We Think Our Way Out of Depression and Anxiety?

When we are depressed or anxious, we can sometimes see, rationally, how illogical and unhelpful our thought processes are – 'Why am I so negative at the moment?' 'Why am I so anxious about something that is unlikely to happen?' Unfortunately, that doesn't automatically mean we can change those thought patterns, or our emotional states. It is very hard to convince yourself to *feel* different.

You can use your rationality to learn what treatments are likely to be effective against mental illness. If you know that moving, exercising or walking is likely to make you feel better, you can try to convince your lethargic self to do them. There are some rational decisions we can make to improve our emotional state.

When people get into emotional difficulties with anxiety, depression and other mental health issues, they are usually unaware of the extent to which their emotional systems are playing tricks on them, leading them into bad places, controlling their thoughts. You might try to explain what is happening, but your rational self is not in the driver's seat. The systems underneath are driving things in dysfunctional ways, and affecting your thinking, and how you feel physically.

A good example is the extent to which people with depression become physically inactive. The rational explanation is that they are tired and therefore need to rest or sleep more. If that tiredness were normal exhaustion, then that strategy would probably work. However, when depressed, the more inactive you become, the more tired you feel. It soon becomes a vicious circle. Paradoxically, becoming more active leads to feeling more energetic and being able to re-engage with the world.

With anxiety, we often cannot understand why we are so preoccupied with a worry that, rationally, we should be able to put aside. They might not realise that their anxiety is not under rational control. Their worries are not a justified response to the world. Combating irrational thoughts with rational ones can help, but there's also a powerful physical and emotional component. Anxiety arises when we perceive a threat. That leads to physical arousal and adrenaline, which we need for optimal performance. There are signs of physical arousal: breathing shallowly, faster heart rate, sweating. It is not just about what you are thinking. It is also about what your body is doing.

Sometimes we get nervous before a speech or public performance, and don't understand why. We think, rationally, 'I've done this a hundred times. I'm prepared. There's no logical reason to be nervous.' But it might have nothing to do with that. It might be that your body has not had enough sleep, or too much coffee, or that it's a very hot day, or that you have a cold, or that you just had an argument with your partner.

Our internal arousal system has taken over, and it is not listening to our logic. For a physical arousal problem we need, not a logical thinking solution, but a physical solution that will lower our level of arousal. That is, some sort of relaxation – deep breathing, progressive muscle relaxation or a walk.

Thinking yourself out of depression with rational thoughts ('I should be happy. I have a great life') doesn't work. An alternative that often helps is to focus on the emotional side and fake being happy. Make yourself smile. Fake the physicality of enjoyment, and your mind might follow.

Moderating Emotional Decision-making

Humans have the capacity to learn from their behaviour, and moderate it. The brain does this via the frontal lobes, a big 'stop-reflect-do different' button. These parts of the brain can see likely events in the future, learn from the past, and override our more instinctive, 'just-do-it' impulses. Our frontal lobes enable us to learn from experience.

When we argue with someone, at some point we might realise that continuing is only going to make things worse, and we should walk away. Yet, often we are unable to stop, because our emotionality is overriding what we rationally know to be the best course of action.

It takes very active frontal lobes to stop. At those points in conflict, there is threat and challenge, and we feel a basic, important desire to protect our self. It is personal and primitive. We should not underrate these drives, but at times they do need to be moderated. Doing so is not simple. It takes active strategies designed to de-escalate both the body and the mind: slow breathing, slow talking, taking a pause, backing off, breaking eye contact, turning away.

It is dangerous to assume you will always have the rationality to override your emotional impulses. The more threatened or angry we feel, the more aroused we get, the more likely our emotionality is to dominate our decision-making, and the more likely we are to lash out.

We all have different capacities to regulate those powerful emotional responses. Children and teenagers do not have fully developed frontal lobes. As a result, they often make more impulsive decisions. The same is true for those who are intoxicated. Alcohol makes the frontal lobes less effective.

Our legal system recognises that in certain situations, passion and emotion can override rationality, and that shortly after doing something terrible, people will regret it, and not really understand how they lost control. Hence, spontaneous, impulsive 'crimes of passion' are often punished less severely than pre-meditated, planned, 'rational' crimes.

If you have on occasions gone further into a conflict than you meant to, and want to control yourself more in the future, you can learn to recognise when you are becoming aroused, and engage your frontal lobes to override, or at least slow, that process. We need to understand that emotionality is within us all, and it isn't rational. On some occasions, like when we get angry, it creates powerful impulses, but it is often not appropriate to act on them. We have to learn, through development and maturity, the best ways to override those emotional impulses.

Stop, disengage, take time out, walk away, defer to someone else who can step in on your behalf. Nothing is lost by de-escalating a risky situation. Often much is gained.

CHECKLIST

- In the modern world, we think of ourselves as being so rational and clever, so unlike the apes. We need to understand we are emotional and physical beings. Sometimes we need to stop and question the 'reasons' we use to justify our actions.
- Big life decisions – jobs, partners – are usually dictated mainly by emotion, not rational thought. 'This *feels* right.'
- We can follow emotionally based big life decisions with a series of smaller, rational decisions to turn a goal into reality.
- We like to think we can logically explain all the decisions we make. However, the rational reasons we give often have little to do with the emotions that really drove them.
- Sometimes emotional responses can take us over and we become aroused or angry. It is good, but not easy, to learn how to engage more self-control. Before acting, can we learn to add in a rational step that might prevent a bad outcome?

3

The Body Clock

There is a wisdom in the body that is older and more reliable than clocks and calendars.

John H. Johnson

There are many reasons we can feel out of sorts, and many things that affect our mental health. One of the most common, and least understood, is the impact of our body clock. Understanding the body clock can help us to live healthier, happier lives, and reduce our risk of anxiety and depression.

What Is the Body Clock?

Our mind and body are connected. What happens to our body affects our mind, and vice versa. One of the body's most important systems for staying fit and healthy is the body clock, our twenty-four-hour sleep–wake cycle. It is a sophisticated system of chemical releases that helps us wake up, be active and alert during daylight hours, and then, after dark, to become less active, sleep, restore and recover.

Most animals live in harmony with the twenty-four-hour light-dark, day-night cycle. Their behaviour, including sleep patterns, feeding time and peak physical activity, is in strong alignment with their internal body clock. Humans are diurnal species, meaning we are built to be most active during daylight. We release cortisol in the morning, which helps us to be active. After dark, we release melatonin, which helps us sleep.

Some small mammals are nocturnal, being most active at night. From an evolutionary perspective, that means they are less likely to be eaten by larger diurnal predators. Internal clocks can be found in plants as well: sunflowers move throughout the day to chase the sun.

Most animals (and plants) have strong behavioural patterns that keep them aligned with their preferred sleep–wake, day–night cycles, and they don't mess with it. Tigers don't do shift work. Goats don't fly to other time zones.

However, many aspects of twenty-first-century human life interfere with our natural day–night cycle. We regularly stuff up our body clock by staying up late, working night shift or flying to a different time zone. That not only makes us feel tired, but can also throw out the orderly functioning of both our body and mind.

How the Body Clock Works: The Chemicals that Get Us Through the Day

Being diurnal, we are built to be awake, physically active, talking, moving, eating during daylight hours.

Cortisol is the basic stress hormone that helps us to be active, energetic, hopeful and to cope with life's challenges, alongside the other adrenaline-like substances our bodies release.

Cortisol release surges in the early morning before we get out of bed. As the sun comes up, we get the signal to release cortisol, which gives us the energy to get going, and helps us concentrate. It gets our blood pressure and body temperature up, signals our other activity hormones to get going and tells other body systems it is time to eat and be active.

By midday, cortisol has started to fall, but another chemical (only recently discovered), orexin, peaks in the early afternoon to keep us going into the early evening.

Come nightfall, a third hormone, melatonin, is released. Its basic message to the brain is: 'It's dark. Go to sleep.' The oncoming darkness of sunset turns melatonin on, and then in the morning, the new day's light turns it off.

In the evening, when that rising melatonin coincides with falling orexin and other adrenaline-like substances, our brain gets quiet, our body temperature starts to fall, and we are ready to head off to deep, brain-restoring sleep.

When we have to get up in the middle of the night or are jet-lagged, our body clock is out of whack, and it is very hard to get going, because our cortisol is very low. We are not naturally nocturnal. Physical and mental activity is difficult because our body and brain are not set up to function at that time of day.

Why We Need to Take Care of Our Body Clock

Have you ever tried to be active, or even just to feel healthy, when you are jet-lagged? It is almost impossible. All the body signals are in the wrong time zones.

When our body clock is out, it is like being jet-lagged all the time. It is just not possible to function, physically or mentally.

When all the body clock's internal functions, such as coordinating the release of cortisol, adrenaline, insulin, melatonin and the activity of immune cells, are chaotic, and all its behavioural signals (like when to eat, rest or sleep) are mixed up, our health quickly falls apart. We feel tired all the time; we fall asleep at the wrong time; we start grazing on food continuously and quickly gain weight; our body's release of insulin to regulate blood sugar moves out of balance.

When our body clock is out, we wake up tired. We become less alert, more moody and irritable, and start making bad and impulsive decisions. Our memory starts to go out the window. Older people often start to wonder whether they are developing dementia. Younger people report more anxiety and depression.

In addition, the risk of catching viral infections or having a heart attack or stroke increases. Muscle pains and aches increase in intensity, and other physical disturbances like headaches and gut disturbances become more frequent.

To prevent this long list of disasters from occurring, we need to take care of our body clock, and keep it well-aligned with the day–night cycle. It is an important part of feeling healthy and well. It can be difficult at certain stages of life, such as after the arrival of a new baby, or when trying to meet tight work or education dead-lines, so we need an active plan to stay in synch with the earth's daily rotation.

Why Do We Need to Sleep?

While we are asleep, our brains are wide awake and actively processing the day's information, rebooting and repairing.

The active, alert and energetic things we do in daylight generate many new connections between brain cells. However, the brain can only tolerate so much activity in a twenty-four-hour period before it becomes 'toxic' and starts killing brain cells.

When we sleep, we are under the influence of more inhibitory brain chemicals that turn down the rate of signals moving between brain cells. Other brain cells actively prune back unnecessary brain connections, creating space for the next day's new activities. Brain processes, including memories and thoughts, are shifted from the working and active centres to storage in other, less active, parts of the brain.

We can do this effectively only by turning off to the outside world and letting the brain focus its attention, and energy use, on these critical 'back-room' activities. When we sleep, we are actively resetting our brains so we will be able to function tomorrow, both emotionally and cognitively.

Starting Up the Brain

Like our teeth and our knees, our body clock ages and deteriorates, until by around age thirty it has pretty much lost its capacity to set itself without reference to the external day-night, light-dark cycle. That means that to reset our body clock, we have to start our brains up manually every day. Soon after we wake up, we have to signal to our brain that that day has begun, and it is time to get going. We do that in three ways:

1. Exposure to Light

Exposure to light sends our brain a strong signal that the day has begun. Once we register light, our body turns off the sleep hormone, melatonin. That is why, when we wake up, we should get quickly into some natural light. Go outside, or look out a window. Exposure to sunlight is much better than artificial light. Sunlight is more intense than any artificial light and sets the clock much more effectively, but if you cannot get natural light, at least get some bright artificial light.

This is why looking at screens just before bedtime is a bad idea. The brain gets the light signal, which tells it that it is time to get up and get going, when actually it should be winding down in preparation for sleep.

2. Movement

Movement also sends a signal to the brain that the day has begun. To get going, we should move soon after we wake up. Don't sit there and watch breakfast television. While the kettle boils, walk a few laps of your living room. Walk to the shop, the cafe or around the block. That will sort out the light exposure, too. Take your dog down the street and listen to a podcast. Do some stretches or push-ups. Go to the park; walk some of the way to work; walk past the nearest bus stop to the one after it, or even the one beyond that. Read a magazine on a bench outside.

3. Set Daily Patterns

The body clock likes regularity – going to sleep at the same time, waking up at the same time. Parents often set fixed bedtimes for kids, but adults can be far less disciplined. 'I was going to go to sleep at 10.30, but the show I was watching was so good I had to watch another two episodes.' Sticking to a fixed bedtime does take some self-discipline, but in return you will experience all the health benefits that flow from taking care of your body clock.

The Body Clock and Age

Newborn babies have a short, four-hour sleep–wake cycle. They have six days, as it were, in every twenty-four hours. Wake up, cry, feed, roll about, feed, back to sleep, repeat.

Midnight to 4 am is a day for them, and their fast-motion body clocks don't care that their parents want to sleep at that time. For the first few weeks, parents have no choice. They have to adjust to their baby's cycle. By doing so, they throw their own body clock way out. The adverse impacts on parents – like post-natal depression – can be dramatic.

By about eight weeks, most babies have at least moved to six-hour cycles and parents are better able to survive. Through their first year, babies might sleep for longer periods, up to about eight hours.

By preschool, the body clock has changed again. Kids operate from about sun-up until sundown, on a cycle of twelve hours on, twelve hours off.

Teenagers start staying up later and sleeping later. Don't blame them. It's built in. The developing brain sends more 'stay awake' signals in the later afternoon and early evening, resulting in later bed times. As they sleep, teenagers release huge amounts of growth hormone causing their bodies and brains to grow.

As adults, the physiological systems in our body – our metabolism, immune systems, hormonal cycles and heart systems – are all orientated towards having approximately sixteen hours high activity, on, followed by eight hours low activity, off. So we should have a sixteen-hour awake, eight-hour asleep cycle.

As you get older, these timing processes start to deteriorate. When our body clock loses its sense of when to be on during daylight and off during darkness, it can be an early sign of dementia.

Older people who develop brain problems often also develop problems with their twenty-four-hour clock. It may become less sensitive to external signals, like light and physical activity. If our clock starts to deteriorate, we need to be even more diligent about having a regular routine, getting lots of light and doing physical activity soon after we wake up. Lots of daytime snoozing and drifting off in front of the TV make it worse.

What If We Don't Get Enough Sleep

If we don't get enough sleep (for example, if you are a new parent), everything becomes hard. We can't function well. The brain just hasn't done the repairs it needs to do every day. Our cognitive function is affected, so thinking is hard. Emotionally, we will probably be moody, irritable and difficult.

Those people who believe they can function normally on very little sleep are just plain wrong. Physiologically, it's not on. Brains cannot put out the right signals to the rest of the body under those circumstances. They also cannot pay attention, be alert, react, remember and plan as well as they usually can when they are sleep-deprived.

If a disturbed sleep cycle goes on for a while, our brain and our body, including our gut, immune system (which fights infection and cancer) and hormonal system, will get progressively worse, because they all run on twenty-four-hour energy/activity/rest and repair cycles. If they are on and reacting to the external world continuously, they become depleted and don't rest and repair.

People do vary in how long they need to sleep. Quality of sleep is more important than quantity. Some can get by on five or six hours' sleep better than others. However, everybody needs several hours of really deep, or 'slow wave', sleep. During that phase of sleep, which occurs between about 1 am and 4 am, the brain is in a really different pattern. The body is quiet, and body temperature is down. The brain's electrical signals are slowing down, using less energy and not attending to the external world. This is when the brain is doing its best internal repair work.

Often when we are anxious and have a lot on our mind, the parts of the brain that send chemical signals to stay awake don't quieten down, and this inhibits deep sleep. You wake up feeling like you haven't slept at all and are not refreshed. Often when people say that they haven't slept at all, they have actually been asleep but they have had very little, or no, deep sleep.

When new mothers are breast-feeding, when they do fall asleep they drop much more quickly into deep sleep. Even though their time spent asleep is short, they recover quickly and survive the new-born period.

So, independent of how many hours of sleep you get, the quality of sleep and the number of hours of deep sleep and dream sleep are more important factors for physical and emotional health.

Some tortures involve sleep deprivation. After a while, your grip on reality slips. You start to have visual and auditory hallucinations, and drift in and out of consciousness. Eventually, if you don't sleep at all for days, you can die. The body is exhausted. The brain stops sending out its normal daily patterns of 'be active' (in daylight) and 'go to sleep' (at night) signals. The whole process collapses.

Changing Seasons

Some animals have a very active body clock that changes with the seasons. In autumn, bears eat a huge amount of carbohydrates and then sleep (hibernate) in winter. Birds migrate. Even if birds are kept in cages, as the seasons change they start to get ready to take off, becoming more active and not sleeping. The way they respond to the seasons is in-built.

Some people are more sensitive than others to a change in the amount of daily light that accompanies the change in seasons. They are more prone to sudden changes in their appetite, weight, daily activity patterns, sleep and mood when the season changes. It is about the changing amount of light, not temperature.

During autumn and spring, when the daily amount of light is changing, they might become unwell. They might put it down to trouble at work, or their partner treating them badly, whereas actually the main cause of their distress is that their brain is very sensitive to the changing amount of light, and it is throwing their body clock out of alignment. When that happens, a cascade of physical and mental health problems can follow. They can gain weight and have no energy. Some say, 'I'm not depressed. I've just got no energy. I just can't do anything, I've got muscular pains and I can't sleep well.' That could be depression, or what is termed 'seasonal affective disorder (SAD) or 'seasonal depressive disorder', driven by a perturbed or changed circadian clock. Professional help may be required.

On short, dark winter days, many of us feel lazy – we lie on the couch, watch TV, eat more and don't feel like doing anything. Winter is particularly difficult for people with a very sensitive, seasonally variable, circadian clock.

People with this sensitivity who move closer to the equator, where there is less light variation between summer and winter, sometimes find that that their general mood improves.

Technology has been developed to help those who live near the poles, like Scandinavians or northern Canadians, where there is hardly any daylight in winter, to get light artificially. Turning on the bedroom light and looking at it can help, but it is not nearly as effective as natural light. Now there are early-morning lamps, head lamps, blue lights (to suppress melatonin) and even glasses that have little lights on the side that shine into your eyes, that help get the body clock going in the morning.

Shift Work and the Body Clock

In some industries, we use the body clock to our advantage. Why does the building industry start work at 7 am? Because it's the best time physically. That is when cortisol is kicking in, giving us physical power, a bright mood and mental concentration.

Seven in the morning is not when you want to be trying to get to sleep. Your body's signals are telling you to get up and get going. Even if you have been up all night and are exhausted, you may only get a few hours of very non-refreshing sleep.

However, if you work night shift that might be what you have to do. Working nights, or hours that are constantly changing (like nurses, airline staff and police) can muck up your internal clock and have adverse effects on body and mind. Those who work irregular and changing shift-work patterns often put on weight, and are more prone to diabetes, more likely to develop heart disease and to have emotional problems like depression. They also have more accidents and injuries. For those with a very sensitive body clock, shift work is particularly difficult.

A problem shift workers can have is that their clock gets lost, and they can't maintain any regular pattern – the worst outcome for our health. A sign this might be happening is if you sometimes can't tell what time of the day it is.

One type of depression is 'circadian depression', when your day is out of whack with your circadian rhythms and body clock. Shift workers are at particular risk of this ongoing misalignment between their internal body clock and the external world. The depression persists until the two are realigned – by changing daily patterns or using light exposure or a melatonin-based antidepressant to target the wayward clock.

If you have to do shift work, try to choose a regular shift pattern that matches your clock. If you are a morning person, do early morning shifts. If you are a night person, do late afternoon or evening shifts. Very few people can do permanent night shift without some adverse effects, but some are much better at it than others. Developing a regular pattern is better than constantly changing the pattern.

The Body Clock, Mental Health and Mental Illness

Swimmers get up early, swim, rest, go to the gym and go to bed each night exhausted. Next morning when they wake up, they are full of energy. When they stop swimming, and no longer have that routine of early-morning physical activity and sunlight exposure, some rapidly put on weight, feel lethargic and get depressed.

Former Liberal MP Andrew Robb has spoken about how, for around forty years, the first two hours of his day were bone-crushingly depressing. He seemed to be describing a circadian depression. He couldn't *think* his way out of it, but eventually, he discovered that if he swam first thing every morning (even though he didn't particularly feel like it), it made a huge difference. He had activity and light exposure. Once he got out of the pool, he was good to go.

If you are feeling out of sorts, check in with your body clock as a potential cause. Are you doing shift work? Are you staying up late? Is winter coming, and the days getting shorter? Try going to bed and getting up at the same time each day. When you get up immediately get some natural light and do some serious physical activity.

Some find an effective treatment for depression is to go camping. Turn your phone off, get up with the sun, be physically active all day, exhaust yourself, go to sleep soon after the sun goes down, and reset your clock. Living like this is much better for us than being active after 11 pm every night gaming, bingeing Netflix, working or clubbing and ignoring the signals from the external world. Yes, we sound like party-poopers. We do remember (vaguely) what fun it was emerging from a nightclub at 6 am – but we also remember how crap we felt for the next few days.

There is strong evidence that a disturbed body clock increases the likelihood of some of the most severe depressive disorders, bipolar disorders and other conditions. Australia's greatest contribution in psychiatry, many argue, is the development of lithium for bipolar disorder. Lithium stabilises the body clock, makes it regular again, and gives a day-to-day pattern to people whose moods and energy have been all over the place.

Circadian medicine has become a big issue in cancer therapy, heart disease and diabetes. Getting the right treatment at the right time of day helps to repair the body and the brain.

In the past, some antidepressants upset a person's body clock and made it more unstable, at least in the short term. Some also disturbed people's sleep patterns, or made them more light-sensitive. Now there is more emphasis on developing antidepressants that don't disturb the body clock.

CHECKLIST

- The body clock is a sophisticated system of chemical releases that gets us going during the day and to sleep at night.
- Jet lag, shift work or keeping unusual hours can disrupt our body clock, which can adversely affect both our mental and physical heath.
- Try to keep a regular sleep–wake routine.
- To signal to your brain that the day has begun, as soon as you get up, move your body and get into light – ideally natural light.
- Some people lack energy and feel depressed during Spring and Autumn, when the amount of natural light is changing.
- For good mental health, take care of your body clock.

4

Autonomy

I don't even want to drink coffee. It tastes horrible. I just want to be able to decide for myself that I don't want to drink coffee.
– One of James's daughters, aged 13, after an hour's argument with her father about whether she is allowed to drink coffee

Autonomy is being able to make decisions about your life, which gives you a sense of being in control. Having a degree of autonomy and being able to exercise some control over our life and work has continually been shown to be an important part of good mental health. Ian sees autonomy as one of the two great pillars that support mental health, the other being social connection.

Any situation where our autonomy is undermined, removed or threatened can adversely affect our mental health.

Autonomy and Social Groups

Humans are social animals, strongly influenced by what the group thinks. We want to fit in with the pack. Often, the dominant behaviour of the group overrides much of our individual autonomy, especially when we are young. A teenage girl might want a crew cut, but everyone in her social group has long hair, and that makes her hesitate. A man in his forties wants to shave his balding head, but fears people will stare at him. Then shaved heads become trendy and James musters the courage to do it.

Most animal packs or groups combine hierarchies of dominance and decision-making with a degree of autonomy. Families try to negotiate the best balance between allowing everyone the freedom to do what they want on one hand, and having rules to ensure the home runs in an orderly and peaceful manner on the other.

Workplaces also face this dilemma. Some bosses say they want employees to use their brains and initiative, but at the same time straitjacket them with inflexible systems and accountabilities that leave little room for individual autonomy.

Centralised, controlling, top-down workplaces, families, relationships and groups might work for a time in a crisis, when decisions have to be made and acted on quickly, but eventually they tend to experience major problems. People get frustrated with their lack of autonomy, and either there is conflict or they leave.

COVID-19 was an interesting case study in personal autonomy versus central control. Some objected to governments limiting their personal autonomy by restricting their movements and social interaction, and requiring vaccination to be eligible for certain freedoms. Many others felt that giving up some personal autonomy to protect the overall health of the population was a sacrifice worth making.

Different societies have different attitudes to autonomy and freedom. In the United States, there has traditionally been a stronger belief in personal freedom and individual liberty, whereas in Australia there is generally more acceptance of the need to act collectively.

With Autonomy Comes Responsibility

While we like to have autonomy, having to make decisions for ourselves can also be difficult and stressful. Sometimes it is easier just to be told what to do. Students in their final year of school are often sick of being ordered around by parents and teachers and crave freedom, but when it finally arrives, it can be scary. 'I can do anything I want! But what do I want?'

After COVID lockdown restrictions lifted, we all got our autonomy back. The responsibility for making decisions shifted from the government to us. *We* decided if we went to the pub or wore a mask, which meant that we had to do our own risk assessment. If we went to the pub, how likely was it that we would get COVID? If we got COVID, how likely was it that we would get very sick? How likely was it we would infect others who were more vulnerable? We had more autonomy but also more responsibility which, for many, was stressful.

Autonomy is not a free ride. Every decision has consequences. If we want to try and get more autonomy into our lives, we have to accept that with it comes the responsibility of learning how to make good decisions.

Developing Autonomy from Birth to Adult

You might think babies have no autonomy. They can hardly move, they can't talk, but they can cry. When a baby cries, parents immediately stop what they are doing and pick them up. The baby is exercising influence on the external world, and getting people to do what she wants. That is the start of autonomy.

Before we can talk, we get what we want by screaming and crying. As we get older, we work out new ways to influence our environment. Around age three to four, we work out that putting on a whingey voice and looking sad often gets our parents to do what we want. Then our parents cotton on and tell us that they are going to ignore the whingey voice. So we try something new.

'No,' is often one of the first words kids learn. It is a powerful, dominant expression of autonomy. 'Will you eat your broccoli?' 'No!' Kids gradually realise they have they some agency and power, and they don't have to live under a dictatorship.

Around age three, kids start asking 'Why?' 'We're going to the shop.' 'Why?' Instead of accepting everything they are told, they are working out that they need a reason to do things, and that they do not have to just accept the rules of the world. They can challenge them.

An important part of human development is moving from total dependency to the expression of preferences about the world. Kids might express their autonomy by wanting to dress or cut their hair differently, in the way they behave or speak, or in what they want to do.

Gradually, we learn how to get our own way, express our preferences and even how to manipulate others. We also learn how to deal with the preferences of others when they differ from ours. If you want to go for a bike ride but I want to play handball, how can we negotiate a solution that keeps us both happy? We are social animals, but still find it hard to put aside our preferred way of doing things.

As teenagers, we gradually move from being members of the family unit to thinking of ourselves as individuals. However, the reality is often that we just shift our focus from fitting in with one group, our family, to trying to fit in with another, our peer group. It might feel like we are exhibiting personal autonomy by wearing tight jeans and sneaking into the pub, but if the main reason we are doing it is because that is what our friends are all doing, how autonomous are we really being?

As we get older we often move from belonging to any group that welcomes us to being more discerning, and start to make choices about which groups we want to be part of. There is a tension between finding our own voice, expressing our views and doing what we want to on one hand, and on the other trying to fit in, be accepted by others, and adopting the uniform and mannerisms of the group.

As adults, we generally become more independent and autonomous. We are more likely to be able to decide, 'Actually, I don't want to fit in with that group. Trying to be like them is not making me happy or content.' Ultimately, we realise we have preferences and choice, but this can be a long and complicated process for humans.

The more autonomy we have, the more important it is for us to keep learning about ourselves: What makes us happy? What makes us unhappy? What groups do we feel comfortable, and uncomfortable, in? Who do we like being around? Who do we find it difficult to relax with? What are the things we will not compromise on? The more we know, the better decisions we can make.

Autonomy at Work

James once had a job stacking bricks onto pallets as they came off a conveyor belt, and was paid by the brick. The faster he stacked, the more he earned. He had a second job as a builder's labourer, where he was paid by the hour and did what he was told. The brick-stacking job was harder, but he enjoyed it much more because he had a financial incentive to work hard and some autonomy over how hard he worked, both absent in his other job.

Many businesses are run with a top-down, command and control structure. The bosses want to exercise quality control over what workers do, and to ensure specific processes and 'best practice' are followed. They might say that they also want workers to have the freedom to exercise initiative and creativity, but often the business is not set up to allow this to happen. This tension between management wanting to control what is being done versus allowing workers to exercise individual initiative and be innovative exists in most workplaces. Teachers all have to teach the same syllabus (control from above) but have some scope to develop their own creative methods to engage students (individual autonomy and initiative).

Some organisations get the balance between control and autonomy right, and trust workers to make the best decisions. Many do not.

When employees have little control over their work, no incentives and are treated as replaceable parts of a machine, they are often unhappy, have poor mental health, low energy and motivation, and there is often low productivity and more mistakes.

Bosses often say they find making lots of decisions difficult and stressful, but it is actually much more stressful for the workers who have no input into those decisions but are greatly affected by them.

The Whitehall studies of the United Kingdom's civil service found that the lower down you were on the seniority ladder, the lower your life expectancy. Workers at lower levels had higher rates of obesity and smoking, higher blood pressure and lower levels of physical activity.

Before these studies, many thought those who had the most decision-making responsibility had the most stressful lives. The Whitehall study suggested the opposite: it was more stressful to take orders than to give them, and that a lack of autonomy, rather than an excess of it, created the worse health outcomes.

We like being in charge. If a CEO makes a bad decision, then the next day they can try again. Those with less autonomy can find it frustrating to watch their bosses exercise power, especially when they think those bosses are doing a poor job. Feeling powerless can lead to stress, frustration, irritation and anxiety.

There are strong human and economic arguments for organisations to decentralise and democratise, and to create teams in which everyone has a role in decision-making. In the past forty years many workplaces have decided that the traditional top-down model is not productive, and have changed. Decision-makers should recognise that for an organisation to be healthy, those who work in it also have to be healthy. That means that those at lower levels have to have some control and be able to make some decisions.

If you have a job where you have little autonomy, what can you do? Ideally, change jobs, but that is not always practical. If it is impossible to quit, there may be a more gradual, strategic way of moving to a job with more autonomy. Can you do further training or study and add to your skill base? Can you set up your own business with the skills that you have? Is there a similar organisation down the road that operates in a different way and gives more freedom to workers?

Can those who lack autonomy at work offset the negative mental health effects of this by doing other activities outside work where they have more control? Can doing sport and exercise, learning a language or gardening, painting or cooking in an autonomous way give us the mental health benefits that we cannot find in a rigid, repetitive job?

The Men's Shed movement is an example: 'I might not be in control of everything in my life, but I am in control in my shed, so that's where I'm going. I've got my toolkit, my woodwork, my car, and I'm in control of them.' You accept that you don't have all the autonomy you want in one area of your life, so you get more in another. It helps to a degree, but work often does take a big chunk of our lives.

Autonomy in Relationships

Through history, in many societies, men have often seen themselves as born to rule, and acted as if the male gender has some sort of intrinsic right to be in charge. Many women have been treated terribly, and lacked the autonomy to fulfil their own needs and desires because of a lack of control over their own reproductive systems, and gender power imbalances in their culture and relationships. As a result, many experienced poor mental health. While much has changed in the past fifty years, many would say that there is still much more to do.

Relationships are about many things, and one of them is power. At the start of a relationship some of us are so eager to keep the other person interested and happy that we give up much of own autonomy, often without realising it. You might hate opera, but when your new partner suggests you get tickets to *La Traviata*, you find yourself enthusiastically agreeing. We can sometimes become so keen to become a part of our new partner's life that we find ourselves ignoring other important activities, and relationships with friends and family.

Any relationship in which you feel pressured to give up things that are important to you, whether it be certain activities, or relationships with family and friends, should raise a red flag. Is that pressure coming from your partner, or from yourself? If it is from your partner, can a frank discussion bring about a change? If not, do you need to have a long think about the pros and cons of being in the relationship?

If the relationship lasts, couples will hopefully learn how to balance their individual autonomy with sharing their lives: separate but together. You might each like different things, and feel secure in doing them, but also share some things and support each other. Your partner goes to the art gallery with friends while you play footy, and then over dinner you share your different experiences.

CHECKLIST

- Having some autonomy and being able to exercise some control over your life is a key pillar of good mental health.
- Being part of groups is also important, so we need to balance our desire for autonomy with compromises needed to fit into groups.
- Having little or no autonomy at work is not good for us.
- If you lack autonomy in a personal relationship, it is worth thinking about what is going on. Can this situation be changed through discussion or not?
- Organisations should devolve power. It is good for the organisation, and for the mental health of workers.
- If you have little or no autonomy in your work, is there something you can do to change that? It might be something quick, or it might take some time.

5

The Importance of Social Connection

Humans need to belong. Humans have always needed tribes.
Today we find tribes in family or clubs or religion. What happens
when we fall out of them?

Richard Paul Evans

'Me' or 'We'?

Much of the focus on mental health and wellbeing in the past few years, and particularly during the enforced isolation of the COVID era, has been on what *individuals* can do to maintain and improve their mental health: meditation, exercise, diet, cognitive strategies, getting counselling. There has not been nearly as much focus on the importance of maintaining and improving the wellbeing and mental health of the groups we belong to, such as our family, household, neighbourhood, workplace, book club and soccer team. Are we missing something?

How Much Do We Need Other People?

Humans are social animals. To be mentally healthy and have a strong sense of wellbeing it is important to be socially connected, and for the groups we are connected to, to be happy and functional.

In days gone by, it was almost impossible for us to avoid being socially connected. We relied on the tribe for protection and support. Three generations often lived together in small communities where tasks, including the raising of children, were shared. There were central meeting places – a clearing, a stream, a town square, a market, a place of worship.

Today, many of us have fewer meaningful social connections than humans have had in the past. If we want to hear human voices, we no longer need to go outside. Instead, television, radio, podcasts and social media provide the illusion of constant company in our lives.

Many live alone. You might be old, with not many surviving friends. You might have a job that does not require much human interaction. You might be young and socially anxious, and avoid interacting with others. You might have just separated, and found that suddenly the social networks you shared with your partner aren't there anymore.

If you do all the things you should to maintain mental health – like daily exercise, being mindful, meditating, doing work that immerses you – but are not connected socially to others, can you still be mentally healthy?

It appears that about five to ten per cent of people can be happy and mentally healthy without social connection. They tend to be people who are quite low on empathy, and don't really understand the experience of others, or how to connect with them. The rest of us really do need to be socially connected to be mentally healthy. If we lack social connection, there is a cost. When we are socially connected, most of us are much happier, have a stronger sense of purpose, and have better physical health and live longer.

Unhappy We = Unhappy Me

We are affected by the mental health of those we are in social groups with. It is hard for people to be very mentally well when those who they are emotionally connected to are suffering, threatened or in trouble. If your child is being bullied at school, your partner is depressed, or your normally friendly boss is anxious and stressed, and taking it out on you, it affects you. It is very difficult for an individual to insulate themselves from the group. If the group is functioning well, we feel better. If it is riddled with conflict and tension, the mental health of everyone in the group is likely to be affected.

When a workplace atmosphere is good, even if you don't love your job it can be a decent place. However, if people are unhappy, complaining, back-stabbing, negative, then even if you like your job, it can be stressful and unpleasant to go to work, and you might find yourself wide awake at 2 am worrying about it.

Today, the average family is smaller than in the past, and people have fewer social networks than they did. We often live further away from our extended family. As a result, workplace-based relationships have become more important in many people's lives. The quality of those relationships matter. During COVID, not being able to connect socially with work colleagues was a major challenge for many.

The quality of our relationships with neighbours is also important. Does your building or street have a good, friendly atmosphere? If there are disputes or people not talking to each other, it affects our mental health.

It is very difficult to be mentally healthy in a toxic situation, whether it be in an intimate relationship, a family or a workplace. Many, perhaps all, families and marriages go through periods of tension and conflict. If those issues are not resolved, we get distressed. For you to be well, your groups needs to be well.

Treating the Individual

Modern psychology focuses on asking if you, the individual, are okay. If you need assistance, it tries to arm you with helpful strategies. It is more focused on 'you' than 'us'. That goes back to Sigmund Freud, who tried to understand the internal plumbing of the mind. This approach was picked up in the USA, and became the bedrock of individual psychology, which has flourished over the last forty years. Individual psychology tries to understand the individual, not the group, or how group dynamics affect the mental health of group members.

If we get depressed and anxious, most of us now know what to do – go to our GP, get a referral to a counsellor, consider medication. But if our family unit becomes dysfunctional, how do we get help, as a group, to fix that?

If you are being bullied by your boss, a Western psychologist would help you understand what was happening in your mind, and give you strategies to reduce your distress. However, they would be unlikely to say, 'Let's get your boss in here and try to work it out.' Individual psychology is not really set up to get people who are having a problem into a room together, or to try and improve the collective mental health of the group.

Ian believes this focus on the individual represents an unfortunate narrowing of the role of psychology. In the past, more group-centred approaches such as relationship and marital therapies were commonly promoted. They still have some place in our system today. For example, it would be unusual for a mental health professional to see a child without also seeing their parents. Generally, however, those group approaches are less commonly known to the wider public.

Having said that, it is true that many workplaces now place a much greater emphasis on creating a healthy culture and ensuring that those who are unhappy within them have a voice to air their concerns.

Showing Distress to the Group

Families tend to naturally focus on the health of their family group, because they care about each other. If one member of a family is unhappy, the others will soon know about it. There is often a ripple affect where, for example, the seventeen-year-old son's unhappiness creates tension between the parents and then unhappiness for the rest of the family. However, his unhappiness will also cause his family members to rally around and try to help him.

One theory is that a purpose of depression and anxiety is to show the group that we need help, and so elicit caring responses from them. By showing distress, whether by being lethargic and withdrawn, or aroused and agitated, we give off clear signs that we need help. There is evidence that this happens in other group animals, particularly monkeys and apes. One ape shows distress, the others notice and try to help.

When we are unwell, we need the group to take care of us. This is true both when we are physically ill, and when we are mentally unhealthy.

Being More Social

Investing more time in social connections can improve our mental health and wellbeing.

What social groups are you a part of? Which ones do you value? Friend groups, work groups, community groups, sporting groups or clubs, churches, bushwalking groups, neighbours, French class, people who volunteer together and take care of other members of the community. A friend of James's was part of a social group made up of people who got to know each other because they caught the same bus each day. They would mix and chat every morning, and sometimes go out to dinner together.

Since the Second World War, the strength of some community groups, including religious groups, has declined. What has replaced them? Netflix, Instagram, phones, online gaming, social media and an increased focus on work. Many of us live in our own individual bubbles, facilitated by modern technology.

Someone told James that the reason you exercise is not to love the half hour you are doing it, but because it benefits you for the other twenty-three-and-a-half hours of the day. Similarly, you don't have to love the actual process of social connection. You might not love walking into a French class where you don't know anyone, but you are doing it because that social connection is good for your mental health and will benefit you for the rest of the day. Just as running is an investment in your physical health, joining the French class is an investment in your mental health.

If you are socially isolated, join a class, or volunteer. It doesn't matter what sort of class – cooking, tennis, art, yoga, whatever. Even if you are not interested in cooking, join anyway, because it is good for your mental health.

If you enroll in a class, or join a book club, a choir or a touch football game, try and get through that difficult initial period when you don't know anyone and feel shy and awkward. Usually, it doesn't last long and you will soon feel like you belong. It's like that first day of school or at a new job.

Some streets, apartment blocks, beaches, parks and suburbs are very community orientated. People talk, look out for each other, kids play up and down the street. However, many streets or suburbs aren't like that. If you live in one of those, maybe you can start the process of change. Pick a date, like Easter, Christmas, Halloween or one of our many long weekends to have a street party. Designate one Saturday or Sunday morning for a neighbourhood BBQ. Have a games afternoon or evening once a month at the local park or beach. A lot of that common street or village stuff helps children develop a social brain, so that they learn to understand how other people, particularly outside the family, think, react and behave. Social activities provide an essential education in how wider social groups can come together to enjoy a shared activity or create a new experience. It's a necessary childhood experience to help develop empathy.

Investing in the Wellbeing of the Group

There is a strong element of self-interest in asking what is best for the group, because our wellbeing is strongly influenced by the overall wellbeing of the group. Doing something for your family, netball team or workmates is an investment, because it benefits the overall mental health of the group, and of every member in the group, including you. Conversely, if your group is unhappy, it is more likely that you will be unhappy.

In tribe and village cultures, the first question is not, 'What will make me happy?' It is, 'What will make *us* happy?' A shared meal, perhaps prepared by several members of the group, can be a daily reminder of the importance of being part of a social group.

Other examples are more complex. Providing safe housing and enabling the creation of a community is much more challenging than just providing individual homes. Smart urban design, public transport and planning of shared spaces promotes both safe and affordable living for a whole community. Delivering such projects, however, often requires us to join community action groups and engage with local councils.

It would benefit our mental health and wellbeing to imitate traditional cultures, including Australian Indigenous culture, by valuing not just individual identity, but also collective identity, and understanding its importance to our emotional wellbeing.

Many of us operate in families or other intimate social groups where the key questions are: What will make *us* safe? What will make *us* financially viable? What keeps a roof over *our* heads? We ask what is best for our family. We should also ask what is best for other groups we are part of. 'What is best for my friend group?' 'What is best for my book club?' 'What is best for everyone at my workplace?'

Many workplaces are based around small teams. When those teams work well, people are happier and more productive, and the organisation is productive. If they don't work well, people become unhappy and less productive. So, even for those who are very individually-focused, it still makes sense to think, 'I want to make my group function well for everyone, because that will ultimately be best for me.'

When we do something nice for someone, we feel good. Many say that they feel better giving, not receiving. If you do little things for others in your apartment block or street, it helps build a sense of community. If you help the old lady who lives alone, and even enlist other neighbours to cook for her once a week, it becomes a shared project, and everyone feels good and talks about it. It adds to the 'mental wealth' of your community.

There aren't as many opportunities in modern Western society to do these sort of activities as there were in tribes and villages, so we need to think about what we can do, and devote some time and effort to it.

Sometimes an event galvanises people. James had a group of friends at university who drifted apart, until recently one of them got very sick. That event brought the group back together. They became involved in each other's lives again in a very positive way, because of this unfortunate event. It would be good if we could work out how to stay in touch and come together without needing a crisis.

What can you do to increase social connection in your community? What can you do to improve the mental health of your workplace? Or of your family or friend group?

Jaky Troy, director of Indigenous Research at the University of Sydney, and one of our guests, has many examples of how First Nations Peoples from around the globe promote social connection, group cohesion and taking care of each other first. The emphasis is on shared dance, trans-generational story-telling and Songlines, in which features and directions of travel are included in a song to be sung and memorised by travellers so they would know the route to their destination. The scaffolding for the whole community is clear. One of her favourite expressions from Australia's Indigenous peoples is 'chuck-a-hand-back' reflecting the obligation to make sure that we always take all of us (not just the most capable) along on the journey of life. Fundamentally, individuals are far less important than the 'mob'. If the mob is not okay, then nobody is okay. She says, 'the Songlines in Australia connect Australia across country. They're like the internet connections. I always think of them as synapses across the country. They connect groups.'

CHECKLIST

- Humans are social animals. Almost all of us need to belong to groups to be mentally healthy.
- Our mental health is partly dependent on the collective mental health of the groups we belong to – family, work, friends, etc. Happy We often means Happy Me.
- What social groups do you belong to? Should you join more, or be more involved with the ones you are in?
- Being socially connected is a form of insurance, because when we are distressed, other people take care of us and help us recover.
- What can you do to improve the collective wellbeing of your groups?

6

How Do Families Work?

The other night I ate at a real nice family restaurant.
Every table had an argument going.

George Carlin

A family is a risky venture, because the greater the love, the greater
the loss . . . That's the trade-off. But I'll take it all.

Brad Pitt

How do families work? How do parents, children, siblings, and partners influence each other's mental health? How do family units navigate conflict and challenge?

The Nuclear Family

For most of us, whether we like it or not, our family has a fundamental influence on the development of our emotional and social life. We are shaped by our early experiences with those we grew up with.

We think of the 'nuclear family' – two parents and a child or children – as normal, but in fact in the history of social animals,

63

and even of humans, the nuclear family is an unusual outlier, most common in the West after the Second World War.

Traditionally, we lived in bigger groups – clans, tribes or villages – where there were fewer fences and doors to retreat behind, and we were much more involved with our extended family and the larger community. Children had regular social interactions with other adult and child members of the group, and formed social relationships with many different people, which helped them develop social skills and empathy.

The nuclear family is smaller, generally more isolated, and less effective at helping children develop social skills and empathy. Children might be social at school, but living in nuclear families rather than larger groups means that we generally have a smaller number of relationships that, as a result, become extremely intense. Because there are fewer relationships, each one – parent/child, parent/parent, sibling/sibling – becomes more significant. If those relationships are going well and people feel secure, that is good, but it is still limited. If one of those relationships starts to deteriorate, there can be a ripple effect that causes problems through the whole family unit.

In the nuclear family, relationships between siblings are important. They are long-term relationships that provide fabulous opportunities for learning and closeness and can be a pathway to later adult relationships. Every day children with siblings are learning about the transactions involved in emotional relationships.

Conflict Within Families

All families have conflict: between parent and child over how much study the child is doing or what time they should get home on Friday night; between siblings over almost anything; between parents over how they should deal with their squabbling children.

If you have an argument with someone at work, tension can linger for days, weeks or even months. Yet families argue and get angry with each other, and then half an hour later sit down and eat lasagne together. We tolerate much more from family members than from friends or workmates. When there is conflict, family members often understand how things went wrong, remember the good things about their sibling, child or parent, and have more empathy for them. 'I kind of know where they're coming from.' (See Chapter 22, 'Forgiveness'.)

Family members realise that they are in it together for the long haul, so everyone has an interest in moving past the conflict and fixing things. They also understand that their own happiness is dependent on the family unit functioning well. That mutual dependency and affection creates a strong interest in moving on from conflict.

People in families say things to each other when they are upset or angry they wouldn't say to others. When a child says something mean and rude (parents – insert your own example here) we simultaneously think, 'That is terrible. How dare you. I'm angry,' and 'They're my kid. I love them. How do we sort out this mess?'

For children and teenagers, trying something new, rebellious and boundary-pushing within their family feels safer than trying it elsewhere, because if it all goes wrong, they know their family will still love them. It is generally safer to tell your mum to 'Get stuffed' than your teacher. There might be consequences, but they won't be suspended from school or labelled a 'problem child'.

Parents continually have to make decisions about how to deal with indiscretions of their children. How seriously should they treat it when one child screams at their sister, or lies, or does not go to school, or smokes or drinks alcohol? Every time a child breaks a rule, parents have to decide whether it is best to take a stand and impose a punishment, or alternatively, let this one slide and maintain family harmony. Where there are two parents, they both have to try to agree on the best course of action. If they can't, then they start arguing, which makes it worse.

Sometimes parents react because they are angry and offended that their rules have been broken. Other times we are able to step back, put aside our disappointment, hurt feelings and pride and simply ask, 'What course of action will be best for my child? What is the best way for our family to collectively deal with this issue?'

Mental Health in Families

How do the adults and children in a household influence each other's mental health? A lot.

Most Western psychology tends to focus on the individual, and rarely assesses the mental health of the group. However, in families, if a child or parent is distressed or upset, there is a ripple effect. The mental health of one member usually affects the mental health of the others.

If a parent has a mental health issue such as anxiety, depression or addiction, it will affect their partner and kids. If an adolescent has mental health issues, it will affect their parents, because they will worry. Sometimes siblings can seem to be the most resilient, and retreat into their own bubble. However, that can lead to other problems. It is much better if, when a problem arises, families work out how to deal with it together.

When a family member develops a mental health issue, you would think that those in the best position to pick it up would be other family members. However, often they are too close and too invested in everything being 'okay', and so they tend to normalise abnormal behaviour. 'Oh, he is just like that sometimes. Lots of kids are.' Kids in distress send out signals, but there needs to be someone to receive those signals. If your child is experiencing difficulties, it is good to discuss it with someone who can bring a more objective perspective – a friend, aunt, uncle, teacher, GP or mental health worker.

Often it takes a teacher to point out to a parent that their child might have a mental health issue such as anxiety, unreasonable anger or very poor attention. Unfortunately, many children who could benefit from specific interventions are in a family where the parents either do not realise something is wrong, or are in denial.

Dealing with Mental Health Issues in Families

When a child is having mental health or other difficulties, parents should step up, engage with the problem, work out the best approach, agree on it, and commit to it. They can explain the plan to their children and let each know what their role is, and try to protect others who may be at risk, such as siblings.

Several types of family therapy put a great deal of emphasis on clarifying roles within families. They emphasise that when a family is experiencing problems, parents should act like parents, and kids should act like kids.

That means parents should not try to become their teenagers' best friend, if that comes at the expense of their parental duties. Parents should be setting boundaries, not thinking, 'If my sixteen-year-old is drinking alcohol, maybe I should have a few drinks with him to try to bond again.'

It also means that parents should not expect their other kids to step in and act like parents to the child experiencing mental health problems. Parents might ask their siblings to cut her some slack because she is going through a tough time, but they should not heap more responsibility than that on younger siblings, or expect them to somehow work out for themselves how to deal with their older sibling's erratic behaviour, especially if it involves violence.

Parents might need to make new rules aimed at trying to insulate siblings, especially younger ones, as much as possible. For example, 'We understand you have lots of problems and often feel bad, and we'll try to help. But one rule is that you can't take it out on your eleven-year-old brother. Ideally don't drink alcohol, but if you do, you cannot involve your fourteen-year-old sister.'

When a child has mental health issues, parents can accept that any plan they make is a work in progress, and not stick dogmatically to it if it is clear it is not working. Everyone is learning how to cope with a new and challenging situation, and the plan might be imperfect. Parents can keep reassessing how it is going, and change it if needed.

What Kids Need Most

Love and Care

When we are young, to develop emotionally the most important things we need are love and care. The degree of positive emotion, warmth, empathy and love between parents and kids is very important. In large families, sometimes kids feel that there is not enough parental love to go around, but they may get it from older siblings, aunts, uncles, grandparents or other close adult friends. When there is a lack of love and care in a family, kids are in trouble. There is a very clear pathway between the depth of love and care children experience, and their success in adult relationships in later life.

It is all about the love. Love is the answer.

If you had a deficit of love and care as a child, what can you do? Sometimes, people blame themselves. 'I must not have deserved love.' We have to try not to do that. Sometimes therapy can help us work out what is going on. Is there something about the way we now behave in relationships that reflects the lack of care when we were younger? If there is, and it is unhelpful or even destructive, can we understand it and start to change it?

Stability

After love and care, the next most important factor for kids is a reasonable degree of stability and predictability. If parents have new partners all the time, if there are lots of comings and goings from the intimate family unit, it can be disorientating. If kids move around a lot, particularly once they reach school age, and especially during the teenage years, it is much harder to form other important peer relationships outside the family unit. Kids that change schools frequently may find it hard to become part of an enduring social group.

If a couple is experiencing problems (and what couple doesn't?) then the fact that they have kids might spur them to try and work through their issues, rather than splitting up. Kids are a strong motivation for couples to get their act together and deal with the sources of their conflict. Often parents are able to work through difficult times and get to the point where they can provide an ongoing, stable and caring relationship for their kids.

However, if the relationship is not working and things do not get better, staying together 'for the sake of the children' is not a good idea. While two parents living together might look stable to the outside world, if there is constant conflict between them, that home environment will not feel stable to the child. This has been extensively studied. It is bad for children to grow up in a home where day after day, month after month, they see their parents arguing, saying nasty things to each other and hurting each other emotionally. If parents know that their relationship is not working, and have tried without success to fix things, they should probably bite the bullet and separate.

When parents separate and ensure that the kids understand that both parents care for them, even though they are no longer all living together, the kids generally have better outcomes than those brought up in homes with two unhappy, constantly arguing parents. The most important factor is not whether or not the parents are together. It is the quality of the care.

If parents separate and re-partner in stable relationships, then their kids have other adult figures in their lives, which can sometimes be positive and beneficial. Parents having new relationships can, of course, be tricky for children to adjust to. New partners of people who have kids from previous relationships should understand and accept that they now have a new relationship not just with their partner, but with their kids as well.

Introducing new partners to older kids is particularly challenging. Younger kids tend to be more accepting of new parenting figures in their lives. Working out when the best time is to introduce a new partner is tricky. It is important to let your kids know just how serious, stable and enduring this new relationship is intended to be. Is it early days? Is it intended to be a permanent rearrangement of the family unit? That sort of openness and honesty helps everyone involved – parent, kids, new partner, ex-partner – get on the same page.

Parents who separate and are not living with their kids can find it extremely distressing and traumatic, especially if there is limited, or even no, access, and ongoing disputes between parents. However, once there are stable arrangements in place, some parents, particularly fathers, say, 'Even though I spend less time with my kids now, I actually have a better relationship with them.'

Teenagers

It is not uncommon for a parent who had a great relationship with their child when they were younger to find things deteriorate during the teenage years. Often the parent has no idea why it is happening. 'When she was ten we had a great relationship. Now we fight all the time.'

The most challenging times for parents can be when their children are in their mid-teens. Teenagers are developing their own individual identity outside the family, but are also still emotionally and physically dependent on their family. They are physically kind of grown up, but not emotionally grown up. It is a testing time for both teenager and parents.

Teenagers want to test boundaries, and their parents are safe people to do that with. To establish their own individual identity outside the family unit, teenagers need to break away emotionally (at least temporarily). Creating some form of disagreement or conflict with parents helps them to do that. It is hard to break away from your family emotionally if you think everything is wonderful. It is much easier if you can find a reason to label your parents unreasonable, stupid and out of touch.

Just because this conflict is playing out does not mean the family is dysfunctional. Conflict between teenagers and parents is normal, and even necessary, for the teenager to move from seeing themselves as a part of a family unit to an individual in their own right.

When there are arguments, they are usually not about whatever is being argued about. Conflict about what time the teenager should get home, the amount of study they are doing, or whether they should emerge from their room to eat meals with the rest of the family, is probably more about power dynamics in the family than the actual issue being argued about. The teenager might seem to be objecting to eating with the family, but perhaps what she is really objecting to is *being told* that she must eat meals with the family. She might not actually want to eat alone in her room, but she does want the autonomy to decide. A lot of parent/teenager conflict is about the teenager wanting to see herself as an individual, rather than as a part of the family unit, and wanting her parents to see her that way too.

For parents, a good strategy is to step back from whatever the argument is about and to try to work out what it is *really* about. If the conflict seems to be about whether the teenager is doing enough study, perhaps what it is *really* about is the teenager feeling suffocated and micro-managed, and wanting her parents to step back and trust her to make her own decisions.

The teenage years are when we move from automatically accepting what our parents and teachers tell us to questioning everything. That is a necessary and important step toward adulthood. If parents continue to guide teenagers through their lives, how will teenagers learn the decision-making skills they will need as adults? During the teenage years, parents should gradually give teens more and more autonomy. Yes, they will make mistakes, but hopefully they will learn from them. Teens can make dumb decisions, so the balance between parents empowering teens to experiment out in the world, and being protective and wanting to keep them safe, is a tricky one. However, if parents try to stay in control of decision-making in this period, there will likely be problems and conflict.

Losing some arguments with your teenager is also a good idea, even when you know you are right. If you are discussing a social or political issue, part of it is about the teenager finding their own identity and learning to articulate their point of view. Even if parents think that their teen's reasoning is flawed or wrong, why not lose the argument now and again to give them some confidence? Or at least draw.

Unfortunately, the parent/child relationship is often damaged during the teen years, and there is frequently conflict over issues that really are not that important. Pick your battles.

Family Influence in Later Life

Are we prisoners of our upbringing? Are the patterns we learn in our early years so deeply embedded in us that we automatically keep repeating them as adults, even when we know they are not in our best interests? Or, can we recognise how our upbringing led to the formation of unhelpful patterns, and then work to change them?

Our podcast guest, journalist and author Rick Morton, talked about a pattern he thinks he got from his upbringing. He felt that his father didn't love him as well as he could have, and from that Rick 'learned' that being open and vulnerable to others can lead to pain. As a result, Rick was unwilling to open up emotionally to others as an adult, which led to unfulfilling relationships. His book *My Year of Living Vulnerably* describes how he became aware of that unhelpful pattern and tried to change it.

Three More Things

1. Every Year They Get Older

When your first child turns eight, you have no experience parenting an eight-year-old. Gradually you work it out, until (hopefully) you kind of know how to do it. But then the kid turns nine. Some of the principles you worked out for parenting an eight-year-old will still be relevant, but others will have to change, because nine-year-olds are different from eight-year-olds. And so on, every year. Parents have to constantly reassess and change what they are doing. That is the challenge, but also the adventure.

2. Kids Have Different Temperaments

Some kids can be told a hundred times to take their plate out to the kitchen after dinner and still not do it, while others only need to be told once. Kids are different, and it makes sense for parents to have different rules and responses that recognise these differences. It is tricky explaining to kids why rules apply differently, but if they are old enough to understand, it is worth sharing your reasons.

3. Showing, Not Telling

When kids are little, holding hands, hugs, and cuddles between parent and child happen all the time, and are immediate and powerful ways to show warm emotion, and to make the child feel loved, safe and secure. It's nice for the parent, too.

As children grow into teenagers, it is easy to lose these forms of non-verbal communication. Most parents have experienced that sinking feeling when their child decides that they no longer want to hold hands as they walk down the street. Maintaining an appropriate physical vocabulary of hugs and cuddles as children get older is a great way to defuse tension, reconnect after an argument, and for parent and child to help ease each other's stress and worries.

Don't worry if your kids say they are too embarrassed to kiss, hug or hold your hand in public anymore. Within the bounds of what is acceptable and appropriate, try and maintain a physically close relationship with your teenage kids. We all need a hug sometimes.

CHECKLIST

- All families have conflict, and most get good at moving on from it quickly.
- The mental health of each family member is likely to influence the mental health of the others, especially if they live together.
- Sometimes parents miss mental issues in their children because they are so invested in everything being okay. They might need an outsider's help.
- When a child has a mental health issue, the family needs to make a plan on how to address it.
- Kids need love and care, and stability.
- Teenager–parent conflict is normal. Arguments about homework, going out, etc. are often really about power dynamics.
- As adults, we can identify the patterns we learned from our family, and if they are unhelpful, we can change.

7

Self-esteem

Low self-esteem is like driving through life with your handbrake on.
Maxwell Maltz

What determines our opinion of ourselves? What is the relationship between our self-esteem and our mental health? How can we build up low self-esteem?

What Is Self-esteem?

Self-esteem is what you think of yourself. Do you think you are a good person? Do you think you are capable of learning new things, and meeting new challenges? Do you think you are a good worker, friend, partner and parent?

Our self-esteem determines how we predict we will go at activities and tasks. If we get invited to a party and have high self-esteem, we might think, 'Great. I'll meet people, make friends and have fun.' If our self-esteem is low, we think, 'I'll be stuck in the corner by myself and everyone will think I'm a loser.' Such predictions can be self-fulfilling.

Some do not have enough self-esteem. They think, 'I'm a hopeless, terrible person.' Others have too much, and think they are wonderful at everything. Many of us have self-esteem that is high in some areas, and low in others. 'I'm good with people, but terrible at sport.'

How Accurate Is Our Self-esteem?

If you wrote down an assessment of your strengths and weaknesses, and what you are good, bad and average at, how closely would it correlate with the way others see you?

We usually have a somewhat better view of ourselves than others do, which is a good thing. Having a robust, optimistic view of our character and capabilities helps us to get through life and take on challenges, which further builds our character, skills and self-esteem. If you have healthy self-esteem and a strong view of your abilities, it can become self-fulfilling. You are willing to have a go at new things. Doing that helps you learn and grow, which further builds your belief in yourself.

Where Does Low Self-esteem Come From?

How does low self-esteem take hold? Messages we are given when young can be significant. If kids are repeatedly told they are useless, stupid or naughty, it can sink in.

Circumstances can lead us to form inaccurate beliefs about ourselves. If an eight-year-old struggles when thrown into a sporting team with bigger, older, more experienced kids, she is more likely to think, 'I'm bad at sport,' than to take account of the factors that put her at a disadvantage. If a six-year-old moves from a school where reading was taught a bit later to a new school where everyone can read, he might think, 'I'm terrible at reading,' rather than realising that the differing teaching schedules of the two schools is responsible. If a child is a little slower than others to understand some concepts in Maths or English, there may be all sorts of reasons, but he might focus on just one: 'I must be dumb.' Once an idea like that takes root, a child can replay self-defeating messages, and try to avoid the activity they think they are bad at. 'I'm so bad at Maths I won't be able to do my homework, so why bother trying?'

This is where positive feedback from the external world is important. Gentle encouragement to persist, praise for even modest achievements and emphasising the importance of persistence over talent can all help those with low self-esteem to push back at the negative messages they send themselves.

Self-esteem and the External World

If your self-esteem is too reliant on the external world, you can get into trouble. Self-esteem that is truly healthy comes more from within. If we rely heavily on external validation – appreciation and praise from others – then when that validation does not come, our self-esteem suffers. We get a work promotion and feel great. We apply for another role, miss out and self-esteem plummets.

The world is inconsistent. It does not always dole out praise when it is deserved. Sometimes we deserve positive feedback and do not get it. Other times we get positive feedback when we know we have not done a particularly great job.

Self-esteem that comes from within is more robust and less vulnerable to fluctuation. Ideally, we should develop our own internal barometer that tells us when we have done something well, and when we have fallen short. Falling short shouldn't cause to us label ourselves as failures. It just means there is more work to do.

James once appeared at a gala comedy night at Sydney Town Hall. Big audience. Huge laughs. He felt great. Then he noticed that *every* comedian was getting huge laughs. They were just a great audience. Getting huge laughs didn't mean he was fantastic. It just meant he was on stage. The following week he performed to seventeen people at a suburban pub. It could have gone either way but he survived and (kind of) won the audience over. He knew that a year earlier he wouldn't have had the skills to do that. Externally, there was much more positive feedback from the Town Hall show, but internally, surviving in front of a smaller, potentially hostile audience was more satisfying.

Building Self-esteem

Having robust self-esteem is important to psychological health and wellbeing. When we find something we enjoy – soccer, cooking, a new job – and persist with it and improve our skills, our self-esteem grows. That gives the confidence to try more new things.

Conversely, low self-esteem has a triple downside. If we think, 'There's no point having a go at tennis, because I'll be terrible at it,' or, 'I'm not going to the party because I'll have a bad time,' then:
- We miss out on what might have been an enjoyable experience,
- We miss out on building skills at tennis or socialising, and,
- We feel bad that we didn't have a go, which may further undermine our self-esteem. 'I'm so hopeless I couldn't even go to a party.'

Often those with low self-esteem overstate the role of talent and underplay the role of practice and persistence. 'There's no way I could learn to play tennis. I have zero sporting ability.' That is such an absolute, and almost always incorrect, statement. Some are not as naturally sporty as others, but anyone can learn to hit a tennis ball. If you have less natural ability it might take longer, but it can be done, and the process of slowly making progress builds self-esteem.

Being able to give a speech, cook a soufflé or build a chair is not determined by whether you were born with some innate speech-making, soufflé-cooking or chair-building ability. It is about trying, failing, trying again, failing again, learning and persisting. Through persistence we improve our skills, which reinforces our belief that we are capable of doing things, which builds our self-esteem. That self-esteem then makes us more confident to try the next new thing.

The danger is that those with low self-esteem let their (irrational) belief that 'I'd be hopeless at that' stop them from even having a go, which then supports their (incorrect) belief that they are incapable, and reinforces their low self-esteem. An initial tentativeness at sport, perhaps at school, can grow into a belief that you are not sporty, which can cause you to deliberately avoid sport, which cements the belief that you are hopeless at it. To reverse this cycle, find a sporting activity you enjoy, accept that it will take time to learn, persist, don't put pressure on yourself to be as good as everyone else, and view 'failure' as part of the learning process, not as a judgement that you are hopeless.

If you tell yourself that you must be a boring person because the last time you went to a party, no-one wanted to talk to you, then even if you muster up the courage to go to another party, you will probably walk in having already labelled yourself as unworthy of attention. That will lead you to stand awkwardly in a corner looking nervous and uneasy, which will make it harder to meet people, which will strengthen your 'I'm boring and bad at parties' belief.

To break the cycle, try to find someone, anyone, to talk to. Maybe someone else who looks uneasy. Maybe you can offer to walk around with food or drink to break the ice. Once you have one even mildly interesting conversation, you can start to change the narrative. 'I wasn't the life of the party, but I had two conversations, one of which was quite interesting. I might be quiet, but I'm a good listener, and people appreciate that. Maybe I'm not a loser.' Next time you go to a party this is the message you have in your mind, rather than the earlier, more negative one. This is 'cognitive restructuring', and it can be very effective. Take unhelpful thoughts and change them into more helpful ones. Just because you have a thought that you are incapable or hopeless does not mean it is true. Thoughts can be right or wrong. James used to have a thought that the capital of Switzerland was Zurich.

Sometimes we blame ourselves, when really we are just in the wrong situation. If you are in a friend group with people who are very different from you and have different values, you might think, 'What's wrong with me? Why don't I fit in?' Nothing is wrong with you. You just haven't found a group in which you feel comfortable yet. Keep looking. Find your people.

One way to build and maintain self-esteem is to find some things that you are quite good at, and do them regularly. This gives us a feeling of satisfaction and achievement, which is good for mental health and wellbeing. It may also elicit positive feedback from others.

So, what are you quite good at? Something work-related? A hobby like gardening, cooking, running or building model planes? Being a good parent, friend or sibling? Whatever it is, keep doing it.

We all have strengths and weaknesses, and often our self-esteem is more invested in our strengths. If someone told James or Ian they were hopeless at fixing things around the house, they would heartily agree. If they were told this book or their podcast was crap, it would cut deeper.

Failure

'Failure is simply the opportunity to begin again, this time more intelligently,' said Henry Ford. 'Success consists of going from failure to failure without loss of enthusiasm,' is how Winston Churchill put it.

Failing does not mean you are incapable of doing something, or that you are not a worthwhile person. It just means there is more work to do.

Sometimes, failure is deserved. Other times it is not. When we receive criticism or negative feedback, our first reaction is often to get defensive. 'What would those idiots know? How can they not understand my genius?' Despite our bravado, deep down our self-esteem might be wounded. 'Maybe I'm not as good as I thought I was.' Most of us suffer from 'imposter syndrome' at one time or another. Often it helps to let a bit of time pass, and then try to look dispassionately at the negative feedback. Were there some points that, on reflection, have some merit? What can we learn, so we can do it better next time?

When Ian writes an article that gets published in a well-regarded journal, he feels good. External validation. Then he writes what he thinks is an even better article, and it doesn't get published. Of course he is disappointed, but tries to keep it in perspective. It is an opportunity for him to have a fresh look at the article. Was it as good as he thought it was? Could it have been better? Was he just unlucky? There are a lot of articles competing to be published in scholarly journals, and only so many slots. Perhaps the editor was looking for something different, and this time his article did not quite fit the bill.

If we honestly think criticism is completely wrong and unfair, then we can disregard it and it should not damage our self-esteem. Many people operate under the irrational assumption that all the feedback we receive should be fair. In reality, sometimes life is fair, other times it is not. Sometimes criticism is fair, justified and useful. Other times it is not. Often it is somewhere in between.

Failure, knockbacks and criticism are tough to take, but when we think negative feedback is valid, we can take it on board. If we stick at something long enough, the odds are that, sooner or later, rewards will flow. It can take persistence and even endurance, but that builds resilience and a robust self-esteem capable of learning, recovering from adversity, and bouncing back. We all have abilities and skills, even if the world doesn't always recognise them.

Building Self-esteem in Children and Teenagers

With kids, there is a knock-on effect. Self-esteem gained from one activity can then flow onto others, even if they are quite different. 'I did a good drawing. Maybe I'll be good at riding a bike, too.'

While getting positive feedback helps, automatically praising *everything* your child does can lead to your praise being devalued. 'Dad told me my drawing is great, but he says I'm also great at soccer, and I know that's not true.'

For young people to build self-esteem and a belief that they can do things, it is great if they have the opportunity and feel free to have a go at anything. That way, they can discover the areas where they might have more ability, and if they then persist, can develop a genuine sense of competence – even mastery.

Self-esteem can get shaky in the teenage years as we struggle to find our place. The outside world can become more critical, and at times, quite cruel. Not everyone thinks we are good-looking, smart and funny. Teenagers might think, 'All that stuff my parents told me about me being good at things isn't true.'

Persistence in developing skills at schoolwork, sport, music, cooking and other activities and interests in those years is important.

If you fail a Maths test or get excluded from your friendship group, it is good to know that there is something else you are good at.

Mentoring and support for teenagers from someone – an aunt, uncle, footy coach, teacher, family friend, even another kid – who can provide positive but realistic feedback and help teenagers find activities that suit their attributes, can be very helpful. For example, if someone is very sensitive, they might be prompted toward expressing themselves in poetry, literature, art, music or drama. If a teenager is struggling, a mentor can encourage and support the teen to keep looking and experimenting until they find the right path.

Too Much Self-esteem

Some people seem to think they are great at everything, and feel the need to constantly brag about their achievements. They may appear to have too much self-esteem, but it is often a sign of insecurity. Their need for unending external reinforcement is not healthy or robust. This self-esteem is brittle and unable to cope with reality. 'If I keep telling people how good I am, maybe that will make it true. It will help me to drown out the little voice inside saying that I'm no good.'

Those with rather brittle egos can come crashing down, often after an adverse event, like a partner leaving or losing a job. The balloon has been pricked and their self-confident boasting is revealed to be a façade.

Such times are an opportunity for reflection – 'Who am I? How do I act? What am I really good at? What am I not so good at?' Reflection can be followed by insight, and then change.

Others who have this need to keep telling people how great they are grow out of it as they get older and wiser. When young, as we build an identity, we might feel the need to puff up our achievements. As we get older, hopefully we develop a more realistic confidence in our abilities born of experience.

CHECKLIST

- Self-esteem is what we think of ourselves.
- If our self-esteem is dependent upon external praise, it is fragile.
- We can build self-esteem by finding things we enjoy, persisting and getting better at them.
- Practice is more important than talent.
- Failure doesn't mean *you* are a failure. It just means there is more work to do.
- Those who boast may sound like they have an excess of self-esteem, but they are often insecure.

8

The Subconscious and Instinct

I don't trust him. Something about Oliver is off.

The O.C.

What is the subconscious? What is happening in your mind, apart from the thoughts and feelings you are aware of? What is instinct? Should we trust our instincts?

What is the Subconscious?

Our subconscious is a collection of automatic brain processes that occur without conscious thought or effort. Breathing is an obvious one. We don't direct ourselves to breathe. We just breathe. Other built-in systems keep our blood pumping, our eyes blinking and our sleep–wake cycle operating. We do not consciously decide to release melatonin in the evening to help us sleep. It happens automatically.

Our subconscious is constantly capturing information about our environment through our five senses, and using that information to influence our decision-making and behaviour. While the real work of keeping us alive and moving goes on beneath the surface, our conscious mind is left free to talk, work and cook lasagna.

Physical Actions

Walking down stairs might look easy, but there is a lot going on: the use of muscles, movement, weight transfer and balance. We learned how to do it when we were young. Through experience, it became encoded in our central nervous system, until we no longer had to consciously think about it.

When we move from walking to running, we are completely unaware that if we do not lean further forward, we will fall backwards. This, too, has been learned, is encoded into our subconscious and happens automatically.

Tying a shoelace is a complex process that requires calculation and precise movement. Most of us couldn't describe how we do it. All we can do is *show* someone. When we see a puddle ahead on a path, we find our stride automatically adjusting, shortening or lengthening, throwing in a little half step or shuffle so that as we get to the puddle, our foot comes down exactly at its edge, allowing us to step over it. How does that happen without our conscious mind having anything to do with it?

To *consciously* get your foot to land exactly at the edge of a puddle, you would have to calculate the length of your stride, the constantly decreasing distance between you and the puddle, and then work out the exact combination of longer and shorter steps that will bring you to the edge. You would need a tape measure, a calculator, pen and paper, a few minutes and maybe a friend who is good at maths and physics. Unconsciously, we do it instantly.

For this and many other complex motor movements, the brain builds up very specific circuits between the sensory information coming in, the coordinating centres, and the instructions going out to the parts of the body that make all the fine adjustments required to make it work smoothly. Importantly, the thinking part of the brain doesn't need to get involved. These subconscious paths are fast and accurate.

When a magpie swoops us, before we have time to think, we react and duck away. For these very fast reflex responses, the brain has direct circuits that go straight from the visual (or other sensory) input to the motor commands, and they get us out of the way. Once we are safe, we engage the thinking brain and our thoughts try to work out what happened.

'I Just Don't Trust that Guy'

Sometimes we meet someone and get a feeling that we shouldn't trust them, but cannot work out why. It is just a feeling. We have come to a conclusion, but don't know how we got there. Is it rational? Or is it prejudice?

Our minds contain an ever-expanding memory bank of faces, expressions, tones of voice, phrases, hand gestures and patterns of speech that we have seen over the years. We even analyse how much eye contact people make. From experience, we learn that some actions are associated with particular characteristics. For example, a lack of eye contact may indicate someone is trying to hide something, or that they are disinterested, or shy, or embarrassed, or just that they are thinking deeply or trying to remember something.

Whenever we meet someone, we analyse what they say, how they say it, and their body language and facial expressions. Our brain compares all this data with past experiences, and then spits out a conclusion, like:
- 'He is friendly and open. Keep talking to him,' or
- 'He is not being genuine. Don't trust him. Move away.'

Often these sorts of judgements are useful and reliable. However, our subconscious minds can also carry unjustified or irrational prejudices and biases that can lead to inaccurate and unfair judgements of others.

Some biases are built on experience. If we once had a bad experience with someone who had a moustache, we might develop an in-built bias against anyone who has one. When we meet someone with a moustache, our biased subconscious gives us that 'There's something about this guy I don't trust,' feeling.

Other biases are built-in and instinctual in origin, and may be reinforced by experiences. We tend to trust those who look and sound like us, and like those who protected us as we grew up. By contrast, we tend to be less trusting of those who look, sound and behave differently, because our subconscious sees them as less familiar and, hence, less predictable.

We are also more trusting of those who have voices, faces and speech patterns that we are familiar with and have previously trusted. However, just because someone looks and speaks a bit like your favourite aunt does not mean they are more likely to be more trustworthy than someone who looks and sounds less familiar.

So, if you meet someone and get a feeling that you should not trust them, how do you work out if your subconscious has come to that conclusion based on rational evidence from past experience, or from irrational bias and prejudice? Should you trust your gut or not?

Being aware of our in-built biases against those who look and sound different can help, as can a diversity of experiences. Spending time with lots of different people who speak, act and express their emotions in very different ways helps us to develop a more rational, less prejudiced view of the world.

If you meet someone and get a feeling that you should not trust them, investigate the feeling. The more different the person is to you – in race, age, gender, accent and so on – the more likely there is some unconscious bias involved.

Shortcuts

Acquiring a new skill, whether it be kicking a ball or playing guitar, requires conscious effort. When learning to type, we start slowly and clumsily. 'Where's the "G"?' Through experience and repetition, our movements gradually become encoded in our brain until we are able to stop thinking and type almost automatically. Our subconscious does the work, and our fingers fly effortlessly across the keyboard.

When learning to drive, gradually our movements become more automated. We learn which events present a risk of danger and require action (a cyclist veering in and out of the traffic lane), and which events don't (a cyclist staying in the bike lane).

Riding a bike, shaving, playing tennis, cutting vegetables, cleaning teeth, buttoning a shirt, juggling and using a knife and fork are other physical skills that get encoded into our brain through learning and repetition.

We encode non-physical skills too, like when we learn a new language, or how to solve algebra. At first we struggle with every French word. Eventually, they come automatically. We also encode some interpersonal skills. The first time we have to have a difficult conversation with someone at work is, well, difficult. We spend hours agonising and preparing. After we have had a few such conversations, we have worked out what works and what doesn't, we need less time to prepare, and we do a much better job. At work, we learn the best way to get things done, and how to most efficiently prioritise tasks. These shortcuts also get encoded.

When learning to play piano, drive a car, cook pancakes or efficiently do a new job, we have all felt clumsy and frustrated.

'I'll never get it.' However, beneath the surface, slowly but surely, our subconscious is encoding the information and skills we need. Then, one day, we *can* do it and the idea that we ever couldn't seems ridiculous.

Instinct

When people say 'instinct', they are often referring to those subconscious conclusions we have discussed above. Instincts are actually things we are born with. When a baby is hungry, she has an instinct to cry. That instinct helps her survive by attracting attention and signalling she wants something.

Babies' instincts draw them towards food, comfort, shelter, warmth and protection. Through childhood and adolescence, different instincts push us in different ways. Young children have built-in separation anxiety. They become distressed when separated from those who normally protect them from a dangerous world. As we get older, we are drawn to form close bonds with others, which prompts us to learn how to communicate, listen and learn to make facial expressions that create closeness, like smiling. Then, as teenagers, our developing sense of competency in the world and desire to experience new things pushes us to go out and explore, look for excitement and novelty, and take risks. During the teenage years (and after) this instinct to explore can override our other instinct to stay close to those who we feel safe with.

Instincts also grow out of our relationship with the environment. We are born with instinctual fears of things that are dangerous, such as heights, snakes and spiders. When we encounter them, we have the physiological response of arousal – our heart rate rises, we breathe quicker and sweat.

Sometimes that response is sensible. When we see a snake in the bush, that physiological arousal helps us to take action swiftly and move quickly away from it. However, if we see a snake at the zoo behind a glass wall, we know we are not in danger, but that physiological arousal might still come. Our deep-seated instinctual fear of snakes is coming up against our rational knowledge that we are safe. If you abseil down a cliff in a secure harness, held by two ropes, rationally you know you are safe. Nonetheless you are terrified. While walking across a high, narrow pedestrian bridge, our instinct says, 'Being up this high is dangerous,' while rationality argues back – 'Hundreds of people walk across this bridge every day. I'm safe.' They are fighting. Sometimes rationality wins, other times instinct.

Those who have a less anxious disposition and a lower general level of arousal are more likely to be able to overcome their fearful instincts. Those with a more anxious disposition and a higher level of arousal find it harder.

Exposure can help us overcome our instinctual fears. As we do more abseiling, the fear recedes, and we learn to enjoy the adrenaline rush. We discover an activity that feels dangerous can actually be done safely, and our fear is repackaged as thrill.

We call a fear of spiders 'arachnophobia' as if it is a medical condition, but there is nothing unusual about being afraid of spiders. Some can kill us, so being afraid of them is sensible. In fact, the reason we are alive is that many of our ancestors were afraid of spiders, snakes, heights and wild animals, and so kept away from them. We are more descended from those cautious ones than from the reckless ones, who often died young.

Who Are We Attracted To?

Why do we find some people attractive and not others? Sexual attraction is complex. You might have noticed.

Some instinctual and subconscious factors prompt us to be attracted to those we share similarities with. People with similar temperaments and emotional characteristics are often attracted to each other, partly because we see those who are similar to us as being more predictable and less anxiety-provoking than those who are different to us. While we *might* be conscious of the conclusion we draw ('I like this person because they are similar to me') our *reasons* for drawing that conclusion (we feel safer with those similar to us, as they are less likely to act in ways we are not comfortable with) are subconscious and instinctual.

So, in this modern, image-obsessed Instagram age, it is nice to know that we are *not* that shallow. We look at much more than a person's physical attractiveness. If we are going to live with someone, it makes sense to find someone who is similar to us in how they think, react emotionally and look at the world. That seems more likely to create a harmonious and sustainable bond than pairing up with someone who thinks and feels in a very different way to us.

On the other hand, in terms of species survival, diversity is also important. Historically, to survive, groups of humans have required lots of different attributes: physical strength, dexterity, intelligence, creativity, logical planning, caution, a capacity for risk-taking and novelty, and many more. No-one possesses them all, so ensuring we meet and mate with those who have different attributes that complement our own has been important. This has also meant that collectively we have avoided in-breeding, which has also been good for our species.

So, there exists a tension between the safety instinct, to mate with someone who is similar to you, and the instinct to ensure the species is strong through diverse mating.

Big Decisions

People often use rational thinking to arrive at what turns out to be to a bad decision. Perhaps they start with a flawed assumption and from that, build up a rational argument. Someone who got good results in year 12 might start with the assumption that they shouldn't 'waste their mark', and from that build up an argument that they should study medicine. Ten years later they are an unhappy doctor who wished they had become a teacher. Perhaps at the time they sensed that their decision to do medicine didn't quite feel right, but they let the logic of their argument take precedence over that feeling.

Sometimes people realise they feel more comfortable and confident in a particular job, despite there being a strong logical case for change, like a pay rise or the extra status that comes with a promotion. They might not be able to articulate their reasons for resisting what looks like a very attractive offer, but their reluctance is often based on their subconscious knowledge of their own characteristics and of how they act and react in the world.

On the other hand, some instinctual feelings push us to prioritise safety, security and maintaining the status quo over change, adventure and risk. Our instinct or gut feeling can sometimes be over-protective and push us to be fearful of new experiences.

If you are trying to make a big decision, and get some sort of gut feeling, it might be for a good reason – or it might not be. You should at least investigate the feeling, and try to work out where it is coming from. If you have a gut feeling about a decision, the way to investigate how much you should rely on it is to ask if the gut feeling is being driven by:

1. Fear of the unknown
2. Past bad experiences that may no longer be relevant
3. A reluctance to engage with the more rational pros and cons associated with the decision.

CHECKLIST

- Our subconscious is a set of automatic brain processes that we are unaware of that keep us sleeping and breathing, and our blood pumping, and much more.
- Physical actions like walking downstairs and cleaning our teeth can get encoded into our subconscious.
- Our subconscious builds up a memory bank of how people speak and act, and uses it to draw conclusions about people we interact with.
- Sometimes those conclusions are reliable; other times they may be a result of in-built biases.
- Instincts are in-built and throughout life push us in different ways – often towards safety, and away from spiders.
- Sometimes our rational knowledge that we are safe comes up against an instinctual fear. If rationality wins, we do the bungy jump. If instinct wins, we don't.
- If you have an instinct about something, it may be right or wrong. Try to work out what the instinct means.

PART 2

WHEN THINGS GO WRONG

9

Anxiety

When I look back on all these worries, I remember the story of the old man who said on his deathbed that he had had a lot of trouble in his life, most of which had never happened.

Winston Churchill

Anxiety's like a rocking chair. It gives you something to do, but it doesn't get you very far.

Jodi Picoult, *Sing You Home*

Worry often gives a small thing a big shadow.

Swedish proverb

Anxiety is essential. It prompts us to lock the front door, prepare for job interviews and look out for snakes. It drives us to our peak performance at work, home and on the sporting field. Turning adrenaline on through anxiety is an essential bit of normal physiology. It's the rocket fuel of life.

However, too much anxiety can paralyse us. Repetitive thoughts can run around our brain creating distress and preventing us from enjoying life. Anxiety can lead us to avoid new challenges that may be exciting and rewarding. It can freeze us in fear when we need to act, and inhibit our ability to think clearly.

How do we know when we are experiencing more than a normal amount of anxiety? What can we do when anxiety gets out of control?

Why Do We Get Anxious?

Anxiety is built in. If you don't get anxious at the right time, you'll die. If a car is about to run you over, it is anxiety (an emotion) and adrenaline (the fuel) that makes you move. If you have an exam coming up, anxiety motivates you to study.

Anxiety leads to physical arousal. Your pulse rate goes up, adrenaline surges and your breathing quickens, all of which help you to focus on a potential threat. That arousal is the precursor to one of two effective actions – to stand and fight, or run. Our level of arousal is usually proportionate to the size of the risk. The closer the bus, the more arousal, the faster the heart rate, and the quicker we move.

How We Assess Risk and Consequence

Ideally, we would all assess risk, and the consequence of our actions, accurately and dispassionately. However, we all appraise situations differently and come to different conclusions about what is at stake. It is that subjective assessment of risk, of the likely consequences, that affects our degree of arousal and anxiety. If you are scared of snakes, you will probably assess the risk of being bitten by one on a bushwalk as higher than it is. If you are scared of flying, you will perceive the risk of the plane crashing as higher than others on board.

When we accurately assess risk or consequence, we react more appropriately. An exam worth five per cent of our yearly mark poses a lesser threat of disaster than one worth seventy-five per cent. It is rational to have higher arousal and anxiety for the exam worth seventy-five per cent. If you have an upcoming exam worth five per cent and think, 'My whole career depends on this,' you have assessed the risk incorrectly. It is catastrophic thinking – an unwarranted conclusion that leads to bad choices and a more miserable existence.

Those who suffer severe anxiety often perceive risks that others don't even consider. 'What if I go for a swim and get attacked by a shark? What if a murderer breaks into my house? What if I have a panic attack in Woolworths?' People with severe anxiety also typically overestimate the magnitude of consequences. 'If I lose my job, I'll never get another one.'

In many situations people have different levels of arousal and anxiety. When an exam is four weeks away, some will start to work steadily. Others will delay. Some will try to study, but whenever they start, will anxiously think about the possibility of failing, and how terrible that would be. The anxiety they feel every time they sit down to work may lead them to avoid their desk completely.

Anxiety Set Points

We all have our own built-in set points for anxiety. Some of us are naturally easy-going, others are more uptight. Those temperaments are set by both genetics and our past experiences.

Those with higher set points are more likely to think ahead, worry about what can go wrong, and plan. When things do go wrong they are likely to feel more stressed and, if they cannot fix things, distressed.

People with higher set points are valuable. They have been critical to our survival as a species. They anticipate what can go wrong, and plan to prevent it happening. They are sensitive and more considerate about the consequences of ill-considered actions on others.

Those who have a lower set point are less anxious, and take life more as it comes. People with low set points are great to have in some real-life crises but they can also be annoying to live with, as they may appear not to be too concerned with the possible outcomes of various dangerous actions.

When Does Anxiety Become a Mental Health Issue?

If some degree of anxiety is normal and productive, how do we know when it has become a mental health issue? There are three big signs:

- When we attach disproportionate levels of worry to the possibility of events whose true risk is low.
- When we assume disproportionate, or catastrophic, consequences will occur if an averse event happens. 'If I lose this job, my career will be over.'
- When we often experience severe physical symptoms of arousal and anxiety: a racing heart, shallow rapid breathing, profuse sweating. There might also be muscle tension, headaches, back and neck aches. The body is tight. These symptoms use up lots of energy, creating fatigue, even exhaustion.

When someone is in an ongoing stressful situation – financial problems, relationship issues, an upcoming court case – their general level of arousal rises. You might find yourself reacting strongly to little things, like traffic jams, neighbours' noise or your child not eating their vegetables – things that have nothing to do with your underlying problem. It is chronic stress, and it can have the same effect as sleep deprivation. You are on edge, constantly on alert, having trouble sleeping, anxious and unwell. It is like having a fever rather than a normal temperature.

That kind of chronic, ongoing anxiety is accompanied by intrusive, unwelcome, distressing and repetitive thoughts. You just can't stop thinking about the things you are worrying about, which are often things that matter, and which are not easily solved. You find yourself continually going back over every detail, and still cannot find a solution.

Panic Attacks

When those who have a higher anxiety set point go through something that further increases their anxiety level they might start having panic attacks. If you think panic is all in the mind – forget it! There are physical signs: it can become hard to breathe, your pulse pounds, heart races, you sweat profusely. You can feel as if you are about to faint, be physically overwhelmed, not be able to think straight, and have no idea what to do.

During a panic attack, your body functions have all moved their settings to high alert, adrenaline has gone through the roof, and your mind can't make sense of it. Many assume that something very physically bad is about to happen, like a heart attack or a stroke, and they urgently need medical help. While some medical people have been heard to say 'it's just a panic attack', research that Ian participated in has measured how much adrenaline gets released directly to the heart. In some people, it's extremely high. It's real, serious and terrifying.

Typically, people have their first panic attack in a supermarket, a shopping mall, or a cinema. Somewhere where you are a bit disorientated and cannot easily find your way out, often with lots of other people around and no windows, or view of the outside world. There is a sense of an impending disaster or threat, and a lack of access to any of the usual or familiar things that would offset that anxiety at home or in some other smaller, more intimate setting.

When the attack ends, most people assume the episode happened *because* they were in a supermarket or a mall, and that it is supermarkets or malls that trigger their anxiety, and that therefore they should avoid them. In fact, retail is not the cause.

The real cause is within the person – their set point was already very high, and the place where it went right off was incidental. Just the straw that broke the camel's back. The underlying problem – their deteriorating marriage, difficult work situation, chronic financial difficulties, or excessive alcohol use – has elevated their already high anxiety levels, and they just happened to be in a supermarket or a mall when they were overwhelmed. Sometimes it's other things, like a very hot and humid day, a physical illness (like a virus) at the same time or a new medication that sets it off.

Nervous Breakdowns

If waves of extreme anxiety are washing over someone, eventually they may not be able to cope and might have what used to be called a 'nervous breakdown', where the brain (which controls the whole of the nervous system that regulates all your body functions, movements, speech, feelings and thoughts) just can't keep it all going. A collapse into an almost child-like state can follow. Completely exhausted. Can't make even simple decisions. Back to bed and withdrawn from the world.

At that point, your brain has stopped processing information from the outside world (like time of day, ordinary schedules, and the need to eat or move or respond to others) and is entirely internally focused and consumed by its own distress. A retreat into that internal world is designed to support survival, to stop engaging in things that are only making matters worse. In a good way, it invites others who are still functioning normally to take control of the situation and provide care and support.

Treating Anxiety

Dealing with Anxious Thoughts

If you are in the ocean and you see a fin, it's rational to be anxious about a shark attack. You need to be aroused by anxiety to swim for shore, fast. However, if you don't see a fin, it's irrational to be overly anxious, because the risk is incredibly low. To never swim because sharks live in the ocean, or to never drive a car because sometimes they crash, is not a reasonable justification.

While anxious thoughts may have their basis in some true statement, they are often irrational. We can overestimate both the risk of an event happening, and the scale of the consequence if it *does* happen, and not realise we are being irrational. For example, we think our fear of the plane crashing is entirely reasonable, or that if our marriage ends we'll never have another relationship. When experiencing chronic anxiety we fail to identify pessimistic, anxious thoughts as being such. We think they are normal, reasonable and well-justified thoughts.

Cognitive therapy encourages us to take those anxious thoughts out, study them, and have a good, hard look at them. Just how reasonable are they? Often people are unaware that they are operating under various dubious or overly restrictive assumptions. Many chronically anxious people are too scared to even begin this challenging process on their own.

A) Over-estimating the *risk* of an event occurring

If you have trouble working out if your worries are rational or irrational, try sharing them with someone you trust, and get their opinion. It is often helpful to collect and write down arguments and evidence that support the more rational, less anxious view. For example, you can find out how many beaches there are in Australia, how many people go to the beach, and the very small number of shark attacks there are each year. You might find that the beach you swim at last had a shark attack eighty-six years ago, and that over a million people have swum there since. Next time the irrational, anxious thought comes, you can start to push back at it with a more rational argument. And try to get in the water. Each time you do, the anxiety about doing it again may reduce. When the anxiety starts to settle, the pleasure can begin.

B) Over-estimating the consequence of an event occurring – catastrophising

James has an irrational fear of huntsman spiders, even though they are not dangerous to people. Whenever he sees one, he is terrified, unable to act and has to beg his teenage daughters to save him. They shrug their shoulders, get the huntsman into a Tupperware container and put it outside as James cowers in the corner.

What consequence is he scared of? Huntsman run away from people. Yes, they can bite, and that might hurt a bit, but they are not poisonous. He is catastrophising the consequence from 'slightly unpleasant' to 'disaster'.

Sometimes people get very anxious if they are running late. If you are late for a meeting, or miss a plane, does it really matter? What is the consequence? Write down what you think will happen if you are late for a meeting. Maybe you fear the person you are meeting will think you are a bad person, and that you don't respect them, and the relationship will be damaged. Elaborating on the feared consequences can reveal common themes and shed light on the deeper or distorted thinking that is driving the anxiety.

The active process of confronting a feared consequence is empowering. This is called the 'what if?' strategy. 'What if' the thing I'm anxious about actually happens? Can I cope? 'If I miss the train, does it matter that much? I can wait for the next one. I'll be late, but that's not disastrous.' 'If I don't get that job, does that really mean I won't get other work?'

This strategy can work in real time and help you reduce your heart rate, breathe more slowly and cope better. Ian often uses the 'what if?' strategy when he feels stressed to get things back in perspective.

Anxious thought patterns can become templates that people drag around with them and attach to all sorts of situations. Most people don't realise the extent to which both their thoughts and behaviours are driven by those patterns. The actual situation is almost irrelevant. It's the way we appraise situations that really matters.

Many people with chronic anxiety have selective memories. They count as evidence only the times bad things happened. They never count the times nothing bad happened (the hundreds of times they went swimming and never saw a shark, the thousands of car trips with no accidents, the countless times they caught the train on time). It can be helpful to collect evidence that the pessimistic predictions you've made don't often come true.

C) Distraction in thought and action

Some find the strategy of collecting evidence and arguing back against anxious thoughts effective. Others, however, find continually having internal arguments that go back and forth, and around and around, to be exhausting. 'A shark will attack me.' 'No, the risk is tiny because . . .' 'But there's still a risk.' 'Okay, but that risk is less than driving to work . . .' 'But you can't prove to me it won't happen,' etc.

An alternative strategy to arguing back at your anxious thought, is to simply move on. Let the anxious thoughts float past without engaging with them. Anxious thoughts are only powerful when linked with strong emotions. Thoughts on their own aren't that powerful. If we can resist the temptation to engage with them, they might just wither away.

When an anxious thought comes, try not to give it any attention, because the more attention (and emotion) you give it, the bigger it will get and the more of your brain space it will occupy. Instead, distract yourself. Take your mind somewhere else. Think about something else or, better still, do an activity that requires your attention. Cook, exercise, play piano or work. If you starve anxious thoughts of attention, they will often pass.

Initially, this is difficult because the anxious mind desperately wants to engage with the anxious thoughts. We get anxious because we perceive a threat, and we want to think about the threat so we are prepared to deal with it. It is like knowing there is a tiger behind you but being told not to turn around and look at it.

However, if you persevere, you might be able to achieve a key change – uncoupling the anxious thought from the physical and emotional arousal, so that the thoughts no longer distress you in quite the same way. The anxious thoughts come, and then they go. They are just thoughts. No racing heart, no shortness of breath, no sweating profusely, no panic attack!

Dealing with the Physicality of Anxiety

The other part of reducing anxiety is to reduce your background level of arousal. Turning the set point down to a lower resting level. When we deal with a lot of anxiety, it's as if we are heating up. Our heart beats faster, we breathe more shallowly and faster, we sweat, we twitch. We are constantly on alert. Tiny things can trigger us.

If you are scared of taking a flight in a week, you might be triggered whenever you hear a plane overhead, or when you see an airport in a movie. All the energy we expend on this constant vigilance leaves us exhausted. We need to turn the temperature down.

Some strategies that can help are:
- Mindfulness. Anxiety is all about what will happen in the future. Mindfulness is about focusing on (and enjoying) the present moment.
- Meditation.
- Slow breathing exercises.
- Progressive muscle relaxation, where you repeatedly tense different groups of muscles, and then relax them. The process is repeated in a calm and organised progression.
- Physical exercise.
- Walking – and if you find anxious thoughts come while walking, listen to music or a podcast.

When James started doing stand-up comedy, he was terrified. He noticed his physical symptoms – fidgeting, talking and walking fast, breathing shallowly – so before going on, he tried to control them. Instead of pacing, he sat still. When he got up he would walk slowly and casually, he spoke slowly and tried to focus on the present, not what would happen when he stepped on stage. People would say 'How come you're not nervous?' He *was* nervous. He was just acting calm, and doing so helped make him feel less nervous inside. He was controlling his physiology in order to control his thoughts, instead of allowing the physical signs of nervousness to control him.

For doctors, like Ian, there is a well-known saying: 'When you're the first to arrive at a cardiac arrest, check your own pulse first!' To be helpful, you need to know how to turn your own arousal level down when you are in threatening situations.

We need to work out which strategies work best for us. Ian is hopeless with meditation. He keeps falling asleep or getting distracted, but he really goes for pulse monitoring, slow breathing, walking (with friends who talk!) and challenging expected consequences (the 'what if' strategy – What if I don't get this grant? Is it really the end of my research career?).

Behaviourial Strategies – Exposure

Exposure is when we try to reduce our anxiety about something by gradually and slowly exposing ourselves to the situation or thought that is creating discomfort. For James, it would be a gradual, repeated process of moving closer to a spider, keeping his anxiety under control at each step and making sure he doesn't get anywhere near being bitten or attacked.

If you are anxious about going to the supermarket or a mall, slowly work your way up to it. It won't go perfectly first time. The aim is to get as close to the supermarket as you can, and then stay as long as you can, without panicking, keeping your pulse rate and breathing rates slow. At first, it may be as simple as planning to go, then stopping and moving on to something else. Next time, it might be driving to the carpark but not going inside.

On each occasion, if you keep breathing slowly, monitoring your pulse and relaxing your muscles, then, when nothing overwhelming actually happens, you start to get used to it. It might take a couple of visits, it might take more, but every time you succeed, you are accumulating more evidence and experience that going to the supermarket or the mall does not lead inevitably to disaster. You uncouple the experience of being in the supermarket from the experience of overwhelming physical and emotional arousal. Gradually, you move from thinking 'I'm in extreme danger!' to 'I feel vulnerable, but I can bear it a little longer,' to, 'I'm having anxiety-provoking thoughts, but they are just inaccurate predictions. I'm going to try to ignore them.'

Through repeated exposure, you may eventually get bored of feeling in danger, and then your anxiety reduces. The treatment of fear of flying used to be take a plane to Los Angeles, because thirteen hours is such a long time that almost inevitably you'd get bored of feeling anxious.

Repetition can also slowly build comfort. Each time we do an exam, we build up more familiarity with the process and feel more in control, until exams become a normal part of the academic calendar, rather than extreme, terrifying events. In addition, the more exams we do, the more evidence we have that any one of them won't decide our whole future. Each time we give a speech, we become more familiar with that process, and gradually our anxiety should decrease.

'Putting It Off' – Safety Behaviours

Actively distracting yourself from repetitive, anxious thoughts can be useful, but we must be careful not to go into denial, especially when a real problem exists. If you are getting anxious about an upcoming exam or speech, it is probably a sign that you should be preparing for it. If, when you start studying and realise how much work you have to do, your anxiety spikes, you might be tempted to shut the book, eat a biscuit and watch Netflix until your anxiety recedes. That is hiding from anxiety by pretending the exam doesn't exist, until eventually it is too late to get the work done.

Typically, people with chronic anxiety develop a whole range of safety behaviours. If you are afraid of going to the supermarket, a safety behaviour is to ask someone to go shopping with you or getting home delivery. This can work in the short term, but it doesn't solve the underlying problem.

Long-term problems

For long-term problems – court cases, financial hardship, lengthy illnesses, relationship issues – it is important to acknowledge that the problem isn't going away, and learn how to reduce your higher-than-usual stress level.

Any type of litigation involves delay, and the waiting and uncertainty are terribly stressful. Long-term problems raise your set point and make you more likely to tip over into these great tides of anxiety. There are three things you can do:

A) Try to resolve the problem

We often put off resolving the problem because when we start to think about it our anxiety spikes. Try and move towards resolution. Can you sort out your relationship problems by going to counselling, or even by making the decision to separate? If you are involved in a court case, can you settle it? Once you start to take effective strategies to solve the problem, even if they don't immediately solve it, your arousal and therefore your anxiety will usually decrease. Moving towards resolution can have an immediate and dramatic effect. Further procrastination only makes things worse.

B) Reduce your physiological response

Through mindfulness – meditation, yoga, relaxation, exercise as described above – you can reduce your physical arousal. Do it every day, not just when you feel anxious or are already overwhelmed.

C) Use cognitive behavioural strategies

As discussed, these strategies can help control anxious thoughts:
- Re-examining the risk
- Re-examining the consequence
- Distracting the mind.

The most important aspect of these strategies is learning the capacity to separate emotions and feelings from thoughts and beliefs. Anxiety can create a vicious circle whereby distorted thoughts pour more petrol on anxious emotions. Using strategies to ignore, challenge and control those thoughts increases the chance of bringing the anxious emotions back under control.

Thoughts and beliefs can be challenged and replaced by new thoughts. For example, 'This court case is going on forever and I'll never recover,' can be replaced by, 'It will be over one day, maybe soon if we can settle it, and then life will be fantastic again.' Most of us never really think about changing our underlying thought patterns, but when our thoughts are driving us to chronic anxiety and distress, the following strategies can be effective:

- Structured problem solving – consciously mapping out the pros and cons of various solutions and then choosing one that is both feasible and personally acceptable.
- Challenging the assumed impacts of a fear – the 'what if' scenario. 'What if I do miss the train?' Another one will come soon. 'What if we are late to the family birthday?' It will still be going. 'What if I don't get this job?' Another, better job might come along.
- Identifying our underlying and recurring patterns of thoughts, especially unhelpful ones, and questioning them. For example:
  • 'Everybody thinks I'm no good.'
  • 'Everyone's out to get me.'
  • 'If I don't take care of everyone else first, no-one will ever take care of me.'

Medication

What role does medication play in reducing anxiety? In the past, sedative drugs that dampened the reactivity or excitability of the nervous system, like valium (and the general class of benzodiazepines), were widely prescribed. Before that, there were really dangerous barbiturates. People have also treated themselves with alcohol, cannabis and other natural sedatives for centuries. Being asleep or sedated has always felt better than feeling anxious.

While sedatives may be useful in a crisis, long-term use is definitely not good. Often there is a rebound effect when you take the sedatives away and anxiety increases. There is also a tolerance effect – over time, you have to take more to get the same result.

The newer medications, specifically the selective serotonin reuptake inhibitors (SSRIs, like Prozac) are not sedatives. They act on different brain chemicals to turn down the set point and reduce temperamental anxiety. They can help to moderate severe temperamental anxiety, panic attacks, as well as reducing ruminative thinking – repetitive thinking where you can get stuck on the same, very unpleasant thoughts.

At times people have been prescribed medications that directly block the increase in heart rate or rising blood pressure that accompanies severe anxiety. It is hard to feel very anxious, or have a panic attack, if your heart is only beating at fifty beats per minute. The medication does this by blocking the effects of adrenaline on the heart, airways and blood vessels. However, they often have side-effects (causing low blood pressure, fatigue, fainting or asthma symptoms) and should only be used under medical supervision.

'Tough day at work. I need a drink.' Many have used alcohol, cannabis or other recreational drugs to de-stress after work, relax with friends, get to sleep or reduce periods of anxiety. When you start doing this every day, and more and more on your own, it soon becomes a physiological as well as a psychological problem.

Alcohol (and most other sedatives) really messes with normal sleep patterns. The less well you sleep, the more likely you are to wake up anxious the next day. This can soon become a vicious cycle where the chosen cure rapidly becomes the main problem. Lots of other non-drug strategies (meditation, progressive muscle relaxation, yoga) to reduce anxiety, after work or before going to bed, provide much better long-term solutions.

The Relationship Between Anxiety and Depression

If anxiety is the emotion that demands you act, depression is the state that says it's time to stop. When all that anxiety and arousal doesn't work, and all that adrenaline is being pumped around the body day after day, the brain and the body eventually says 'Stop'. It is exhausted. The fuel tank is empty. Thoughts soon switch from finding solutions to helplessness and hopelessness. The body just stops. That's depression.

Anxiety and depression often co-occur. If you are anxious, you are more likely to be depressed. If you are depressed, you are more likely to be anxious. People are more likely to have their first-ever panic attack during a depressive episode. Being chronically anxious can soon make you depressed. Being depressed can make you anxious and concerned that you will never get better.

The most common forms of depression in adults are preceded by separation anxiety in childhood and social anxiety in the teenage years. To prevent depression, treat anxiety early and effectively in childhood and in adolescence. For those whose anxiety was not treated when they were young, there are still effective strategies that can help you learn to control it and live a happy life.

CHECKLIST

- Anxiety is essential, but if we have a high anxiety set point we might assess:
  - the risks of adverse events happening as being higher than they actually are, and,
  - the consequence of those events as being worse than they actually would be, and we can become over-anxious.
- Physical arousal usually accompanies anxious thoughts and can wear us down.
- To treat anxiety:
  - Challenge anxious, irrational thoughts.
  - Distract yourself from anxious thoughts.
  - Try to uncouple anxious thoughts from physical arousal.
  - Calm the body through relaxation strategies and mindfulness.
  - Try gradual exposure to the object of your anxiety (e.g. spiders).
  - Try to resolve the underlying source of anxiety.
  - Alcohol is very unlikely to help in the medium and long term, but prescribed medications can be effective.

10

Depression

*Depression is being colour blind and constantly being
told how colourful the world is.*

Atticus

*Try to understand the blackness, lethargy, hopelessness, and
loneliness they're going through. Be there for them when they
come through the other side. It's hard to be a friend to someone
who's depressed, but it is one of the kindest, noblest, and best
things you will ever do.*

Stephen Fry

What is depression? Everyone feels sad and out of sorts sometimes, but at what point does normal distress, low mood or low
energy start to become depression, a mental illness?

Distress Is Normal

Adversity happens, and our normal response to it is some degree
of distress. If we lose our job, distress is normal. We might feel sad,
bad, wronged, a sense of loss, or miss the job and our colleagues.

Distress is unpleasant, but when something bad happens, it can also be the appropriate attitude. It can help us deal with adversity, and learn and grow from it.

Feeling distressed can also be a signal. If we feel distressed at work, or in a personal relationship, it might be a sign that we need a change. If we get distressed after losing our temper, it might be a signal we need to learn to keep calm.

Showing our distress or sadness also signals to our social groups – our family and friends – that we need help. They see that we are upset and suffering, and respond by offering comfort and support. The warmth and kindness of others helps us deal with our problems and recover. If we do not show distress, others will not know we need help. In this way, social groups continue to function: I take care of you. You take care of me. We all survive. Expressing distress is a normal and important part of that reciprocal process.

Why Now? Why This?

It is difficult to pick what events or situations will prompt us to become distressed. Sometimes we cope with challenging situations without distress, and then later something that seems less significant floors us.

Given all that we have dealt with in the past, why has this particular event caused such a big reaction? The answer is not always obvious. However, when things go wrong, we always propose an explanation. Whether it is actually true is another matter.

Often, the particular event is just the straw that breaks the camel's back. There has been a build-up of personal difficulties and chronic stress over a longer period. Prolonged financial, relationship, work or health-related stress is more likely to lead to depression than a one-off disaster.

Sometimes particular events hit us very hard. 'Why now? Why me?' The explanation, to the extent that there is one, is often a complex combination of our biology, our genetics, our individual characteristics, and our personal history. Some events can feel very important, particularly in our personal life, like a dispute with a close friend, or our professional life, like a failure to get an important job.

Sometimes things just happen at a difficult time of life – after childbirth, during menopause, or while we are recovering from a major physical illness, like cancer. At times like this, we are more vulnerable. At some point in our life, we are likely to be rattled by something.

When Does Normal Distress Become Depression?

Usually when we are distressed, upset or unhappy, people support us, we gradually rally and before too long, we start to improve. If our distress has been prompted by change – a job lost, a dispute with a friend, the end of an intimate relationship – we slowly adjust. We start looking for another job, seek new friends or get used to being single again. It is a tough time, and we might still miss what we have lost, but we are coping. We see a future.

Other times things don't get better. In fact, they get worse. We take another step down, perhaps a few steps, and end up in the deepest hole we have ever been in, with no idea how to get out. That hole is depression.

At what point should you recognise that a period of unhappiness might have gone over the edge, and become depression? There is no definitive brain scan, blood test, X-ray or nasal swab for depression. There have been many attempts over the past forty years to develop a simple test to diagnose it. To date, none work well enough. Other tests can check if there is a related medical problem (eg stroke, thyroid disease, anaemia) that is causing the depression, but they can't definitively tell if someone is depressed.

We need to look at the features, the severity and the duration of distress.

Features

We can look at four factors:

- Feelings: How do you feel? Are you are miserable and unhappy? Withdrawn? Uninterested in, and not enjoying, things you usually do, like family, job, activities and socialising?
- Behaviours: What are you doing? Staying in bed more? Deliberately withdrawing from social and other activities? Smiling less?
- Thoughts: What are you thinking about? Are your thoughts pessimistic? Do you assume bad outcomes?
- Physical symptoms: Depression is as much a physical as it is a psychological illness. What is your body doing? Is there fatigue, pain, headaches, weight changes, disturbed sleep?

People we live with or see a lot often have a good perspective. While we might tell ourselves we are just reacting normally to a bad event, a partner might say, 'She's withdrawn. She doesn't smile anymore, or enjoy things, and isn't interested in anything. She is staying up late, doesn't get up until midday, hardly eats and has stopped contacting anyone outside home.'

Severity

Is rating your mood on a scale from 0 to 10 useful? To a degree, but people have different ways of rating themselves. Ian's '8' is probably different to James's. Try to remember back to the worst you've ever felt in your life. How bad was that? How bad is this feeling now, compared to it? Have you ever been in a hole this deep before?

Starting to rate each day from 1 to 10 is a good way to chart progress. Establish a baseline – 'My average day is about a 7 out of 10'. If you find that most days feel like a 2 or 3, it is a good indicator that something is seriously amiss.

The intrusion of really dark thoughts about the whole value of living is a clear sign that the severity of this distress has gone way beyond our normal response to daily adversity.

Duration

We can all have bad days, but if serious distress continues for two weeks or more, it is getting to the point where it may well be depression and you should seek help. If the symptoms are severe, don't wait more than a week. When episodes of depression are left untreated, they can go on for months or even years, so simply hoping that things get better soon is not a great strategy.

What Happens When We Have Depression?

Most of us describe depression as psychological. We can feel sad, pessimistic, irritable, self-critical, numb, angry, and worthless. But depression is an illness – it is not just a psychological response, it is also physical. We feel tired during the day and lack energy, but then cannot sleep at night. We might lose our appetite, or eat more than usual and put on weight. We might not want to get out of bed, and feel permanently jet-lagged because our whole day–night cycle has lost its rhythm.

In severe depression, our in-built stress response (releasing the hormone cortisol) is in overdrive. Our arousal systems that release adrenaline are ready to overreact at any moment. This uses up a lot of energy and puts our whole system under great strain. That is fine for a few hours or, at most, a few days, but after that, it starts to take a real toll. If they do not get time to recover, our hormonal, immune and heart systems start to deteriorate.

Not everyone has every symptom. Different types of depression have different characteristics. Some can eat and sleep okay, but their waking hours are just miserable. Depression in young people often has more fatigue, oversleeping, late sleeping and weight gain. Depression in older people often has more impact on memory and concentration, weight loss and the slowing down of physical actions.

Just like headaches, back pains and fevers, not all depressions are of the same severity. Some have depression that is less severe, but lasts longer. Others have episodes that are very deep and dark, but rebound out of them more quickly. Some depression can be more anxiety-orientated. Some is more body-clock orientated, and will often respond well if body clock problems are addressed. (See Chapter 3, 'The Body Clock'.)

A common characteristic is that people often do not understand what is happening. 'Why am I in this deep hole? I'm lost in anxious thoughts. I can't sleep. I'm losing weight. I've got no appetite. I feel terrible. I have no energy. 'What is going on?'

What Is Happening in Our Brain

When we are depressed, we don't just feel bad. Our brain is functioning differently. As the brain controls most body functions (heart, gut, hormones, immune system), it is not surprising that lots of other things go astray as well.

A brain that is depressed is much less active in some areas. There are fewer thoughts, and less response to the outside world. In other parts of the brain, there may be overactivity, reflecting increased anxiety.

When depression lasts for some time, we lose connections between brain cells, which can affect short-term memory and make us more prone to mood fluctuations. However, these changes are not permanent, and can recover when depression is effectively treated.

Chemically, within the brain, three chemicals – serotonin, noradrenaline and dopamine – play critical roles in regulating mood, energy, sleep, appetite, concentration and physical activity. We know that bumping up brain concentrations of these chemicals when someone is depressed can be an effective treatment.

A brain that is depressed loses its normal feedback response, so it just keeps pumping out more cortisol, our stress-response hormone, and adrenaline, causing us to feel constantly anxious and unable to relax. Depression can also put strain on the heart, and put us at increased risk of heart disease, infection and in the long-term, possibly cancer.

For some types of depression, the internal body clock that releases chemicals to help us to get up and active in the morning and go to sleep at night, loses its daily rhythm and gets out of synch, causing us to feel jet-lagged all the time.

Withdrawal and Inactivity

When depressed, we usually become less responsive to the world. We withdraw and lose interest in things. There can be an absence of emotionality – a feeling of numbness, of being separated from the world and everyone in it, and not being able to cry, or respond in any emotional way. We might feel lonely, but also have no desire to talk to anyone. Being with other people can feel strained, and like hard work.

Related to withdrawal is inactivity. Lack of energy and disrupted sleep create a vicious cycle where even the thought of exercise is exhausting, so we end up lying on the couch all day. This lack of activity and movement make it harder to sleep, which further disrupts our body clock and drains energy even more.

Pessimism and Loss of Pleasure

When someone is depressed, there is hopelessness and helplessness. The glass appears to be totally empty, and we cannot see any way our situation can improve. Partners might say 'I keep telling him he will probably get another interesting job soon, but he just says the same ridiculously pessimistic, untrue things about how hopeless it all is and how he has no hope of a good future.'

People often feel that no matter what they do, it will go wrong. They cannot see a way out.

Those with depression often lose the ability to enjoy things, and no longer get any pleasure from things they used to love doing. It is like trying to enjoy something while you are jet-lagged. You are too tired to have any fun. You might go through the motions, but the pleasure is gone.

When this state persists for a while, the next step is often to think 'If I don't get any pleasure from playing tennis, or going out with friends, or cooking, or sex anymore, why do it? I might as well stay in bed.'

Pushing Through It

Most people with depression try to cope, at least initially. They have family and work responsibilities and they try to put on a brave face. They think, 'Maybe I can push through it,' but their body and mind are not in the right place to keep going.

Is trying to push through depression a good strategy, or will it wear us down and make it even worse? Having purposeful activity such as work, having social contact, being physically active and exposing ourselves to sunlight are all effective ways of treating depression, so maintaining as much of that as is bearable is helpful. It is good to try and do things. Even if we don't feel like it, we should urge ourselves to do some of the activities we usually do, but not to the extent of hiding how we are feeling and pretending we are not depressed, because that will wear us down.

When we are distressed, it is important that we signal it. When we try to behave as if everything is normal, others think, 'He seems fine.' If we collapse and stay in bed, it sends a strong signal of distress. Everyone will realise that we are unwell, and start to provide support and help. If we do not signal our distress, we might not get the support we need. Don't be 'brave' and pretend you haven't got a problem.

Some people cope with depressive episodes for months. They pretend to be okay, don't get any help, and things get worse. Six months later something happens – they lose their job or their partner leaves – that pushes them to see their doctor. At first it appears the lost job or partner leaving has prompted the depression, but the depression has been going on for much longer. The lost job or partner leaving didn't cause the depression. They happened, often, *because* of the depression.

Sensitive People

Those who are more sensitive to personal interactions are more likely to become depressed. They are often on high alert, and overanalyse every social situation. 'What is that person thinking? Did I offend them? Do they think I'm stupid?' They can over-react to everything, which becomes exhausting, and then they become worn down and overwhelmed, and feel they can't cope anymore.

One way for people who are very sensitive to reduce their risk of depression is to recognise their over-analytical tendencies early, and seek out Cognitive Behavioural Therapy, anxiety reduction treatments or other interpersonal therapies that can arm them with behavioural and psychological strategies to help them to change. (See Chapter 9, 'Anxiety'.)

Depression and Young People

Children get anxious, sad and distressed, but the type of clinical depression we are discussing does not really occur before puberty. Normal childhood development involves the development of moodiness, but before puberty children predominantly have anxiety, and only rarely persistently depressed moods.

When puberty arrives, it brings rapid brain, hormonal and social development, along with moodiness. Moods, which are our general feeling about the world, can change quickly, and not necessarily because of anything external. 'I was in a bad mood. Now I'm in a good one.'

As the brain develops, identity and an internal world start to emerge, as do emotional centres and the regulation of them. Teenagers are often developing a sexual identity, interacting with others in new ways, trying to fit in with peers and discovering what groups they do and don't belong in. Sometimes they are bullied.

There is a lot going on in brain development right through the teenage years. Key connections between the thinking structures and the emotional circuits are being refined. Those new connections underpin new thoughts about personal identity and our place in the world. When that development goes wrong, or is delayed, it can lead to the first onset of significant depressive syndromes, often including extreme moodiness and self-destructive thoughts.

While the essential nature of the depressive experience is similar whatever your age, teenagers in particular often feel excessively tired and irritable, and oversleep and gain weight.

Teenagers, Technology and Depression

Teenagers' social development is tricky. Today's teenagers also face the online dimension of it, which creates further complexity. Social media can be judgemental and critical. Being shamed or bullied online might mean it is happening in front of hundreds of people, rather than two or three, and that amplification can be very difficult to deal with.

In addition, social media emphasises how we look over other more important social traits such as our personality and how we respond emotionally. It also invites us to compare ourselves with everybody else, and that rarely ends well, no matter who you are or what your age.

In addition, new technology has brought many new and shiny ways we can keep ourselves up beyond a healthy bedtime and disrupt our sleep–wake cycles – streaming services, gaming, apps etc. However, new technologies also have an upside. They can increase social connection. Smartphones enable us to easily stay connected to each other. It can be fantastic for those who don't find it easy to participate in person, and a great way to find people who are like you – emotionally, sexually and socially.

While smartphones can operate in an addictive way (see Chapter 15, 'Addiction'), ultimately we are in control of what we do online. If an app makes us miserable, we can delete it.

Treatments for Depression

Medication
While medicines are still the most common medical treatments for depression, there are also now a range of new brain stimulation and other physical treatments. Here we will focus on common antidepressant medicines.

How antidepressants work
Since the late 1960s the focus of antidepressant medicines has been on increasing the concentration of serotonin, noradrenaline or dopamine, the chemicals that regulate mood, energy, sleep, appetite, concentration and physical activity in the brain.

In people who are severely depressed, increasing the brain concentration of these three chemicals can slowly improve mood, energy and wellbeing, and reduce anxiety and feelings of hopelessness. This does not mean that a lack of these chemicals causes depression, but it does mean that increasing their concentration via antidepressant medication often helps people with depression to recover. Aspirin is a good analogy. Taking aspirin relieves headaches, but that doesn't mean that *not* taking aspirin *causes* headaches. However, while aspirin works in less than an hour, antidepressants take longer. Because they induce changes in the brain's nerve cells, it takes some weeks for them to reach full effectiveness.

Antidepressants also help the adult brain to grow new nerve cell connections. That may help not only short-term recovery, but also with long-term protection from depression. For those with body-clock based depression, new antidepressant medicines based on melatonin try to reset the daily clock.

Social acceptance of antidepressants

Since the late twentieth century, society has become more educated about, and accepting of, antidepressants, but some still fearfully think, 'They will control my mind. They will turn me into a vegetable. I'll get addicted. I won't ever be able to stop taking them.'

Antidepressants do not change your personality, or who you are. In fact, they do the opposite. When we are depressed, we are fundamentally different from who we normally are. We are unhappier, less energetic, more pessimistic and withdrawn, and overly sensitive to criticism and disappointment. Antidepressants, along with other psychological and behavioural treatments, help restore us to our normal selves, and to normal wellbeing.

Part of accepting medication as one aspect of treatment involves accepting that we are sick. Depression is an illness, not a failure of character. Whether or not we get asthma, heart disease or cancer has nothing to do with our strength of character or will power, and neither does depression. We don't question doctors prescribing us medication for other conditions. If a doctor tells us about the benefits of taking a pill every day for our blood pressure or acne, or of the benefits of an insulin injection for diabetes, or of an inhaler for asthma, it is highly likely we will do it.

People sometimes think they should stop taking antidepressants as soon as they feel a bit better. However, a big part of *why* they feel better might be *because* they are taking the pills. You don't say to someone with asthma, 'No asthma attacks for two week? Great. You're cured. Chuck that puffer in the bin.'

Some people only need to take medication when they are really unwell until they get better. Others, particularly those who have had recurrent episodes, may need to take it for longer periods to get well, allow the brain to recover fully, resume their social and work lives and greatly reduce the risk of another relapse.

If someone has two or more episodes of depression in under five years, they are at serious risk of further bouts of depression. If they don't fully recover, and have continued severe anxiety, poor sleep, daytime fatigue or other symptoms, sticking with prescribed medications – along with other psychological therapies – is usually the best approach.

Counselling and Other Therapies

Counselling with a skilled therapist, clinical psychologist, mental health nurse or mental health-trained social worker is very effective for treating depression, and other common mental illnesses. While there are many other general counsellors out there who provide support, they are less likely to teach the skills that are of greatest use to someone with more severe depression. (See Chapter 15, 'How Therapy Works'.)

When we have counselling, we should begin to look more objectively at our depression, understand what is happening to us, and learn practical strategies and skills to help us through the tough times.

For depression, a number of therapies work well. They include:
- Cognitive Behavioural Therapy, where the emphasis is on changing negative thought patterns
- Interpersonal therapy, with an emphasis on improving close personal relationships
- Behavioural therapies focused on engaging in pleasurable personal and social activities, and having daily activity schedules aimed at improving sleep, increasing physical activity and reconnecting with the social world.

No matter which type of therapist you see, there should be a clear focus on a careful analysis of the situations that have led to the depression, and on any factors causing stress in your life. The therapist should help you schedule daily activity to include regular bedtime and getting-up time, more physical activity, less alcohol or other drug use, more intimate contact with key people in your family and social world, and re-engagement with work or study. Where people have been made particularly vulnerable to depression by previous trauma, or lifelong anxiety, the therapy may need to deal specifically with that.

As we start to recover, we should also learn what we can do to help prevent further episodes. These skills are not the same for everyone. Some skills may be psychological, such as focusing on past trauma and restructuring unhelpful thought patterns, while others may be behavioural, focusing on daily physical activity, managing the sleep–wake cycle, and reducing alcohol and other drug use.

Using these psychological and behavioural strategies can help restore brain connections and rewire pathways, and reduce anxiety and ruminating, and that helps us recover. However, just as with medication, psychological and behavioural strategies can take some time. Therapists encourage patients to put their anxiety-reduction, social engagement, and thought-control skills into action in real-life situations. For many, it's a chance to lead a better life than previously.

Physical Activity

Physical activity is an essential part of recovery. It leads to improved energy levels, motivation and better moods. It is paradoxical, but when you feel tired, sleepy and overwhelmed during the day, the best way to lift your mood for the next four hours is physical activity, preferably outside in sunlight. We feel that doing any physical activity will completely wipe us out, but, counter-intuitively, when we do it, we often feel *more* energetic.

Being physically active doesn't necessarily mean swimming twenty laps. Even a walk around the block can help raise your mood. When we lack energy, we feel like we won't make it to the end of the street, but doing even a small amount of daily exercise helps, especially when it is outside.

If we are depressed and lack energy, we need more, not less, daytime activity, including exercise, more sunlight exposure and less time being inactive or in bed. Exercise drives hormones like cortisol and adrenaline up during the day. The higher they go, preferably in the morning, the higher the chance that they will drop quickly at night and help us get to restful sleep.

The Body Clock

All forms of depression disrupt the body clock to some degree, and impact our sleep, tiredness and related behaviours, like eating patterns. Attention to the body clock's needs – regular sleep, morning sunlight, and daily physical activity and exercise – helps us recover.

Some types of depression are probably caused by disruption of the body clock. Working nightshift, or shifts whose times are constantly changing, can lead us into a state of continual jet-lag which can require specific therapies and medication, such as melatonin-based antidepressants, to return it to normal. (See Chapter 3, 'The Body Clock'.)

Social Connection

Those with depression usually withdraw from social contact, at least to some extent. Starting to once again connect with friends, family and our other social groups is vital to recovery.

Humans are very social animals, and our brain function relies heavily on constant interaction with others. However, for most people with depression, social contact is the last thing they want. But if we do manage to make the effort, we often enjoy the interaction more than we expect to, and get lots of the positive personal comments on which we all depend. Pushing those we are closest to away during these periods only makes the hole deeper and darker.

It is often important to involve partners and families in treatment. Rather than expecting someone with depression to reach out to others, we all need to reach in and grab the person who is suffering. (See Chapter 5, 'The Importance of Social Connection'.)

Purposeful Activity

One of Ian's favourite sayings is, 'We don't get well to go to work, we go to work to get well.'

Purposeful activity can mean work, but it does not have to be work. It can be anything that requires us to be mentally or physically active, ideally both, and is directed toward a goal we think is meaningful, and in which we invest our thoughts and plans. It can be gardening, volunteering, cooking, painting or trying to write that novel you have never got around to attempting.

Purposeful activity is an important part of recovery from depression and good for our mental health more generally. If we retire with the intention of just moving up the coast and lying on the beach without any purposeful activity, we will be at heightened risk of depression. There are more antidepressants prescribed on the Gold Coast than anywhere else in Australia.

CHECKLIST

- Our normal response to some degree of adversity is distress, which signals to the group that we need care and support.
- When distress continues and deepens, and we withdraw and feel lethargic, pessimistic and unmotivated to do things we usually enjoy, for a week or more, we may be depressed.
- While continuing to be involved in activities can help, it is not a good idea to put on a brave face and pretend everything is okay.
- Depression can be treated by:
  - Medication
  - Therapy
  - Physical activity
  - Fixing body clock issues
  - Social connection
  - Purposeful activities.

11

Burnout

Burnout is what happens when you try to avoid being human for too long.

Michael Gungor

What Is Burnout?

Burnout is a loss of motivation and satisfaction at work. A job that might previously have been enjoyable becomes exhausting and dull. Every day is hard to get through, and we just want to stop.

Why does burnout happen? Can we prevent it? If we experience burnout, does it mean we are psychologically unwell, or do we just need a rest or a change of scene? How do we recover?

How Do We Burnout?

Burnout is often associated with those who put a great deal of energy into stressful jobs, but it is not limited to high-flying doctors, lawyers and executives. Those who have monotonous work with little autonomy are also vulnerable.

Sometimes, burnout occurs when we are 'on' all the time. Constantly experiencing lots of stress can wear us down. We have used up all our energy, the tank is empty, and there is nothing left. Our nervous system is exhausted.

Common signs of burnout are a loss of energy and enjoyment at work, increasing cynicism and scepticism, being detached from our work, and feeling that what we do is not important. Workdays become a series of tasks to try to get through, rather than something that might bring us some satisfaction or enjoyment. We can lose any real interest in our job, our co-workers and the organisation we work for.

For those whose job involves helping others – health and aged-care workers, teachers, lawyers and so on – one sign can be a loss of empathy. After years of willingly shouldering the burden of helping others to solve their problems, you find yourself wishing they would all just go away and stop bothering you.

No-one can expect to love their job all the time. Almost everyone goes through ups and down at work. Some days are diamonds, some days are stones. How, then, do we tell the difference between being a bit bored or unenthused for a while, and being burned out? What are the signs that our disengagement has got to a level that we need to address?

We should look at two things: the symptoms, and how long they last for. Feeling disengaged and unmotivated sometimes at work is normal, but feeling like that constantly for weeks is not. If you experience burnout symptoms consistently for two weeks or more, it should be addressed. If you have a break from work during which you sleep well and have a nice time, and then as soon as you return, you feel bored and detached again, that is a problem.

Prevention is better than cure. How can we reduce our risk of burnout?

Reducing the Risk of Burnout

Before You Experience Symptoms

No matter how exciting you find your job, it can't give you everything you need. If your life revolves entirely around your work, and you lack other social relationships, activities and stimulation outside it, you are at increased risk of burnout.

If you have a challenging, stressful job, then to maintain enthusiasm and energy at work, you need to take care of yourself by creating good habits and routines. Good sleep, good diet and exercise are important, as is regular downtime, family time, socialising and doing other activities you find rewarding and refreshing. Try to do something outside work that you enjoy each day. Look for activities that take your mind to other productive pursuits away from your work.

It is important to have a realistic attitude. A friend of James's with a high-powered job said that a turning point was when he realised that no matter how hard he worked, he would never get everything done. There would always be more work to do. He had to change his expectation from, 'Get all your work done, then go home,' to 'Get some useful things done each day, then go home.'

Recognising when you are near full capacity and learning to say no to further demands is also important.

If your job involves helping people – social worker, nurse, aged or child care, doctor – then always expecting to completely solve everyone's problems is unrealistic, and sets you up for frequent failure and disappointment. Raging at the injustice of the system might only increase your stress and likelihood of burnout. There is no end to the number of people who need help. Rather than beating yourself up every time you don't get a perfect outcome, having the more realistic expectation of doing the best you can, given each person's circumstances, and understanding both what you can and cannot control and influence is more likely to be sustainable.

If you have a job that you find boring, look for ways to find some pleasure in it. If you are bored working in a shop or at a supermarket check-out, can you get some enjoyment from chatting to customers or workmates?

These days, our working life can last fifty years. Variety is important. Ian thinks he may have avoided burnout and feeling stuck by frequently changing what he is doing, and taking up new challenges – like our podcast and this book.

Those who think of themselves as the 'key person' often experience burnout. They believe that only they can do certain tasks. 'I must keep working or something terrible will happen.' Often they have some obsessional, controlling and perfectionistic qualities. Some surgeons think, 'No-one can do this type of operation as well as me.' This belief puts enormous pressure on them, and often makes them reluctant to heed early signs of burnout. 'If I don't keep working, people will die and it will be my fault.'

'Key person syndrome' is also common in executives, small business owners and lawyers. When they are finally persuaded to go on holiday, they ring the office all the time: 'Is everything okay?' When told that it is, they sound disappointed. 'Things aren't falling apart without me?'

It is much better for the long-term health of both the individual and the organisation to recognise that no-one is indispensable and to ensure that the next generation is always being trained.

Work-life balance is often discussed as being important in preventing burnout, but the term suggests there is work, which is non-life, and life, which is non-work. Ideally we want our work to be a satisfying, engaging and a very pleasurable part of life.

And for goodness sake, take your holidays. You get *paid* to have a *holiday*! What's the bad bit? For some reason, many let months' worth of holiday leave bank up, and have to be shoved out of the building by HR. Holidays are good for you. A surgeon who has recently had a holiday and is well rested will probably do a better job than one who has been working non-stop for a year. We are not machines.

This is all about minding your mind pre-emptively. Do some planning to try and make sure you have a good life.

Taking Early Notice of Symptoms

If you find yourself losing motivation and enthusiasm, and lacking energy at work, it is important to take notice. Ignoring early signs can lead to the problem worsening. These early symptoms are a sign to step back and think about what is happening. Have you been going through a particularly busy and stressful period? If so, perhaps when things calm down you will feel better. On the other hand, if you are just normally very busy, you might be experiencing the early signs of burnout.

Are there things you can do to get a bit of enthusiasm back? Can you focus on the things you enjoy about work and do more of them, and less of the stuff you dislike?

Are you getting enough sleep? Do you have downtime? Time with family and friends? Exercise? What can you do to give yourself more pleasure outside work?

Many of us have busy weeks, even months, but if working long days and most weekends has become your norm, you are feeling drained and are not using your non-work hours to refresh yourself with exercise, socialising and fun, you may be heading toward nervous exhaustion and burnout.

Check in with yourself regularly. The earlier you notice signs of burnout, the more likely it is that you can address them, and the less likely you are to fall into a more serious psychological disorder.

Dealing with Burnout

Burnout might feel unpleasant, but it can sometimes serve the useful purpose in forcing us to step back, re-examine our relationship with our work and make decisions we might have otherwise avoided. Burnout can be our brain and body's way of signalling that something is seriously wrong, and that we need to engage with it and make some changes.

There is a sliding scale from those who just need some time away from work, and to make some minor adjustments, to those for whom it has become a psychologically more significant event, and who need to consider bigger changes.

Our brains want novelty, difference, challenges and new stimuli. They want to do different things, not the same things over and over again. If we do not give them enough novelty, we can struggle.

Those struggling with burnout, and who find that holidays bring only temporary relief, may have been doing the same job for too long. They might be good at it, but be bored. It might be time for a change. 'Yes, this is a good job and pays well. But is it what I should be doing at this point in my life?'

Deciding to change jobs or careers can be difficult, particularly when we have financial and family commitments. Many who feel stuck in jobs are also scared by the uncertainty of change. We might be nervous about money, feel we only have one skill, or be scared of starting out all over again. However, if we have become chronically stressed and the pleasure has gone out of both our work and then the rest of our life, change might be the best option. It might not be easy but that does not mean it is impossible. If you have twenty, thirty or even forty work years ahead, perhaps making some difficult decisions in the short term might, in the long run, prove to be a worthwhile investment.

The question then becomes, 'What *sort* of new job or career change?' These are hard questions and require planning. No-one is going to appear magically and parachute you into the perfect job, but advice from others can be helpful. Maybe you know someone who knows someone who has made a similar change and can give you advice. Reach out and tap into the accumulated wisdom of your groups.

Some have more options than others. Focus on the options you *do* have, rather than on those you don't. These days, many qualifications can be obtained part-time or online, or both, so it can be easier to change jobs or careers than in the past.

Some can move sideways, using the skills and experience that they have in a new way: a lawyer goes to work for a client, a teacher moves into administration at the Department of Education, a surgeon becomes an educator, researcher or administrator.

For others, burnout may be more about changing the circumstances in which they are working. Some find leaving a big company to work for themselves reinvigorates them. For others it is the opposite. They are sick of running their own small business and doing quarterly GST calculations, and want to work in a bigger organisation. For some, the problem is the culture of their workplace, or the personality of their boss. If you can work out where the dissatisfaction and stress is coming from, then you know what you need to change.

Sometimes the solution is less drastic. In the 1990s James worked as a criminal lawyer by day and a stand-up comedian by night. He loved both jobs, but they both burned adrenaline and as the decade wore on, he got more and more tired, until every day became a series of tasks to be ticked off. The pleasure was gone. He thought about becoming a part-time lawyer, but never followed through. Eventually he got burnt out and sick, had a couple of weeks off and realised that his current life was not sustainable. That forced him to engage with the idea of working less. He reduced his lawyering to three days a week, and with the extra downtime, his enjoyment and motivation returned.

Can some adjustments to your daily or weekly cycle help you deal with burnout? Doing more exercise, getting more sleep, eating better, drinking less alcohol, spending more time with family and friends and ensuring you do something you enjoy each day might improve how you feel about work. You might realise, 'It wasn't the job. It was me.' Again, this requires reflection and planning.

Burnout and Mental Illness

Sadly, when people do not respond to those early indications that something is amiss or out of whack, they are often heading toward something worse. Their whole world can start to crash in around them, and they cross over into serious psychological disorder: severe anxiety and depression.

This can be more than temporary exhaustion and disengagement, and might not be fixed simply by tinkering with work-life balance, or rearranging how you do things. There can be chronic stress, distress, alienation and detachment. We cover some treatments in the chapter 'Depression'.

CHECKLIST

- Burnout is a loss of motivation and satisfaction at work. In 'helping' jobs, one sign can be losing empathy.
- Both those with high-flying, demanding jobs and those with monotonous jobs with low autonomy can experience burnout.
- To reduce your risk of burnout, ensure you do things outside work that you enjoy – activities, socialising, family time, exercise, etc.
- Sometimes, burnout can be cured by some time away and reasonably minor lifestyle changes. Other times, it might be a sign we should change jobs or careers.
- Take early notice of symptoms. Don't wait until a more significant mental health issue develops.

12

Insomnia

The worst thing in the world is to try to sleep and not to.

F. Scott Fitzgerald

Dear Mind, please stop thinking so much at night, I need sleep.

Unknown

Getting enough sleep is important to both our mental and physical health. When we don't get enough, everything is worse. Enjoyable activities become draining chores, tiredness is constant and our mind and body cannot function properly. (See Chapter 13, 'The Body Clock'.)

For many, sleep is a given. You go to bed, fall asleep quickly and wake up refreshed. Perhaps, now and again, something is running around your mind and keeps you awake for a while, but it doesn't happen often enough to be a problem. If you have had a few late nights, you go to bed an hour or two early, and the next day you feel fine again.

For some, however, restful sleep is elusive. They lie there and lie there, worrying about work or money or the state of the world.

Then they start worrying about how much they need to get to sleep, and how tired they will be the next day.

Why does insomnia happen? What can we do about it?

Why Can't We Get To Sleep?

Around ten to twenty per cent of the adult population say they consistently sleep poorly.

Two factors influence the timing of sleep. The first is sleep pressure, a biological response that makes us want to go to sleep. After a certain period of being awake (for most adults, about sixteen hours), if the brain has an opportunity, it will go to sleep. The longer the period of wakefulness, the stronger the sleep pressure. If you get up at 7 am, by 11 pm sleep pressure will start to make you feel very tired.

Sometimes we feel sleep pressure but deliberately override it because we are working late shift, have a crying baby, want to watch the next episode of a show, or are out at a party.

The second factor that impacts the time we go to sleep is the body clock. It sets our daily timing for wakefulness (typically in the morning and with sunlight) and sleepiness (typically in the darkness and at night). Some people have in-built clocks that push them more towards waking early and going to sleep early ('morning larks'), while others have clocks that push them towards waking later and going to bed later ('night owls').

In addition to our in-built clock, the circadian system in humans responds strongly to light and darkness, promoting physical activity during daylight and low activity in the evening. It likes to keep things regular, so the more predictable your daily pattern of activity and sleep, the better the quality of your sleep.

Anxiety is the most common cause of initial insomnia and difficulty falling asleep. When we are anxious during the day, activities like answering emails, meetings, shopping and making dinner often distract us from anxious thoughts. Lying in bed, there is nothing to distract us. We are alone with our worries. To sleep, the brain has to turn off, but anxious thoughts run around and around, overriding sleep pressure and circadian timing. Anxiety leads to physical arousal, elevating our heartbeat and keeping our body temperature up, all of which make falling sleep even harder.

Often we are tempted to distract ourselves by turning on the light and reading a book, listening to a podcast, or looking at our phone. But when we stop, our anxious thoughts are still there, fighting the sleep pressure and keeping us awake.

Physical Activity, Body Temperature and Melatonin

Insomnia is not caused just by what happens at night. Being physically active during the day is important. Physical activity keeps us alert and awake during the day, and leaves us tired out at night and ready for sleep. If you are inside and inactive all day, you are more likely to have trouble sleeping. When people are recovering from surgery, they spend a lot of time in their hospital bed, and often find it impossible to get to sleep at night, because they have hardly moved during the day.

If you sleep during the day, you will probably find it hard to get to sleep at night.

While being active is good, playing sport at night increases your body temperature, which makes it harder to get to sleep. It is good to tone down physical activity – especially more vigorous sports – a few hours before bedtime. If you want to go to sleep at 11 pm, no gym workouts in bright light after 9 pm. A quiet relaxing walk, in the semi-darkness, is a much better option.

At night, our body releases melatonin, which lowers our body temperature and helps us get to sleep. The signal for the body to release melatonin is darkness. Ideally, melatonin should come on in the early evening and then peak at about 10 or 11 pm.

Melatonin is sensitive to light and physical activity. If you turn on the lights, look at your phone, watch television, or get up and walk around, your melatonin levels will go down, which will make it harder to get to sleep on time.

Waking Up in the Night

Sleep is not just the absence of wakefulness. It is a very active brain process. If you are exhausted and get to sleep, the brain usually goes, 'Thank God. We're going to stay here a while. We're not going to let him wake up until we've done a bit of work behind the scenes.'

However, when anxious people get to sleep, they often wake up before morning because their anxious brain is still on high alert, staying active, even when they are asleep. We know from the brain's electrical activity and the body's physical movement during sleep that people can worry while they are sleeping. Sleep has several stages of 'deepness' and people who are anxious remain in light sleep and so tend to wake up a lot.

When people wake up at 2.30 am they can feel anxious that they won't be able to get back to sleep which, of course, makes it harder for them to get back to sleep.

Try to work out why you are waking up in the middle of the night. Do you have a physical health problem, like joint or back pain? Is it a new breathing problem, like sleep apnea, often seen in those who snore heavily, where people momentarily stop breathing? Have you been drinking alcohol more heavily in the evening? Those who do so often wake up when the alcohol wears off.

People who have been waking up during the night for a long time often develop other behaviours that might actually perpetuate the problem. Instead of trying to go back to sleep, they turn on the light and read, listen to a podcast, watch an old movie or get up and do housework. If this becomes a habit, the body clock and the sleep system will adapt to this new pattern. It then takes some time to deconstruct it and reinstitute an all-night sleep.

Chronic Insomnia

If we have trouble sleeping for a while, we often start to operate in ways that make it even worse. As bedtime approaches, instead of gradually becoming more relaxed, we become more anxious. 'I'm not going to be able to fall asleep again. I'm going to lie awake for hours. Tomorrow I'll be exhausted.' Our heart rate goes up, and worrying about not sleeping keeps us awake.

When we are sleep deprived, we often feel hungry a lot of the time, and are more likely to graze and eat more, so there tends to be weight gain. Because we are physically and psychologically tired, we do less physical activity during the day, which in turn works against a good night's sleep.

Insomnia and Mental Health

The relationship between insomnia and our mental health can become a vicious circle. If we don't sleep, we are more likely to become anxious and depressed, and if we are anxious or depressed, we are more likely to sleep badly.

Historically, it was thought that mental health conditions like anxiety, depression, bipolar disorder and schizophrenia caused sleep problems. The evidence now suggests that it is often the other way around. The sleep problem comes first, and can lead to depression, anxiety and other conditions, particularly if we have a propensity or vulnerability to them. It can happen the other way around, too. Minor anxiety or depression can lead to troubled sleep, which can then become major anxiety or depression.

Insomnia at Different Ages

Children and Teenagers

Getting children and teenagers into regular sleep–wake cycles is important for their later life, particularly when they go through periods of anxiety, which most of us do at some point.

Often children do not get enough physical activity because they are sitting in classrooms all day, looking at screens. They should be outside when the sun is up, running around kicking balls, chasing things and playing with frogs. If a child is having trouble sleeping, tire them out, outdoors, during the day.

The sleep–wake cycle shifts for teenagers. They go to bed later and get up later. That's normal. There's a release of growth hormone, often as they shoot up, and other major changes in brain development, a lot of which occurs during sleep.

School or work can keep them in a good routine but when they don't have those, like during school holidays, it can be bed at 3 am, up by 11 am. The timing of this is all wrong. Sleeping during daylight hours is inefficient and often associated with less deep and more disturbed periods of dream sleep. The end result is waking up feeling more tired. How long sleep lasts is only one factor. What is also important is getting the right patterns of sleep.

These days, it is easier for teenagers to become sleep deprived. Television stations used to shut down at midnight. Now there are an almost infinite number of movies and television shows available 24/7, not to mention social media and gaming.

Teenagers should sleep eight hours or even a bit more, and do it in darkness, but the evidence suggests that during the week, many sleep six hours or less each night. They build up a huge sleep debt and on Saturday, try and make up for it in one go, and don't get up until lunchtime. That is understandable, but is not a good biological strategy. It makes the body clock even more confused and chaotic, which puts the rest of the week out.

If a teenager is sleep deprived, it increases their risk of anxiety, depression and other mental health problems, and is also not good for their physical health. It can lead to weight gain, metabolic changes linked to diabetes and reduced functioning of the immune system, which fights infection. Added to that, you feel terrible.

Menopause

Menopause interferes with the body's regulatory systems, particularly body temperature. Many women experience night sweats and disrupted sleep because their body temperature is not falling during sleep as it did when they were younger, due to the hormonal changes.

Older People

As we age, sleep tends to become lighter, shorter in duration, and come on earlier in the evening.

Your internal body clock starts to wear out after about thirty years, so it becomes more important for us to manually start our body clock each morning by exposing ourselves to light and moving about. Being physically active during the day (even if it hurts a bit) and having a regular bedtime help with sleep and are good for brain health.

One obstacle for many older people is physical pain, especially musculoskeletal pain, which is often exacerbated when you are horizontal or less active. Inadequate management of pain, particularly musculoskeletal pain, is a big cause of insomnia in the elderly, especially among those who have done a lot of physical work or played a lot of sport.

Chronic pain can disrupt sleep. Older people sometimes say they don't want to have their knee or hip replaced. The key question the orthopedic surgeons ask is, 'Does the pain wake you up?' If it does, you should get the replacement, because your brain needs to sleep.

Treating Insomnia

It's Not Just About Bedtime

If you are having trouble sleeping, the cause might arise earlier in the day. Start your body clock properly by getting up at a set time, getting into some natural light and moving. Be physically active during the morning and later in the day while the sun is still up, so that by sleep time you are tired.

Distraction

If we are worrying about money or losing our job, it can feel sensible to keep thinking about the problem, because it is a threat. We want to think about what might happen, and what we can do about it. However, you can't do much about it at midnight, except tire yourself out for tomorrow.

Worrying thoughts go around and around in a non-productive way, and keep us awake. They cause physical arousal – increased heartbeat, shallow breathing – which also makes it more difficult to get to sleep. We have to reduce that arousal before sleep will come.

Sleep comes on when our pulse is slow, our breathing is deep and relaxed and our mind has moved away from the thoughts of the day.

So, one strategy is to distract yourself from anxious thoughts by taking your mind elsewhere. Sometimes this can be achieved by deep breathing exercises, slow yoga, meditation, mindfulness or progressive muscle relaxation, which also helps to de-arouse and relax your body.

Other distracting strategies are visualising a pleasant time or place, or reliving in your imagination a great day you once had. Reading a book (for a short period) that takes you elsewhere can help. James finds counting sheep boring, so if he has trouble sleeping, he picks a day from an overseas holiday he has been on, and recreates it as fully as he can. Where did he go? What did he see? Or he challenges himself to select some sort of unusual sporting team, like the best Australian cricket team since 2000 featuring only left-handers, or the best Canberra Raiders NRL team. This takes just enough mental effort to keep him involved, but there are no stakes, which means no stress or anxiety.

Making lists can work: your top-ten favourite books, films, holiday destinations or activities.

Engaging in an alternative cognitive activity can distract us from what we are worrying about, and thus lower our physical arousal. Hopefully, while we do it, the sleep pressure comes rushing in and we are off to sleep.

If you are having trouble getting to sleep, it makes sense to have a couple of cognitive strategies that are ready to go if you need them.

Don't expect them to work immediately. Some people try one strategy for a few minutes on two or three nights, then say 'It didn't work'. Stick with one or more strategies for at least two weeks. Find the specific strategy, or combination of things, that works best for you.

People often find these behavioural and cognitive strategies hard, even boring, and quickly jump to medication. However, if you are trying to get to sleep, being bored is much better than being anxious. You are more likely to bore yourself to sleep than you are to worry yourself to sleep.

We are trying to get to the absence of active, anxious thoughts, a racing heart, tense muscles and short and shallow breathing that keep us awake.

Sleep Restriction

When we are sleeping badly, and wake up feeling tired all the time, we often try to cope by sleeping more. We go back to bed after we have got up, or have a daytime nap. Very good sleepers actually sleep for less total time, but spend a much higher proportion of that time in deep sleep (the most refreshing type) and dream sleep. Contrary to most people's expectations, there is an inverse relationship between duration of sleep and its efficiency.

In practice, this means setting a very specific schedule for going to bed (often later), getting up (often earlier and with the sun) and reducing the total number of hours asleep. While seven to eight hours of sleep is normally recommended, in these circumstances we can reduce the number of hours down to about six (midnight to 6 am) until a new fixed habit of sleep is established.

Interestingly, sleep restriction and other forms of short-term sleep deprivation often have a positive effect on mood, particularly when people are depressed. But, this is all short-term. It is not a long-term solution.

Identifying Anxiety Triggers

Preparing for sleep should be a time when we wind down and relax, but if we are sleeping badly, the brain might have got into bad habits around sleep. Going to bed may trigger anxiety. Specific actions – putting on pyjamas, cleaning teeth, climbing into bed – can lead to a racing pulse and anxious thoughts. 'I'm not going to be able to get to sleep again and tomorrow I'll be wrecked.'

Those behavioural patterns need to be identified and broken. We need to separate the stimuli (entering the bedroom) from the actual problem, which is the anxiety. We have to change our reaction to the physical environment.

Make sure your bedroom is not too warm. Some find it relaxing to have quiet music or comforting background sounds such as running water or the sound of the sea rather than their normal background noise or silence. Try to arrange things so you are woken up by natural light.

At times, people can go further to break up a bad phase of disturbed sleep. Can we sleep somewhere else for a few nights? A spare room, on the couch, at a hotel or a friend's place? Some go camping, which is great for getting your sleep–wake cycle back in synch with the sun rising and setting – no television, hopefully no phone, and a lot of physical activity.

If entering your bedroom at night starts to make you anxious, become aware of that. You can usually feel the physiological signs, like your pulse rate increasing and shallow breathing. Focus on slowing and deepening your breathing before you get into bed.

Doing this over and over again helps to break the anxious pattern. Don't expect to get it right in one night. If you are lying awake for an hour every night before you go to sleep, it will take more than one relaxation session to cure the problem.

Pre-emptive Action

If you know something is coming up that may challenge your sleep and make you vulnerable to insomnia, such as a new baby or a job that will be demanding, stressful and may involve long, irregular hours, it can be useful to look at strategies beforehand.

Setting up a new routine and getting into the habit before the disruption happens is important. For a new job that finishes later in the day, you may need to get light exposure and physical activity earlier in the day. You may need to shift your main meal each day to lunchtime so that you are not eating a big meal and drinking alcohol after you finish work at 10 pm.

For a new baby, you may need to sort out who is going to do what, and when, in the twenty-four-hour cycle (assuming that you have at least one other person to help). Making sure that everyone (including the new mum) gets some regular sleep, daylight exposure and physical activity is critical. If you are on your own, then getting some help may be critical.

Getting Help

About twenty per cent of those with sleep problems have some other major physical health problem like heavy snoring, sleep apnea, or restless leg syndrome. Sleep specialists, sleep assessments and overnight sleep studies might have a role to play. First, discuss with your GP whether a sleep specialist referral or a sleep study is needed.

A good cognitive or behavioural therapist can help. They will ask you specifics. What is your sequence of events before you go to bed? At what point do you start to get anxious? What behaviours have you put in place that may be making things worse?

Competent therapists deconstruct the whole process and then help you reconstruct it, step by step, in a way that will increase the chance of it working. They examine your whole daily pattern, and how that influences your sleep.

Online cognitive, behavioural and monitoring programs, where you record what you are doing, and what effect it has, can also be useful. Sometimes, however, people are reluctant to monitor themselves, particularly if the information they start to record – for example, how much alcohol they are drinking in the evening – is inconsistent with what they would prefer to believe.

It is easy for us to tell ourselves that we don't drink much alcohol, tea or coffee in the evening or that we are very physically active during the day. It is also easy to believe that we stick to a regular schedule for going to bed and getting up in the morning. When their recordings start to show that people are not sticking to the program, often they abandon their recording.

The online programs are full of helpful information, smart tips and strongly suggest that keeping accurate diaries and using monitoring devices are likely to help.

They also make it clear that actively dealing with anxiety and other psychological problems is critical.

Medications

Starting with simple psychological and behavioural approaches are strongly recommended. However, when insomnia is more severe or persistent, medication can work hand in hand with them. The medication might help you to get the behaviour right, which can lead to a long-term, medication-free solution.

If you only use medication, and don't engage in the behavioural and cognitive strategies, you might end up back with the same problem, and possibly with a drug dependence problem as well. People with insomnia sometimes develop alcohol or prescription medication problems. When they have both, treatment can then get very complicated.

None of the sedative drugs, including those prescribed by doctors (mainly benzodiazepines these days) or those that are self-prescribed (mainly alcohol or cannabis) induce normal sleep. They cause unconsciousness, but that is not normal sleep. Normal sleep has many stages, deep sleep and dream sleep being particularly important, and progressing through those stages during the night is essential to waking up feeling refreshed.

Self-medicating

Alcohol

Some find that their insomnia is less bad when they have a couple of glasses of wine before bed. 'It stops me worrying about things and seems to knock me out.' Good or bad?

Alcohol is a favourite go-to-sleep drug, and has an upside and a downside. Alcohol is a sedative. It makes us sleepy half an hour to an hour after we have it, and that helps us fall asleep. However, as the effect wears off, our falling blood alcohol level creates a stimulating effect, which can wake us up an hour or two after going to sleep, which is the time we *should* be progressing to deep sleep.

Often people initially think that treating their insomnia with alcohol is working, but then they start waking up at three in the morning, and find that, due to the disturbed sleep pattern and lack of deep refreshing sleep, when they wake they don't feel refreshed.

In addition, using alcohol every night to aid sleep is not great for our overall health. More calories, leading to weight gain, is bad for sleep and increases snoring and sleep apnea. There is also an increased likelihood of liver damage and heart problems, including disturbed heart rhythms. Overall, a bad strategy for our health.

Cannabis

Cannabis is, like alcohol, a sedative. For many, it is their preferred way to relax in the evening or used as a pre-bed sedative. While it has less immediate rebound effects than alcohol, it causes similar sleep problems. It interferes with deep sleep, meaning we wake up feeling less refreshed.

Prescribed Medications

Prescribed medications can play an important role in treating some forms of insomnia. Ideally, you and your health professional can decide what will best get you through the crisis and back into good habits, without medication becoming a long-term solution.

Benzodiazepines

Benzodiazepines such as diazepam (Valium), and temazepam (Normison) have been used a lot to help people get to sleep. They can also help reduce anxiety.

Like alcohol, they turn the activity of brain cells down. When the brain is less stimulated, and sending fewer messages between cells, you are much more likely to get drowsy and drop off to sleep.

Most medicines prescribed for sleep, like temazepam, have short 'half-lives'. That means they are metabolised in the body in a few hours, so their effect doesn't last too long. However, other benzodiazepines (like diazepam), tend to remain in the body and the brain for longer, which can cause a hangover effect the next morning.

These medicines are intended to push us over the edge into the first stages of sleep, but if they are active for too long they can interfere with deep sleep and cause us to be drowsy the next morning.

Importantly, these medicines can lead to dependency. If you take them for a while, the effect tends to wear off, so you tend to need to take more, and that can create problems. There are likely to be withdrawal effects when you stop taking them, which might cause even more insomnia than when you started.

As they are sedative drugs, they can also affect cognitive function by affecting our memory and making us slower to react to the environment (like when driving a car or operating machines). This happens because of the direct effects the drugs have on normal alertness, and because the drugs interfere with the way the brain normally stores memories when we are asleep.

When you are dependent on these drugs, you are not getting normal sleep. You are being sedated. That is better than being awake all the time, but is not nearly as good as natural sleep. The normal sleep stages that are critical to brain and body health, deep sleep and dream sleep, are being disrupted. It is important that these drugs are seen as a short-term treatment to help restore a healthy sleep pattern, not as a long-term or permanent solution.

Melatonin

Recently, melatonin has been more commonly used as a sleep medication. Melatonin is the natural body hormone that is most responsible for the timing of the onset of sleep, and our progression through the normal stages of sleep. So, it is the medication that most resembles what the body normally does. If you take it when your body is naturally producing the most melatonin, about 9 or 10 pm, it adds to the body's own dose, and can aid the onset and depth of sleep.

Some of us, either genetically or during periods of brain-related illness (including depression), don't produce melatonin in the normal way at the normal time. Taking additional melatonin, which is available over the counter from pharmacies and comes in short and longer-acting versions, can assist this natural process. However, we do not yet have an easy way of telling whether someone's melatonin release is normal or less than it should be. We try to guess from their patterns of activity and sleep.

Another advantage of melatonin is that we do not become physically dependent on it.

Orexin Antagonists

We produce another chemical called orexin, which comes on in the afternoons to help keep us awake through the late afternoon and early evening. A new class of sleep drugs are orexin antagonists. They help turn this orexin arousal off at night. They are also short-acting, so don't necessarily help to keep us asleep.

CHECKLIST

- Sufficient sleep is vital to mental and physical health.
- Anxiety often causes insomnia. Then, once it starts, approaching bedtime can itself make us anxious.
- To treat insomnia:
  - Be physically active during the day.
  - Distract yourself from anxious thoughts. Prepare other things to think about.
  - Try to break patterns of 'getting-ready-for-bed' rituals that cause anxiety.
  - Don't use alcohol or cannabis.
  - Medication may be helpful in the short term, but don't let it become a long-term solution.
  - Melatonin is the medication that most resembles our body's natural rhythms.

13

Schizophrenia

If you think this Universe is bad, you should see some of the others.

Philip K. Dick

Schizophrenia may be the most misunderstood mental illness. We all have some idea of what depression and anxiety are like, because we have all felt sad and worried to some degree, but hearing voices that aren't there sounds like science fiction. What is it like to have schizophrenia? Why does it happen? How is it treated?

What Is Schizophrenia?

A person with schizophrenia can hear voices when no-one else is speaking, and see and smell things that do not exist. These sensations and signals appear to be coming from the outside world but, in fact, are being generated inside their own head. What is happening?

Psychotic symptoms, or hallucinations, are more common than we think. They can occur when we are severely sleep deprived, when falling asleep or waking, and with epilepsy, drug intoxication and alcohol withdrawal. Those experiencing extreme traumatic stress can also have psychotic symptoms.

Brain scans show that when someone with schizophrenia says they hear a voice, the part of the brain that hears and processes sound is active. That means the brain is having exactly the same experience as it would with a real external voice. The person *is* hearing something. The voice sounds like it is coming from the external world. They turn around to see who is talking, or talk back to it, but there is no-one there.

Often the voice says horrible, disturbing and threatening things. Sometimes there is more than one voice, and they talk to each other about you: 'He's a useless, terrible person.' The voices might discuss private thoughts that you have not shared with anyone else. It is disorientating and very frightening.

Other common symptoms of schizophrenia are:
-   A flat affect. There is little emotional engagement or variation. Often families report that this loss of emotional responsiveness is the most distressing part of the illness.
-   Unusual thinking patterns and ways of piecing thoughts together. These odd thought patterns and misinterpretations give rise to delusional and untrue beliefs about the external world and how it functions.
-   Disjointed thinking and the loss of logical connections between thoughts. As a consequence, it becomes increasingly difficult to understand the thinking processes of the person with the illness.
-   Disorganised behaviour. Without apparent explanation, a person's behaviour can become chaotic and progressively less connected to the external world. When extreme, this can result in almost complete withdrawal.

About one per cent of adults will have a schizophrenia-like episode in their lifetime. The most common age for a first episode is from fifteen to twenty-five, when the brain is changing and maturing, and new and complex connections are being created.

At the start of the illnesses, it is usually only active for brief periods and sometimes manifests by the person becoming pre-occupied by something that is of little or no importance. A painting you have seen a hundred times suddenly seems to be more important than the person you are talking to. Or you might hear a voice for a short period. As the illness progresses, the hallucinations can become more elaborate and persistent.

Once schizophrenia takes hold, it is usually quite severe. There is less of a spectrum than with anxiety and depression. For some, symptoms will come and go. For others, they persist.

Who Gets It?

Our vulnerability to schizophrenia is largely determined by genetic and developmental factors that occur before birth or in early child-hood. Only a small proportion of us, probably about five per cent, carry a high genetic risk, and only about one in five of these people will have an episode of illness.

If you have genes that make you vulnerable, some specific environmental factors can increase your risk, including:
- Viral infections while you are in the womb
- Physical trauma during childbirth
- Some childhood exposures, such as viral infections or extreme emotional trauma
- Brain infections at any age
- Heavy cannabis or amphetamine use, especially in the teenage years
- Severe emotional stress.

How People Respond

When something unusual happens, we try to make sense of it. The symptoms of schizophrenia are often both extraordinary and confronting, and to explain them people come up with rationalisations that are unusual but nonetheless have some logic. 'Where did that voice come from? There's no-one around. There's no television or radio. Is it coming from inside my head? How could that be? Could there be some sort of transmitter in my head? Who put it there? How? Who is conspiring against me?'

People with schizophrenia often think they have been interfered with by an external agency. In trying to make sense of the strange, scary things that are happening, they take something real and go from there. It used to be, 'Aliens have inserted a chip in my brain.' In 2021, it sometimes was, 'The COVID vaccine has taken over my brain.' Two hundred years ago, the explanation was that the voices came from God or the Devil. 'The Devil is in me. It has to be exorcised.'

Those with schizophrenia are often scared to tell anyone what is happening. They think, often quite rightly, that no-one will understand what is happening to them. While the idea that someone has seized control of their brain makes sense to them, they know others will consider it a paranoid fantasy. 'If I tell anyone, they'll think I'm crazy.' Instead, they keep it to themselves, retreat into their room, go online and find other people who have experienced something similar.

Why Does It Happen?

Our brain receives information from the outside world via our five senses, and then processes it. When we talk to someone, our eyes are interpreting light, our ears are interpreting sound, and our brain is turning all that into the perception of a conversation.

From the mass of sensory data it receives, our brain draws our attention to that which is most relevant. So, we pay more attention to what the person we are talking to is saying than to the painting over her shoulder.

This all takes a lot of brain wiring, and sometimes that wiring can go haywire. Brain-imaging studies in those with schizophrenia have shown that the way that wiring is set up during childhood, or the way that it rearranges itself during adolescence, can go wrong. In those with psychotic and some other mental disorders, the normal process of 'pruning' connections between brain cells, particularly in the frontal lobes that oversee complex thoughts, is exaggerated. What drives this process is not entirely clear but there is often brain inflammation during acute episodes, which has the potential to seriously disrupt the normal ways cells are connected.

Normally, when our brains draw our attention to something unusual, like the smell of smoke, we switch our attention to it, and then our cognitive processes come into play. 'What does that smell mean? Is it a fire? Should I get out of here?' With schizophrenia, there is a breakdown in the brain's filtering mechanisms and the relevant and the irrelevant can get mixed up. All sorts of information gets in, in the wrong order. Our perception becomes muddled and loses coherence. In addition, the mind can generate hallucinations of things that are not there at all.

The search to understand exactly what is happening is ongoing, and remains a big target in research.

The Myth of the Split Personality

Schizophrenia is derived from Greek and means 'fragmented mind'. It describes how the rational, emotional and perceptual functions of our brain are no longer working in harmony, but have become split. The brain can no longer make sense of things.

Its functions have become dislocated, like a dislocated joint. However, when the term went to the United States, the 'fragmented mind' was misinterpreted as referring to a split personality.

Diagnosis and Treatment

People with schizophrenia do not often say, 'I am hearing voices that aren't real.' More commonly, they describe the reality of what they are experiencing: 'I'm hearing voices. They must be coming from a chip in my brain.'

They can make odd associations, jump between unconnected ideas in unpredictable ways and string together different concepts in unusual ways, sometimes on the sound of a word or some other odd association which they then try to explain, as if it is something that the rest of the world hasn't quite caught onto yet.

Diagnosing schizophrenia is not just about listening to *what* people say. It is about listening to *how* they say it, observing their expressions, or lack of them, and the emotion they show. Is the emotion consistent with what they are saying? How do they string a sentence together? In severe cases, words and sentences are put together in a disorganised, almost haphazard way, that is hard to make sense of.

There is now a focus on the early identification of those with schizophrenia. It is complicated because only a small proportion of those with psychotic symptoms go on to develop schizophrenia, so you have to pick up a lot of people early to find those who are at most risk. It is a bit like screening for cancer. However, progress is being made. Any young person who has psychotic symptoms or very odd behaviour should be assessed and followed up to see if they start to hear unusual things, behave in bizarre ways, hold strange ideas, or their school performance or social situation changes.

Treatment

People can learn that the voices they hear are being generated by their own brain, and to recognise them. They can try to learn to live with the voices and, when they come, to think, 'Okay, this is that thing that happens to me. I've just got to continue on.' There are other things that happen to us, like ringing in our ears or chronic pain, that we can't get rid of, but we can adapt to and live with.

Medication

Before the development of effective medication in the 1960s, people with schizophrenia would have episodes that lasted weeks, months or even years. If they were unable to function, they often stayed in asylums and mental hospitals until they recovered. Charities created asylums, and churches provided convents, monasteries and other places of safety and quietness for people whose mind had become dislocated to stay in while they waited to recover.

Now we know that, for those with a genetic vulnerability to schizophrenia, the release of a lot of dopamine (for example, following the use of amphetamine-releasing drugs) can bring on hallucinations. Dopamine-blocking agents have been developed to stop these symptoms, and work reasonably well to halt hallucinations and delusions. However, they are not as effective at rectifying other symptoms, such as the impairment of emotion and cognitive function that goes with the illness.

Many of the medications also have anti-inflammatory effects that may help to protect the brain from the damaging effects of acute episodes. Reduced inflammation appears to be associated with preservation of connections between brain cells and retention of longer-term cognitive abilities. It may also help to reduce recurrence or progression of the illness.

A side effect of early schizophrenia medication was that it slowed people down, and could cause trembling. People looked and felt very medicated and sedated, and had reduced facial expression. They could also get restless, and not be able to sit still. As a result, as soon as they were able to leave hospital, many stopped taking their medication.

Now, the medication is better, but there can still be side effects of weight gain, increased risk of diabetes and over-sedation. Some medications still have significant motor side effects with restlessness and agitation.

Today, the overwhelming majority of younger people who are well-treated in their first episode will recover. They will be at risk of a recurrence (as with many severe illnesses, such as cancer), and may have some ongoing impairment or symptoms that they have to learn to live with. It may be that the illness does most damage to the brain in its early period, so ways to stop the illness progressing and preserve the brain are being looked at.

Many people with schizophrenia who take medication can recover to the extent that they return to their jobs, lives and relationships. Lots of people with high-pressure and difficult jobs have been treated for psychotic episodes and returned to work. However, people are less likely to talk openly about schizophrenia and the medication they take to control it than those suffering depression or anxiety, as there is still a stigma attached. Hopefully that will change.

Nonetheless, schizophrenia is not the terrible life sentence it was even a couple of decades ago. The situation has radically improved. It is still a severe illness and needs good, specialised care to get the best outcome, but treatment is improving.

As with many other mental disorders, the use of medications is only a part of effective treatment. Other psychological, family and social therapies can play a critical role in promoting recovery. These treatments help people with schizophrenia to maintain personal and family relationships, obtain and retain employment and maintain their own homes.

Reducing the use of other drugs, especially cannabis, amphetamines and alcohol, is critical. Additionally, a much greater emphasis is now placed on maintaining better physical health, through a better diet, exercise and reduced cigarette smoking.

CHECKLIST

- A person with schizophrenia can hear, see and smell things they think are coming from the external world but are, in fact, being generated by their own brain.
- They can also have little emotional engagement and unusual thinking patterns.
- The brain actually hears voices in the same way it hears them from the external world.
- About five per cent of people have a genetic vulnerability to schizophrenia, and about one in five of them get it.
- Schizophrenia is extremely confronting and distressing.
- Treatment, especially medication, has greatly improved, and recovery from an episode is very common.
- Early diagnosis is important for effective treatment.

14

Obsessive Compulsive Disorder

It is like you have two brains – a rational brain and an
irrational brain. And they are constantly fighting.

Emilie Ford

Obsessive Compulsive Disorder (OCD) occurs when we have repetitive, intrusive and obsessive thoughts or feelings, and feel anxiously compelled to repeat routines, like washing our hands or checking doors are locked.

There are two distinct phases:
- Obsessive thought: 'If I don't wash my hands now, I might get a disease.'
- Compulsive behaviour: washing hands, again and again.

When do everyday routines and personal hygiene habits tip over into compulsive behaviour? How do you treat OCD?

Routines and Rituals

Most of us have routines and patterns. We do things in the same sequence, and in the same way, every morning: wake up, sigh, get up, go to toilet, shower, choose outfit, get dressed, make coffee, have breakfast, search for keys, clean teeth, pat dog, walk to bus stop.

Some have obsessional personalities – lives that are full of habits, rituals and specific ways of doing things. The house must be tidy. Plates should be washed before cutlery. The iPad must be kept on the second shelf. The red cushion goes at the far end of the sofa, the green one in the middle and the yellow one at the close end. Anything else just isn't right. Others may find all this a bit odd.

This sort of behaviour, however, has some advantages. Being obsessive about having a neat home prevents chaos and untidiness. Double-checking the front door is locked at night ensures intruders are kept out. Handwashing after being in the bathroom makes sense. We want doctors who triple check that they are injecting you with the right drug and pilots who are obsessional about safety. That kind of cautious, careful and appropriate checking before doing something dangerous makes sense. If you are about to abseil down a cliff, you don't want the person checking your harness to shrug and say, 'It'll probably be okay.'

When people have routines and rituals, and follow them, they feel fine. However, if they cannot do things 'the right way', they get anxious. Their anxiety is a consequence of them not doing the behaviour: if they want to wash their hands, but there is nowhere to wash them, anxiety rises. If their partner rearranges the cushions and says, 'Let's just try it this way for a while,' they get anxious. It feels like something terrible is happening.

When Do Rituals and Routines Become OCD?

James was once at a dinner of ten people where someone said, 'Everyone tell us their OCD behaviour.' Everyone had one. James's was, and is, about leaving hotel rooms. Before he checks out, he has to check the room – under the bed, under every pillow – several times to make sure he hasn't left anything. He starts to leave, then comes back and checks again. It delays him a few minutes, but eventually he can leave. As soon as he shuts the door behind him, he feels fine.

Some, however, have to check their room so often, they miss their plane.

People with OCD become good at hiding their behaviours. 'Why did you spend twenty-five minutes in the bathroom?' 'It's personal.' There are people in important jobs who have significant OCD that they are able to control just enough.

How do you know if an unusual routine has boiled over into OCD and you should seek help? Often, people who seek treatment are those to whom someone has said, 'You probably should do something about that. You could save two hours a day.' Or, there has been some consequence that shows them that their behaviour is interfering with their life. They might miss several planes, or wash their hands so much that they become red and raw.

Three factors to consider are:
- Frequency: how often do you do the behaviour?
- Extent of interference: how much time do you spend doing the behaviour? If you feel a compulsion to touch your elbow, it only takes a second, but having to continually go and wash your hands takes longer.
- Inability to stop. Can you stop the behaviour for a day? If you can't, then you might need help.

How does OCD Start?

There is a strong genetic component with OCD. It can run in families. Children often do things repetitively, in an obsessional way. They wash, check and count things excessively, or try not to step on cracks. However, as they get older, these tendencies often diminish.

Part of brain development is creating inhibitory pathways, whose job is to stop us doing things. For example, in a hotel room, the inhibitory pathways help us to think, 'I've checked the room three times and I want to check it again, but I have to catch the plane. I'm leaving.' The inhibitor overrides the desire to check. With OCD, the problem is that the inhibitor fails to override the desire to check. There is no stop button.

When people develop OCD, often the inhibitory pathways that turn those repetitive checking processes down have not developed as they should. Why? Some infections can interfere with brain development and might limit the growth of inhibitory pathways. Traumatic experiences can also play a part. We can become conditioned to think, 'Something terrible happened, and it might happen again. Therefore, I have to keep checking to make sure it doesn't.'

Brain development can get stuck, leaving people with a vulnerability to obsessional thinking and compulsive behaviour through life. Some might usually have their OCD under control, but if they become depressed or develop anxiety, it flares up.

The early months of COVID were difficult for many with a vulnerability to OCD. They might have been trying to resist urges to continually wash their hands, and then suddenly were being told to wash their hands every time they went out, and that touching any doorknob or kitchen bench could expose them to the virus.

The Two Components of OCD – Thoughts and Behaviours

Obsessional Thoughts

People with OCD have intrusive thoughts that something terrible will happen. They think they might *do* something terrible, like punch a stranger, or that something very bad will happen if they *don't* do something, like check doors are locked.

At some level, people rationally understand that the chances of the imagined catastrophic event occurring are incredibly low, but they still want to react to the thought. Just in case. They know they are being irrational, but that does not stop the thoughts coming.

Compulsive Behaviours

The only thing that will reduce the anxiety that obsessional thoughts create is to carry out a particular behaviour. If the thought is, 'I might have germs on my hands', the behaviour is to wash the hands. If the thought is that the front door may be unlocked and allow in an intruder, the behaviour is to check the door is locked. Once that is done, anxiety immediately reduces, until the thought returns, and the pattern repeats.

At some point, people try to push back. 'I don't need to wash my hands again.' However, resisting the behaviour causes their anxiety to skyrocket, until they give in. The volcanic anxiety OCD induces is worse than ordinary anxiety.

Ian used to treat people with severe OCD. Some would wash their hands forty-five times in the morning before doing anything. The more the cycle repeats, the more anxiety increases. Eventually, the intervals between the Thought/Behaviour cycles shorten, and people are continually checking, while their anxiety keeps increasing. 'I've checked six times. I need to check again.'

They have to do the behaviour to relieve their anxiety, but the periods of relief get shorter and shorter. Every time they repeat the pattern, they are reinforcing the 'Feel uncomfortable/Reward/ Feel better' cycle. It is like being on a playground roundabout that is going too fast to get off. Somebody has to slow the roundabout down.

There are some parallels with addictive behaviour. People try to stop drinking alcohol, but then feel uncomfortable. That increases their desire to drink because they know it will relax them, so they have one. The next day, stopping is even harder. (See Chapter 15, 'Addiction'.)

OCD can come to dominate people's lives, but it is possible to get things back under control.

Treatment

OCD in Children

If kids are showing OCD-like behaviour and it continues, brain circuits will build that increase the risk of similar behaviours occurring through life. Sometimes parents and others can help kids stop.

Offering rewards can work. 'If you only wash your hands once, I'll give you ten points. When you get a hundred points, you get a new book.'

Instead of just talking about it, the most effective treatment for children can be for someone else (usually an adult) to intervene and quietly, safely and effectively stop the behaviour. A parent can lead a child out of the bathroom. A grandparent can turn a kitchen tap off when the child is about to wash their hands a second time. An older sibling can take a child's hand and lead them out of the house without checking the doors are locked again. A teacher can lead a child away from repeating a checking behaviour in the classroom and on to the next activity. The more times the child safely stops doing the behaviour without getting more distressed, the more likely they are not to engage in the same action again.

Punishment – 'If you wash your hands again, you can't have dessert' – does not work well. It doesn't decrease anxiety. It just makes the whole process even more traumatic. That additional

174

distress caused by the fear of punishment may actually make it more likely that the unwanted behaviour might increase in frequency.

OCD in Adults

For a long time psychologists and psychiatrists have come up with all sorts of psychological explanations for OCD, and ways to cure it. The traditional mixture of talking-based therapies, which have been successful with other mental illnesses, do not work as well with OCD. It appears the best outcomes arise from behavioural therapy. That is, working to change your behaviour, stopping the repeated actions, reducing the anxiety, and confronting the weird thoughts about what may happen next.

Dealing with Obsessional Thoughts

Stopping ourselves having unpleasant thoughts is difficult. Brains are creative. They throw up ideas, make associations and see links. We are imaginative, and there is a huge advantage and upside to that. Tall buildings, Netflix and spaghetti bolognaise would not exist without our imagination. We can also imagine scenarios that are terrifying and unpleasant, but that, too, can have advantages. Just ask Stephen King.

It is quite common for us to have strange and disturbing thoughts. 'What if I punch that guy as I walk past him? What if I pushed him in front of that car?' Having thoughts like that pop into our head does not make us dangerous psychopaths. It is just a thought. When we have such thoughts, we should not get preoccupied with them. We should just let them go.

However, some of us have a vulnerability or predisposition to have more of those unpleasant thoughts, and to get stuck on them. When an unpleasant thought comes, we think about it, and examine it. The more we do that, the more the thought takes root in our brain, and the more likely it is to return.

When trying to deal with obsessional and unpleasant thoughts, such as, 'If I don't check the doors are locked again, someone will come in and murder us,' should we aim to:

1. Never have the thought again?, or,
2. Not be distressed by the thought?

People usually pick option 1. They want to get rid of the thought entirely, but that is very difficult. Thoughts come, and it is hard to stop them. Once you become stuck on a repetitive, obsessional thought, it is hard to unpick the circuits and let it go. It is like someone telling you not to think about a blue elephant. Often the thought becomes part of our thinking pattern, or we become conditioned to have it in particular environments. For example, every time we see a public toilet sign we start to think it may be a new source of infection. Or, every time we eat in a restaurant, we start to imagine that all the kitchen staff have an infection that has got into the food.

Option 2 is easier. Accept that the thought may come, but try and avoid becoming distressed by it. Remind yourself that it is just an unusual thought, not reality. You don't need to get upset by the thought, or act on it. You can practise trying to reduce the distress and anxiety that is associated with the thought. You can re-label the thought. Instead of seeing it as an indication that something real and terrible is about to happen, remind yourself that it is 'just a random thought'.

We often feel that our thoughts are us. That if we think some-thing, it must be true. That is wrong. Our thoughts are just thoughts. We have thousands of them. Some are meaningful. Many are not. One of Shakespeare's thoughts was to write a play about a Danish guy called Hamlet. He latched onto it as meaningful. Then he had another thought about writing a play about a talking dolphin, and let that one go. We can choose the thoughts we give attention to, and the ones we do not.

When we attach great importance and emotion (such as fear and distress) to a thought, we make it more powerful. Say two people both have the thought that they need to check that their front door is locked. One reminds herself she has already locked the door, and dismisses the thought as irrelevant. The other knows he has locked the door, but because he attaches great importance to the thought, he checks it again, and starts to create a repetitive thought/action pattern that could grow into something harmful. Anxiety makes us think more about the thought, and explore all its possible consequences: 'If the door isn't locked, what would happen? Who would come in? A robber? How many? Would they steal from us? Kill us? Kidnap my son?' This creates more anxiety, and around and around it goes.

Intrusive thoughts happen. If we do not get preoccupied or distressed by them, they do not tend to come back. Trying to decrease the amount of anxiety associated with the thought is a much better strategy than trying to get rid of the thought, and never have it come back. But how do you do that?

Dealing with Compulsive Behaviour
1) Exposure
The way to uncouple an unpleasant and intrusive thought from anxiety is to accept that you will have the thought, but not act on it. You think, 'I need to wash my hands so I don't infect my family,' but then resist the urge to wash your hands. This is hard because you can almost feel the dirt on your hands.

Resisting the urge to do the action while still experiencing the thought will eventually override the thought. Then the anxiety will get back under control. This is exposure therapy.

However, the process is difficult. When someone resists the urge to carry out the behaviour, their anxiety skyrockets. It feels horrible, and they have to do it not just once, but many times, because it takes time to rewire the brain. Exposure takes courage. Support from others, including the therapist, is crucial. The person will think their anxiety will never come down, and the therapist (or parent) has to instil confidence and belief that eventually it will.

If the person repeatedly refrains from doing the behaviour, they will pass through the period of very high anxiety and then their anxiety will start to reduce. They will build up more and more experiences of not washing their hands *not* leading to them getting an infection. Eventually, they will be able to leave the bathroom after two hand washings, or leave the house after two checkings of the door.

In some ways, exposure is easier than trying not to have the thought, because we have more control over our body than we do over our mind. We cannot stop thoughts, but we can restrain our body. In behavioural therapy, a therapist can ask for permission to, in an appropriate way, physically stop the person from, for example, washing their hands.

2) Positive reinforcement

When you manage to go to bed without checking the front door more than once, and then the next morning wake up un-murdered, take a moment to connect the fact that you did not re-check the doors with the outcome that nothing bad happened. Do the same whenever you resist washing your hands and do not get an infection. Use that as positive reinforcement. It *is* possible not to do the behaviour, and everything to be fine.

However, those with OCD often say, 'Okay, that time I didn't get infected. I got lucky. But it might happen next time.'

People come up with elaborate explanations as to why the feared event did not occur, and why it could happen next time. We are very creative. Some people imagine that the infective bug has suddenly mutated, so that now it can hide from the soap they are using to wash their hands. Consequently, they decide they must use a more powerful cleaning agent, but then imagine that the bug has already developed resistance to that, and so on, with even more elaborate and unlikely explanations as to how powerful the bug really is.

The potential to go down those rabbit holes is there, but we have to try and leave the thoughts out there without recommencing.

OCD and Medication

If someone is struggling with behaviour therapy, good psychologists will suggest medication, as well as therapy. Often the best treatment for severe OCD is combining both behavioural therapy and medication. There are types of antidepressants, particularly those that affect serotonin in a big way, that seem to work best on OCD. The drug reduces the person's anxiety level, which helps them cope enough to work through the exposure therapy.

CHECKLIST

- OCD consists of repeated, obsessive thoughts followed by compulsive behaviour.
- If your routines and repeated behaviours are interfering with your life, you may have OCD.
- To treat OCD:
  - It is very hard to try to stop having the obsessive thought. You can try to downplay the significance of the thought or lessen the distress that the thought provokes.
  - Often the most effective treatment is to try to stop doing the behaviour, but it is not easy. Resisting washing hands or checking that doors are locked can cause anxiety to spike. However, if you can keep resisting, anxiety will start to reduce.

15

Addiction

First you take a drink, then the drink takes a drink,
then the drink takes you.

F. Scott Fitzgerald

It was the hardest boyfriend I ever had to break up with.
Fergie from the Black Eyed Peas on drug addiction

What can we become addicted to? Alcohol, drugs, gambling? Definitely. Online shopping? Porn? Can you really be addicted to sex? Exercise? Food?

Are some of us more prone to addiction than others?

If you are addicted to something, what can you do about it?

What Is Addiction?

Historically, the label 'addiction' has been attached to two different types of problems. The first involves alcohol or other drugs, where there is a clear and continued use of a substance, despite the harm that repeated intake is causing to our health or welfare.

The second is much broader, where there are no chemicals involved, but a certain behaviour, such as gambling or shopping, is repeated endlessly, despite the obvious harm being caused to the person or those they are close to. While professionals will often call this an obsession (see Chapter 14, 'OCD'), many prefer the term 'addiction' to indicate it is beyond voluntary control.

The reasons why these quite different problems get lumped together is because of what they share in common. First, that despite the strong desire to stop, and the harm being caused, the person feels compelled to repeat the behaviour. Second, the same brain systems, involving the release of the chemical dopamine, are involved in driving these repetitive patterns. Dopamine is the main pleasure chemical in the brain. Its release gives us a natural high, and it is particularly active in those centres of the brain that drive repetitive behaviours.

How Do We Get Addicted?

When we do something pleasurable (eat ice-cream, perform on stage, have sex), our brain releases a range of chemicals, including dopamine, and starts to connect engaging in the activity and feeling pleasure. Most animals like pleasure, and it is a strong motivator of behaviour. That's why we walk to the shop in the rain to get more chocolate.

A pleasurable activity or substance drives dopamine release, which can make us want more. When we do not get that pleasure, and feel low, we may well come to believe that to feel good again, we need to do the activity (for example, gamble) or take the substance (for example, ice-cream). Before long, we may come to think we don't just want more, we *need* more.

Chemical Addiction

When we take some drugs such as alcohol, cocaine, opiates, amphetamines, marijuana, caffeine and nicotine, there are a range of feel-good chemical substances, including opiates, cannabinoids and serotonin, that are triggered in our brain, as well as dopamine. Each of these substances has the potential to induce a chemical addiction.

The brain becomes progressively accustomed to having the substance, which means that we need to keep taking more to get the same effect. The brain then adapts to high daily doses by reducing its response to those chemicals, which means that we respond less even when we take a higher dose.

Because the brain has adapted to the substance (coffee, heroin, sleeping tablets) that we are regularly taking, if we suddenly stop or reduce the amount, the brain believes it is being deprived and we get unpleasant withdrawal symptoms. If the substance normally wakes us up (like coffee or amphetamines), then we will feel drowsy, slow and sleep-deprived, with a bad headache added in. If the substance normally makes us sleepy (alcohol, sleeping tablets), we will feel agitated and be unable to sleep. The good news is that over a few days, the brain will readjust to the absence of the daily hit by returning to its pre-addiction state.

Initially, having coffee, alcohol or heroin might make us feel better, brighter, and happier. After taking them for a long period, however, part of the reason we want them is because if we stop, we will experience those withdrawal effects like pain, low energy, depressed mood, irritability, or even an epileptic seizure (after alcohol withdrawal), a migraine (after caffeine withdrawal) or cramping and vomiting (after heroin withdrawal).

Historically, heroin, nicotine and methamphetamine are at the top of the list for addiction potential. On a day-to-day basis, in terms of harm done, alcohol also rates very highly.

Shopping Addiction and Heroin Addiction – The Same or Different?

There is a difference in degree, and basic physiology, between a chemical addiction to heroin where there are severe physical withdrawal symptoms, and a behavioural addiction to shopping or exercise. Historically, shopping, gambling, sex and exercise 'addictions' would have been called compulsive behaviours, because when we stopped, there was no physical withdrawal.

However, if online shopping or sex causes your body to release dopamine, or other chemicals that make you feel really good, and then you suddenly stop and no longer get that dopamine hit, some argue that that is just like withdrawal.

Some people exercise every day and feel better when they do. If they miss a day they feel bad. Is that withdrawal, or just frustration and disappointment? Exercise is good for us, and provides relief from anxiety or stress. What is the downside of that repeated and pleasant behaviour? If our exercise habit is not so compulsive that it interferes with other parts of our life, runs us down physically or is linked to other conditions such as body dysmorphia or anorexia, then it is not really an addiction. It is just a well-entrenched habit.

You could argue that shopping addiction goes further, particularly if you cannot stop and are spending more than you can afford. Then it starts to look more like drug addiction, with the same sorts of behaviours, and being triggered by similar environmental cues like exposure to the opportunity.

Both compulsive shopping and alcohol addiction arise from basic systems that cause us to want to repeat pleasurable behaviour. We want more, because it makes us feel good. The more we experience that pleasure, the more we associate three things:
- The environment (shops or pubs) reminds us of . . .
- The behaviour (shopping or drinking), which gives us . . .
- The pleasure (the thrill of owning something new, or intoxication).

At that point, what is and is not technically an addiction becomes a bit of a semantic argument. Whether it be taking heroin or shopping online, what matters is that you recognise that you are behaving compulsively, and that the behaviour is out of control and causing harm, and take steps to address it.

Are You Addicted to Your Phone?

'What do I have to do today? What's happening in the world? What's new on Netflix? What have the Kardashians posted on Instagram? What are my friends saying on WhatsApp? Has anyone swiped right on my Tinder profile?' Your phone will give you all the answers. Smartphones are full of reminders, schedules, calendars, emails and messages that we easily become dependent on.

Both smartphones and social media use intermittent reinforcement. That is, as with poker machines, we get rewards, but the timing of those rewards is unpredictable, which means we have to keep checking. 'The last fifteen emails I got were rubbish, but the next one could be life-changing.' 'I just scrolled through one hundred Twitter posts without seeing anything interesting, but the next one could be gold.' And occasionally it is gold. The next life-changing email or golden tweet *will* come. We just don't know when. The only way to find out is to keep checking. Intermittent reinforcement makes it much more likely we will become addicted to our phone.

How Do You Know if You are Dependent or Addicted?

If not taking the substance or doing the activity for a day makes you feel very uncomfortable, then you are probably becoming dependent.

If you are willing to risk real harm by going out of your way to do the behaviour, or get the substance, you are probably addicted. If you are willing to steal, get into fights, deceive those close to you and get arrested to get more, addiction is the appropriate label.

A word health professionals like is 'dependent', rather than addicted. For example, if Ian and James don't have coffee every morning they lack energy, feel tired and irritable, and get head-aches. They are both dependent. If many things in your life revolve around the activity or the substance, you are probably dependent.

If a health professional is trying to find out if someone is addicted, they might ask:
- Have you tried to give up?
- How long for?
- Have other people said to you, 'This is really a problem'?
- Have you said that to yourself?
- What does your family say about it?
- What do others who care about you say?
- What does your doctor say about it?

Once an Addict, Always an Addict?

The American idea is that addiction is not your fault. It is an illness. You were born an addict, and you are an addict for life. To treat addiction, you need to stop forever, because if you ever do it again, you'll be addicted again. The only treatment is abstinence.

That is very absolutist, and while it might make sense for some addicted to alcohol and heroin, or for those who have lost their home and family due to gambling, how do you abstain from other compulsive behaviours like shopping or sex? Never walk through a mall or buy milk from the corner shop again? No sex, ever?

An alternative view is that, even with physically addic-tive substances like alcohol, it is possible for some to return to controlled drinking, and learn to drink in moderation. After all, the overwhelming majority of drinkers aren't addicted.

The point of difference between the two schools of thought might arise from different ways of thinking about the brain. If we view the brain as fixed and unchangeable, it makes sense to conclude that once an addict, always an addict. The more modern view, however, is that the brain is constantly changing, and can be rewired. This suggests that with some hard work, most addicts may be able to rewire their brains and change their relationship to the things they are addicted to.

Are There Addictive Personalities?

A controversial question is, if you are addicted to one thing, like nicotine or alcohol, are you more likely to later become addicted to something else, like heroin, gambling or exercise. Do certain people have addictive personalities?

We are not all equally likely to be addicted. There is considerable individual variation as a result of both genetic and environmental factors. A *propensity* toward addiction often runs in families, which can lead to *actual* addiction running in families.

Our childhood environment is important. Growing up in disrupted or traumatic circumstances increases the chances that we will later become addicted to something. Early exposure to substances also raises the chances of addiction. Those who grew up in a family of smokers are much more likely to themselves smoke.

The teenage years are significant. If you never smoke as a teenager, it is highly unlikely you will take it up as an adult. Those who start drinking alcohol or taking drugs in their teens are much more likely to become addicted to them than those who start as adults.

Teenagers, especially boys, haven't fully developed their risk-assessment systems, or 'Stop' button, in their brain, which makes them less likely to take into account the longer-term consequences of actions. They are more likely to think, 'That went badly. Let's do it again!'

Complicating matters further, early exposure to some drugs, such as amphetamines and alcohol, can affect brain development, and that itself can make addictive behaviour more likely. Teenagers who are more risk-taking are likely to try more substances and risky behaviours than others. Those with attention or mood problems often try substances at earlier ages. Those who use cannabis are more likely to go on and use nicotine. Previously, it was usually the other way around – nicotine use would increase the likelihood of cannabis use.

There can be some patterns of overlapping addictions, but it is also true that each substance and compulsive behaviour has its own set of characteristics. It is not inevitable that people move from one substance or behaviour to another.

'Self-medicating' and Addiction

If life is very challenging, or if we are in psychological or physical pain, we are more likely to seek out those regular dopamine, opiate, cannabinoid or serotonin shots in our brain that addictive or compulsive behaviours provide. People use addictive substances and activities as a way of escaping from and distracting themselves from unhappiness, anxiety, depression or pain.

Alcohol can affect our mood and, in the short-term, make us feel good. Cocaine and amphetamines release dopamine and create pleasure. Heroin is an opiate that connects with the natural opiate pathways in the brain to stop pain. Benzodiazepines connect with the brain's natural 'calm down' systems to reduce anxiety and cause drowsiness. So, if life is unpleasant, these substances can become attractive.

When people have mood disorders and psychological distress, it is very common for them to misuse illegal drugs, prescription drugs and alcohol. When people are in significant physical or psychological pain, including having depression or anxiety, the chance that they will become dependent on a substance substantially increases.

It also runs the other way. The earlier you are exposed to alcohol and drugs, the more likely you are to become depressed or anxious on an ongoing basis. That is because the drugs lead to a roller-coaster of drug-intoxicated highs, followed closely by drug-withdrawal lows, making your emotional life much more unstable than those not using those chemicals.

Typically, those who are addicted promise themselves and their loved ones that they are about to stop, and genuinely mean it. But then they do it again, and wake up the next morning hating themselves. It's a vicious circle. Someone promises themselves not to drink, then they *do* drink, the next morning they feel shame and regret, and quite naturally ask, 'What will make me feel better?' The answer is often another drink.

Addiction and Learning

Usually we are good at learning. We might put our hand on the hot plate once, but not many of us do it a second time. If doing something results in a bad outcome, we usually change our behaviour.

Addiction, unfortunately, is often an exception. Through addiction, people can lose their life savings, job, possessions, friends, family, home, health, and even liberty. Rationally, they understand their addiction has caused all this loss, but they keep going.

Addiction has the power to cause people to make the same mistakes again and again. It is not rational. Once someone is in the vicious, deep hole of addiction and continuous use, despite the negative consequences, the compulsive element of the brain overrides the more rational parts. When people feel the urge to feed their addiction, they get restless, distressed and anxious. That won't subside until they engage in the activity. Once they gamble, drink, or watch porn again, their anxiety goes down and they feel better.

As an addict's life gets more complex – 'I just got kicked out of my house, my relationship is over, I've got no money, I have to go to court' – they know from experience that escaping into their addiction can, for a while, make them feel okay again. People who have been in this situation say they know they are doing something stupid, but they do it anyway. They say to themselves, 'I'm not going to do it again,' and then find themselves doing it. It can feel like they are almost acting independently of themselves. 'I'm at the casino again. How did that happen?'

Triggers

If a gambling addict sees a betting shop, or a heroin addict walks past a street where they have previously scored, they associate that environment with their addictive activity. A bell ringing caused Pavlov's dog to salivate, because the dog had been conditioned to associate the bell with meat. The dog didn't need to see or smell meat to salivate anymore, just to hear the bell. Similarly, after a while, an alcoholic does not need to see a glass of wine to feel the urge to drink. They just have to see a pub or a bottle shop. That will trigger the association with alcohol, and the anticipation of the benefits (such as anxiety relief and improved mood) that will accompany drinking. For gamblers, the sight of the club where they play poker machines is enough to get their pulse racing with the anticipated thrill of landing a jackpot.

Treating Addiction

Addiction causes us to prioritise the short term over long term. 'What do I want now?' becomes more important than 'What do I want over the next five years?' We have seen how powerful it can be, so how do people ever stop?

Rock Bottom and Motivation

At what point and under what circumstances are people prepared to take realistic, prolonged action to treat their addiction?

In the criminal law world, people are often not motivated to deal with their addiction in a realistic way until they hit rock bottom. That isn't when they go to court for the first time and get a good behaviour bond. It is when they go to court for the fifth time and get sent to jail. By then, it can be a long and difficult, but by no means impossible, road back.

Early intervention is much better. The earlier you recognise that you have a problem, the easier it is to change. It is much better to do it before your whole world falls apart.

Finding the Right Motivation

People need to find the right motivation to push them to seek treatment and make a prolonged effort to stop. A doctor might tell an alcoholic that their physical health is deteriorating, but the alcoholic might not care about that. However, perhaps he does care about his relationship with his daughter, and knows it is going rapidly downhill because of his drinking. That might be where he finds his motivation to stop.

The question an addict should ask is, 'What still matters to me?'

To start treatment, we need to think longer term. The rational part of the brain, which is usually in the back seat when we are addicted, has got to assert itself. We need to recognise that the life we are leading is very different from the life we want to lead.

Make a Plan

'You know what? I'm sick of gambling. It's dumb. I'm never going to do it again.' If you say that to yourself, no matter how sincere you are, and change nothing else in your life, unfortunately, it is unlikely to work.

If you have a deep, rational desire to rid yourself of your addiction, accept that you will need more than willpower and good intentions to do it. 'Don't drink anymore', 'Just say "no"', and 'Exert willpower', are great as statements of intention, but you also need a clear, practical plan.

1. Identify triggers

We need to look at the situations that are driving our behaviour, identify what our triggers are, and try and ensure we don't come into contact with those triggers. If walking past a street where you have bought drugs before triggers you to want to take drugs again, then don't walk past that street. Take the long way home.

Our brain has changed over time to create a connection between seeing that street and craving drugs, but we can rewire those circuits, and remove that connection. If you are an addict now, it does not mean you will always be an addict. You can change.

If a teenage boy thinks he might he addicted to online porn, his trigger may be being left alone at home. To break his addiction, he should try and avoid being home alone.

If you think you are addicted to your phone, telling yourself to use it less will probably fail. The trigger is having your phone in your pocket. So stop carrying it around all the time. If you don't have it, you can't use it, and your brain can start to rewire and change.

The environmental circumstances of addiction are important. There used to be poker machines in New South Wales, but not in Victoria. The smartest thing a New South Wales poker-machine addict could do was to move to Victoria. Some did. Suddenly, they had no access to poker machines, and their addiction was cured.

If you are addicted to alcohol, it is hard to remove yourself from triggers because there are pubs, bottle shops and social events everywhere. One advantage of rehab is that it removes you from triggers. You can't drink at rehab because there's no alcohol there. Sometimes, it is best to opt out of society for a while and go somewhere where it is simply not possible to use.

2. Take the pressure off – stop for today, not forever

'One day at a time,' is an excellent motto. If you tell yourself that you are stopping forever, it can feel overwhelming, and pile on the pressure. Psychologically, it is easier to tell yourself that you are just having a break for a while, or even just for today.

Giving up something we are addicted to is hard, so try just to focus on getting things right for the next four, twelve or twenty-four hours, rather than worrying about whether you will be able to maintain it for the next five years.

3. Social support

When seventy per cent of adult men smoked, it was much harder to stop than it is today, now that smoking is much less common and more disapproved of. That negative social pressure now helps people reduce and quit. Alcohol, however, is widely accepted, and associated with fun and social pleasure, and that can make quitting harder.

When we are trying to do something hard, like break an addiction, we need lots of social support. Friends, family and other social groups play an important role. If someone in the family is trying to quit alcohol, it is very helpful if the rest of the family decides to support them by also not drinking at home, so the home becomes an alcohol-free zone. If you are trying to quit smoking, it is much harder if you live with a smoker and there are cigarettes constantly within reach.

The longer and deeper someone's addiction goes, the more that most parts of their social world start to connect to it in some way, and the less likely they are to be engaged in other activities. Alcoholics will tend to socialise with fellow drinkers at the pub, heroin addicts with fellow users and dealers, gamblers with other gamblers. Meanwhile, they withdraw from other friendships and activities that are unconnected with their addiction.

If your social world is heavily connected to your addiction, an important part of stopping is to set up a different set of social practices, and a different set of repeatable behaviours. Alcoholics Anonymous meetings are an excellent example. Instead of going to the pub, you go to the meeting. You are still being social, you are still in a group, and everyone supports each other. A great thing about AA is the peer support, the understanding of people who have been in the same situation, and their mentoring of newer members.

If someone trying to stop drinking didn't have AA meetings to go to, they might feel a need for social connection, and know their friends will be at the pub. Before they know it, there they are, having a beer with them. Ironically, what has caused them to drink has not been an overwhelming desire for alcohol. It has been a need for social connection.

Some smokers enjoy the opportunity to go outside their work building for a smoke break every hour, get some fresh air (kind of ironic) and chat to other smokers, as much or more than they enjoy the actual cigarette. If they are planning to quit smoking, they need to think about how they will meet those social needs in another way. Can they go for a walk around the building every hour with a non-smoking co-worker? Is there something else they can do with their hands? A fidget spinner, worry beads or stress ball, perhaps.

Whether it is something formal like an AA meeting, or something else you can design, it is very important to work out what social needs your addiction fulfils, and find another way to meet them.

4. Drug replacement

Methadone is commonly used as a prescribed replacement for heroin to relieve cravings and remove withdrawal symptoms. But what is the point of replacing a dependence on one drug, heroin, with another, methadone?

Methadone allows people to change their circumstances. Rather than having to do all the things required to finance and run a heroin habit, which can take up most of a person's time, money and energy, methadone allows them to fit their (prescribed) drug behavior into a small window of time, and have plenty of hours left for a job, and activities and relationships that have nothing to do with the drug world. They can start to set up a whole other life, and be physically healthier. Just as importantly, they will be socially healthier, as they start to make new connections outside the drug world. Once that new life is constructed then, if they choose, they can gradually quit methadone.

Relapse and Controlled Use

If someone manages to break an addiction, what factors might raise their chances of a relapse?

We are more likely to relapse when we are stressed, anxious or upset. If our marriage is ending, we hate our job or we are worried about the mortgage, relapse is more likely. If we are not sleeping well due to anxiety or have become withdrawn, we could be headed back down the road to seeking the same short-term relief that we were previously addicted to. So, taking steps to sort those problems out on your own, with the help of others who've been through the same things, and professionals, is important.

Another factor that can increase chances of a relapse is renewed exposure to the substance or activity. An alcoholic who has gone years without relapsing might get offered a job in a pub, where their exposure to alcohol would sky-rocket. For gamblers, a job in a casino is a bad choice. Before taking such a job, you would need to be free of the problem for many years.

If someone who has had an addiction to painkillers is subsequently injured or develops an illness, they might well be prescribed strong painkillers again. In these situations, it helps to be upfront with doctors and other health workers and agree to limit your access to them, or use other non-drug strategies instead.

Another risk factor is exposure to the same triggers. What if, after having avoided the street where you used to buy drugs for years, you get a job around the corner and have to walk past it every day? Will that trigger still have power over you? Not nearly as much as before. The more time that has passed without repeating the behaviour, the weaker our response to the trigger.

If you do relapse, that does not necessarily mean you will automatically become an addict again. Ian hates American shows where someone who hasn't had a drink for fifteen years has one drink and then they are a hopeless alcoholic again. That is rarely the case. People often have relapses, but frequently get the behaviour under control again, because this time they usually already know what strategies actually work for them.

Societal Responses to Addiction – Controlling Supply

Broadly speaking, anything we can do to reduce supply or make access more difficult is likely to lead to fewer people becoming dependent. Societies have tried to lower the use of some drugs by making them illegal and thereby restricting their supply. Another approach is to restrict access by making substances more expensive via taxation. That is used with alcohol and nicotine and it works.

With gambling, there used to a strong relationship between the number of poker machines there were in pubs, clubs and casinos and the amount of poker machine addicts there were. Now, online gambling is an example of the relationship between increasing the supply of, and access to, a problem and the rate of dependence in the community. The use of online gambling sites has exploded in recent years, and the COVID pandemic gave it a further boost. As more people are betting online, many sites spring up to meet this increased demand. As supply increases, addiction to online gambling rises.

There is a currently worldwide debate about whether to legalise cannabis and make it widely available, or stick with restricting supply. It has been legalised in parts of the USA, Mexico, South Africa, Canada and a couple of other countries, and decriminalised while still being illegal in others. Use has immediately gone up in those places where it is easily available and affordable. We will now need to see what happens longer term.

CHECKLIST

- Addiction can refer to continued use of alcohol and drugs, or of harmful behaviours, despite the harm being caused.
- If you think you might be addicted, try stopping the behaviour for a day. If that makes you feel very uncomfortable, you may well be addicted.
- Being addicted now does not mean you will always be addicted. We can change and rewrite our brain.

- To treat addiction:
  - Find something that motivates you.
  - You need more than good intentions. You need a plan.
  - Identify your triggers and stay away from them.
  - Just stop for one day. Then do it again the next day, and so on.
  - Get support from friends, family and, if needed, professionals.
  - If your social world revolves around your addiction, you need a social replacement. If you go to the pub to drink and socialise, consider where you can socialise while you are giving up alcohol.
  - The greater the stress, the greater the chance of a relapse, but relapses can be contained.

16

Trauma

I wish my head could forget what my eyes have seen.
Dave Parnell, Detroit Fire Department

What is trauma? How do our minds process it? How do we deal with it? What effects can it have in later life?

What Is Trauma?

Trauma is a response to a deeply distressing or disturbing experience, such as a car crash, being assaulted or losing your home to a flood or bushfire. We can divide traumatic events broadly into two types:

- One-off events: being robbed, run over, shot, or physically or sexually assaulted.
- Reccurring events: long-lasting childhood or domestic physical or sexual abuse, bullying, harassment, long-term financial stress or bushfires and floods where the danger continues for some time.

Varying Affects of Traumatic Events

If two people both get their leg run over by a car, their physical experience is likely to be similar: a broken leg, weeks in a cast and then gradual recovery and rebuilding of strength. When exposed to disturbing or traumatic events, however, people can react very differently. Some are able to cope and move on quite quickly, while others are still affected years later.

Often, people are very distressed for some time after the traumatic event occurs, but then are gradually able to return to normal life. Importantly, the great majority of people do not develop post-traumatic stress from one-off events. The event will remain in their memory and still be distressing when they think about it, but it will no longer affect their everyday life. Only a minority experience long-term mental health effects.

It can be more difficult when the trauma is repeated over weeks, months or even years, such as with domestic violence, or physically or sexually abusive relationships with a parent or somebody who was trusted, such as a school teacher. Not only is the abuse awful, but during the rest of the day the person will be thinking about the events, feeling unsafe and worrying about when they will happen again. This lack of safety, and unpredictability, causes chronic stress. While many do recover from this type of ongoing trauma, it is more likely to lead to major mental issues down the track.

Trauma in Young People

When children are being physically beaten, sexually abused or repeatedly exposed to other sorts of trauma, the long-term mental health effects are likely to be very severe. It often happens secretly within families and can go on for years. Often it is known to some family members, but they might be powerless to stop the abuse. Sometimes the abuse or neglect is sporadic, and starts up again when the abuser is experiencing financial, relationship or emotional stress, or alcohol or drug problems.

When terrible abuse or neglect is discovered, the first response is often to immediately get the child into a safe environment. If something terrible has happened repeatedly to a child or teenager, they can do very well if they get into a supportive and caring environment. This is what lies behind the notion of child removal from families: getting the child away from danger, to long-term safety and more secure and trusting relationships.

However, historically, we have not always done a great job of doing this. The intention might have been good, but the implementation was often misguided. Many kids ended up in even worse situations, being neglected or abused in institutions such as orphanages or work homes, or in foster families that were unstable. Moving regularly between various homes or families without the opportunity to develop more stable relationships with warm and caring adults didn't help.

Elsewhere, children were removed from their parents, families or communities for racist, religious or ideological reasons, for example, in Australia with the Stolen Generation of Indigenous children. This was highly traumatic. Removing children from parents or families is something that should be considered only in the most extreme circumstances.

Today, when children are growing up in difficult circumstances, there is more recognition that it is often very upsetting and even threatening for a child to be removed from their family, so there is much more emphasis on supporting parents and families to improve the situation, involving other family members well known to the child, while keeping children safe.

If, at a time when a young person is learning about their relationship with the world, they are repeatedly abused by an adult or older sibling, they may start to think that these sorts of abusive relationships are the normal way in which relationships work. As a result, it can affect the types of relationships they form down the track. If a young person trusts an adult who then betrays that trust by abusing them, the learning for the young person might be not that this is an abnormal event, but that it is dangerous to let down your guard and trust people. This may affect their ability to form close relationships later in life. The abnormal event – the abuse – has been normalised.

Childhood trauma can also have an effect on the developing brain and the developing arousal and stress-response systems. If the abuse causes arousal – anxiety, elevated heartbeat, shallow breathing – while the nervous system in the brain is still developing, the trauma can become encoded in the brain's arousal systems. That means that those systems will operate at a higher set-point and be much more likely to be 'on' a lot of the time. Minor events, such as a branch scraping against a window at night, or seeing a stranger outside your home, can put you on high alert and create anxiety.

A person living with this type of over-reactive alarm system can feel constantly on edge, be easily upset and distressed, and often have highly variable moods; at times be angry and prone to emotional outbursts, at other times sad, withdrawn and feeling helpless and overwhelmed. It is physically and emotionally exhausting to be living on the edge; feeling constantly exhausted is common.

Arousal systems that have become abnormal through repeated exposure to trauma can lead to anxiety, depression and substance abuse as adults. However, many children go through war, natural disasters and other terrible things and are not adversely affected in the long term. This is particularly likely if they are surrounded by safe and protective families.

Dealing with Trauma

1. Get Away

When faced with a traumatic, dangerous or distressing situation, the first thing we have to do is to get away. With one-off events we have to get away from the person who bashed us, or the bushfire threatening our home.

With ongoing trauma, such as repeated abuse from family members or a partner, getting away may not be easy. Nonetheless, it is very harmful for people to remain in a traumatic situation where they are being repeatedly exposed to distressing, degrading or abusive events. You have to get away from the situation, whether it be a workplace, a marriage or your family. Often people who stay in those situations do not realise how badly it is affecting their mental health. This, of course, can be difficult, especially for children. Ten-year-olds do not have many options. They are dependent on their family and their wider community.

In the past, some types of abuse have been normalised within some families, as if physical abuse through harsh discipline or even sexual abuse is an appropriate thing to do. Over the past few decades the increase in societal awareness and open discussion of these issues has helped, because it enables people to understand that abusive behaivour is not normal, and not okay. Bashing your kid is never okay. It is not just a matter of individual choice or normal cultural practice.

2. Initial Distress and Gradual Recovery

Right after traumatic events, people usually experience acute distress, which often tapers over time. In that initial period, it is very helpful to have the support and protection of family and friends, the people we trust and are close to.

There might be a physicality to that support. People holding you, being close to you, can help. Often after a traumatic event we feel in danger and the arousal that accompanies that can be scary and exhausting. It helps to be surrounded and protected by those you trust. Getting physical messages of safety from them, such as hugs, helps. In communities exposed to natural disasters like floods and bushfires, sharing experiences with others who have gone through the same experience helps everyone to start to cope and recover.

After traumatic events people usually cope much better in groups than they do on their own. If they have all experienced the same natural disaster, everyone helping each other is very beneficial to moving on and recovering from the trauma.

Once that physiological arousal starts to recede, we can start to think about other things and return to normal patterns of sleeping, eating and general activity, and being with people.

In that initial period, don't rush into psychological therapy. In the late 1970s, the notion of immediately debriefing with a psychologist after a distressing event was popular. However, it often did not help because when we are asked to go over the distressing event repeatedly, it can feel like we are almost experiencing it again. Every time we discuss it, to an extent we relive it, and that can cement those memories in. In fact, if you keep going over the same events, you might actually be creating new memories of them and re-traumatising yourself.

3. Longer-term Effects

A minority of people who experience a traumatic event find that it continues to disrupt their life. Some of the psychological symptoms to keep a lookout for are panic attacks, increased alcohol use to calm down or sleep, and becoming depressed and socially withdrawn. Physical symptoms can include abdominal pain, headaches, muscle aches and pains, and exhaustion. If, after three months, you are not starting to return to normal, if memories of the distressing event keep coming back, and if you are feeling overwhelmed, then it might be time to seek some professional help.

Someone who has experienced trauma as a child and subsequently has a string of relationships that all fail, several jobs that they have left or been dismissed from, and issues with drugs and alcohol, might wonder, 'Has this all got something to do with the abuse I suffered as a child? Is there some pattern ingrained in me that I'm not aware of? Or is that just the way things have turned out? How do I find out if that trauma is continuing to affect me?'

When life has not gone well, and there are breakdowns, unstable moods or patterns of self-defeating, self-destructive or risky behaviour, it can strongly suggest a long-term reaction to trauma. This is where psychological counselling can help. In counselling, it is not uncommon for people to disclose for the first time some abuse that happened to them as a child. They might have never talked about it before because it is difficult to open up about it, and, if the abuser was in their family, they are concerned about the effect raising it will have.

4. Denial

Denial can be very useful in the short term. If you are injured in a car accident it can help to almost pretend that you are okay while you focus on getting help. If your house is about to be burnt in a bushfire, getting upset has to wait. First, you have to get away.

However, denial doesn't work in the longer term, because there will be triggers that remind us of the event – a sound, a smell or a sight – and immediately cause our heart to race. Our mind might be in denial and not be thinking about the event, but our body has made the connection and the stress response quickly returns.

If this continues to happen, it is best to discuss the events with a therapist or counsellor and try to find ways of coming to terms with them without experiencing the same degree of distress.

The solution is not to pretend that the traumatic events are not still lurking in the background. We have to accept that they are. The solution is to know they are there, and work to reduce the degree of distress and arousal we experience. That is, to detach the memory of the traumatic events from that distress and arousal, so that the events continue to exist as memories without causing the same unpleasant physiological response.

Memories

How Accurate Is Our Memory?

We often assume our memories are more accurate than they are. If you ask three people who live together to describe what happened last Sunday morning, you will probably get three different versions. Details of memories can fade, and even be completely wrong. You are certain you went to a party years ago with Chris, but Chris is sure she didn't go.

People who observe the same event rarely remember it in the same way. They jumble up the order of events. If you suggest to them that incident A actually happened before incident B, not after it, they might accept what you say and 'change' their memory.

Sometimes you can even 'see' an event in your mind that didn't happen. 'I'm sure Chris was at that party. I can see her in my memory.' A memory is not something we pull out of the filing cabinet intact from the time it occurred. Every time we reconstruct a memory, we lay it down again, and every time we think about an event, we make it 'new' again, potentially with different details.

Trauma and Memory

Our minds take notice of traumatic events because they are unusual, threatening and very distressing, but the memories we form of them are more chaotic. The more traumatic the event, the less likely we are able to behave like an independent observer making accurate notes about the sequence of events. People often block out key details, make wrong assumptions and link together different parts of the story in inaccurate ways. When you are very distressed, you just grab onto bits of what is happening – you're not focusing on trying to form a precise account of the situation.

The legal system sometimes assumes that someone who experienced distressing and traumatic events has the capacity to describe them as if they were an independent observer, watching themselves getting punched up. Traumatic situations are overwhelming and frightening, and we often detach from the experience to some degree to cope, especially when there is great physical harm.

Someone who wasn't involved in a car accident can usually give a much more accurate description than the driver. If a car hits a pedestrian, the driver will continually replay the time between seeing the pedestrian and hitting them, and think about what they could have done differently to prevent the collision. They might place less emphasis on other factors such as weather conditions, being distracted by their child shouting in the back and having to swerve to avoid another car.

Some traumatic events become strongly encoded in our memory, and are hard to forget. If you put your hand on a hot plate, you remember how much it hurt and that memory acts as a warning not to do it again. If you were frying onions at the time, the smell of onions might also get encoded as part of the warning. Whenever you smell fried onions, you get the message, 'This is what you smelt just before you burnt your hand. There is danger!'

Anything that links to the traumatic experience might bring the memory of it back. If you had Thai takeaway in your car when you had an accident, the smell of Thai food might trigger a memory of it. If a fire engine drove past you just before the accident, you might be triggered whenever you see a fire engine.

In an evolutionary sense, this is a learned warning not to get in this situation again. We share these conditioned responses with many other species, and they help us survive. When rats drink something that makes them sick, they will avoid the tastes and smells associated with that fluid in the future. These warnings are not conscious thoughts. They are sensed or felt. Our body has encoded these usually innocent signals as warnings of danger. When we see, hear or smell them, adrenaline is released, our heart rate increases, and we feel anxious.

Recovered and Repressed Memories

It is very controversial to suggest that, in therapy, trauma *that was previously unknown to the person* can be recovered. In the past there have been cases where a client who has had patterns of troubled behaviour and failed relationships, but who has had no awareness of an earlier trauma, has had a therapist suggest to them that they *must* have experienced trauma, and asked the client if they are sure that they weren't abused. In these circumstances, there is a danger that the so-called traumatic events have been generated by the therapy.

Good therapists approach the subject of trauma without suggesting something must have happened: 'Let's talk about your childhood.' 'What was your adolescence like?' They try to create a safe and trusting environment where clients might be able to disclose traumatic experiences that they had always known about, but not previously shared. People may not have a full memory of past traumatic events, but know that stuff has happened. They need to be in a trusting environment to be able to explore those events and their impact on their life.

As these traumatic events are explored in therapy, links between them and the person's current problems may become more obvious.

Therapy and Memory

Many people exposed to trauma do not ever need to talk about it. If you have coped and moved on, and the trauma is not disrupting your life, there is no reason to explore it again and re-experience every bad thing that happened.

However, if things are going badly in your life, then it is a good idea to try and find out why, and therapy often helps people do that. A past traumatic experience might be relevant to your current issues, or it might not be. If you have been beaten up or sexually assaulted, talking about it can be difficult, but some therapists specialise in treating trauma, and aim to help people to lead productive lives where they are no longer controlled by the traumatic event.

CHECKLIST

- Experiencing trauma does not necessarily mean mental health issues will arise from it.
- People can react very differently to the same unpleasant events.
- Childhood trauma can lead to being permanently 'on alert' and becoming anxious and stressed more easily.
- When faced with a traumatic, dangerous or distressing situation, the most important thing is to get away.
- Acute distress following the event usually tapers over time, especially if we are supported by those we trust.
- When those who have experienced trauma later struggle in life, or repeat patterns of unhelpful behaviour, it can be useful to investigate whether the traumatic events have been a cause.
- Sights, sounds and smells associated with the traumatic event can bring the memory back.
- Professional 'debriefing' immediately after a major trauma may do more harm than good.

17

Hypochondria

After obsessively googling symptoms for four hours, I discovered 'obsessively googling symptoms' is a symptom of hypochondria.

Stephen Colbert

A hypochondriac is one who has a pill for everything except what ails him.

Mignon McLaughlin

Anxiety can show itself in many ways. Hypochondria occurs when our anxiety focuses on our health, and we worry to an abnormal extent about it.

Worrying to some degree about our health makes sense. Being in denial that anything could ever go wrong and avoiding doctors can lead to an early death. If something is amiss, the sooner we know about it, the better. It makes sense to screen for some illnesses, like cancer, even when there is only a low chance we have them.

At what point do we cross the line from sensible monitoring of our health to abnormal, overactive, obsessive vigilance? How do you treat hypochondria?

What Is Hypochondria?

Hypochondria occurs when people repeatedly become convinced that they've got cancer, heart disease, a brain tumour or something else when there is little or no evidence to suggest that is the case. They are usually not easily reassured by investigation or appropriate screening that they do not have that problem. If they *do* eventually accept that they do not have it, their focus quickly turns to another illness or disease.

Those with hypochondria often spend many hours exploring various illnesses and symptoms online, regularly go to the doctor, and can go as far as adopting a sick role, putting themselves to bed and actually treating themselves as if they have a particular disease, even though they do not.

When we are anxious, we want reassurance. If a child worries there is a monster under the bed, they look. No monster. The most common response to hypochondria from health professionals and others is reassurance. 'We've done the test. You don't have cancer. You're fine.' Unfortunately, this rarely stops the worrying, because there are a thousand other diseases and illnesses the person can shift their attention to. 'I don't have brain cancer, but maybe I have another type of brain disease.'

Those with health anxiety are overly vigilant of any tiny, little thing that feels slightly less than perfect in their body. It is similar to being worried about being robbed, and being overly vigilant of people you don't recognise in your street. Every time you see a new face, you get anxious. With hypochondria, every time you have a headache, a sniffle or a small pain, instead of ignoring it, you will be on high alert, and start googling possible causes.

Why Does Hypochondria Happen?

Anxiety plays out in different forms, at different ages. If someone has an anxious temperament and a propensity to worry, their anxiety floats about looking for something to attach to. When they are four, they might be anxious about being separated from their parents, at nine have a fear of the dark, at seventeen be anxious about meeting new people, at thirty their career, and then at forty their anxiety might attach to their health.

One theory is that the brains of those with hypochondria are overly sensitive to feedback from their body. Normal, minor discomforts, aches and pains that most would ignore, or be only vaguely aware of, get right into their conscious mind and attract way too much of their attention.

Another contributing factor for some of us is that we can seek the additional care and positive reinforcement we usually receive when we are sick, from those we live with and others. When we are unwell, people are nice to us, they take care of us, they listen to us, they forgive us more easily, they make us toast. Those things may make it more attractive to continue to be 'sick'.

In some circumstances, there may even be a financial benefit – for example, if you have to reach a certain level of medical incapacity to receive a government benefit.

If you have hypochondria and hate spending your days googling symptoms and continually going to the doctor, you have a strong motivation to do what is needed to get better. If, however, you see some benefit in being classed as unwell, it can be harder to treat.

Hypochondria and the Health System

Those with hypochondria present a tricky problem for the health system. When a person is known to have hypochondriac tendencies, health professionals can be wary and not take them seriously, because the last ten times they came, nothing was wrong. Resources are scarce and precious, but just because someone is a hypochondriac doesn't mean they are not sick. The chance that the person does have something requiring treatment can get minimised or even dismissed.

The irony is that the person definitely *does* have a health problem that needs treatment that won't show up on any scan, x-ray or blood test – they have health-based anxiety.

Can You Get Hypochondria About Mental Illness?

Hypochondria has usually focused on physical illnesses, but now that there is a greater awareness of mental illness, some become preoccupied with the idea that they have symptoms of depression, schizophrenia, bipolar disorder or other mental illnesses.

Sometimes, mental health professionals have to tell people that they are not depressed, or do not have post-traumatic stress disorder. Instead, they have some degree of psychological distress that is a normal part of life. Diagnosing you as mentally ill when you are just experiencing the normal ups and downs of life can attach labels and adverse predictions, and make you feel that you are sick. Only those who are genuinely unwell need to receive mental health treatment.

There is no definitive test or scan that proves that you do, or do not, have a particular mental health disorder, so diagnosis remains a highly contentious area. Life can be stressful. We all have highs and lows, trials and tribulations, and we react emotionally to them. At some point, our thoughts, emotions and behaviours can become abnormal, which may represent the start of a mental health condition or illness. They key question is, 'At what point does someone cross the line from normal to abnormal, and start to need treatment?' Sometimes it is obvious that a person is mentally unwell, but often, people are very close to the line. Mental health professionals have to be very careful that they do all they can to get their diagnosis right.

Treatment

The first step in treating hypochondria is recognising that it might be a problem. Often the first person to notice it is someone who lives with a person who has health anxiety. The next step is to convince them they have health anxiety. To treat hypochondria effectively, you have to at least buy into the possibility that the illness you have might not be a mystery virus or an obscure cancer, but in fact a mental illness – hypochondria. It can be hard to convince some, especially those who have had health anxiety for years. You might reply, 'It's not all in my head. I have real physical symptoms.' That is likely to be true, but the cause of those physical (as well as their psychological) symptoms might be anxiety.

Anxiety and Physical Pain

Some think anxiety is purely having worrying thoughts, but it can also manifest physically through an elevated heartbeat, shallow breathing, sweating and the over-production of adrenaline. Over time, that can stress our entire system and lead to headaches, stomach-aches, a less effective immune system and feeling run-down and worn out. (See Chapter 9, 'Anxiety'.)

These physical manifestations of anxiety are often misinterpreted by those who worry about their health as being symptoms of something else, such as cancer or a mystery virus. It becomes a vicious cycle, as the more you worry about what condition or illness is causing your symptoms, the more anxiety there is to drive those symptoms. It then seems sensible to go back to their doctor to have more blood tests, x-rays and scans.

If you are experiencing physical pain, how do you know if the cause is anxiety, or something else? Try using anxiety-reduction strategies such as mindfulness, meditation and progressive muscle relaxation. If every time you think about your health, or read about a new cancer or rare disease, you feel your heart rate spiking, can these strategies get it down and reduce your physical arousal level?

If you persist with these anxiety-reduction strategies and are able to reduce your physical arousal, *and your physical symptoms abate*, that strongly suggests those symptoms were anxiety related, rather than caused by an undiagnosed illness or condition. The vicious cycle can then be reversed. As the physical symptoms reduce, so too can the anxiety that surrounds them.

There are specific thought-based and behavioural therapies for health anxiety.

Thought-based Strategies

Distraction

Distracting yourself from anxious thoughts is useful for all types of anxiety. Keep busy. Do lots of stuff. The busier you are, the less time and space you brain has to monitor every little thing that isn't working perfectly in your body.

Challenging the thought

If you think you have cancer, can you challenge that thought? Is there another, more likely explanation?

Over time, those with health anxiety can learn that the extreme vigilance they have about any type of physical discomfort they experience is not justified. Bodies are not perfect. Especially as you get older, it is very common to have an ache, a pain, a sniffle, a bit of a headache or a funny tummy. Many of us get out of bed in the morning feeling a bit congested, have a stiff back or lack energy. After a while we warm up, get going, engage with tasks, activities and people, and our conscious attention moves away from our internal physiological world.

Those with health anxiety should practise challenging the thoughts they have that suggest that any tiny physical problem is a sign of a serious physical problem.

Behaviour-based Strategies
Not seeking reassurance

It is important to try to resist the urge to keep checking your body for new symptoms, and then obsessively googling them to find out what they could mean. People with health anxiety often try to stop this behaviour, but that can be very hard. You desperately want to google the symptoms of the latest obscure type of cancer that you think you might have. You try not to check, resist for a while, but then give in. 'I know I checked yesterday, but there might be a new disease they just found that explains my symptoms.'

It is also helpful to try to resist the urge to seek reassurance by going to the doctor and asking to have more tests done. This is tricky because if you really are sick, then you should go to the doctor. How can someone with hypochondria know the difference? To get some objectivity, can you find a trusted person who you can share your symptoms with, and then ask, 'If this was happening to you, would you go to the doctor?'

You should accept that resisting investigating your symptoms and going to the doctor will probably spike your anxiety, and that will be unpleasant. Have faith that if you can continue to avoid seeking reassurance, your anxiety will reduce and you will be able to make lasting behavioural change and break out of the anxiety/reassurance loop.

Calming behaviour

As discussed above, when you feel anxious, slow, deep breathing, mindfulness, meditation, progressive muscle relaxation and exercise can all help. The aim is *not* to never have the anxious thought. The aim is, when anxious thoughts come, to be able to use these strategies to stop them from creating that physical arousal in your body.

Getting healthier

If you improve your physical health through diet, exercise, drinking less alcohol and not smoking, you will feel better, and have the physical sense of the body functioning normally. You will know what it feels like to be normally tired, even exhausted, after physical exercise, understand what normal discomfort and pain feels like during and after exercise, and know what your body feels like when it is physically fit.

Good doctoring

Often there is a breakdown between the person with health anxiety and the health system. Every time the known hypochondriac reappears, the health system rolls its eyes. 'Stop wasting our time.'

It is much better if a GP can say, 'We will meet every three months, and do any appropriate tests and screening. We won't deny the fact that you might get sick, but we will look at it in an evidence-based way. In return, you must stop swallowing stuff I haven't prescribed, because it can harm you.'

A GP and a psychologist working together can make a big difference and, as with other types of anxiety, antidepressant medication can play a role.

Distrusting Doctors

When most of us engage with the medical community, we accept that they know a lot more about medicine than we do, we trust them, and we take the medicine they tell us to. When prescribed antibiotics, we think, 'I have no idea what they are or how they work, but sure.' When told a vaccine might protect us against COVID, we don't really understand how it works, but we trust them and roll up our sleeve.

Some, however, are less willing to accept what doctors, the government and others in authority say and even go so far as to try experimental, unproven and unapproved treatments for COVID and other health issues.

Where does this distrust and suspicion of authority in general, and doctors and the government in particular, come from? Often it is indicative of a general worldview driven by mistrust and suspicion. There may have been childhood or later events where the person trusted an authority figure, and felt that their trust was betrayed or abused. Some may have had bad experiences with government in Australia or elsewhere, that led them to conclude that governments are not to be trusted. Some may have had adverse experiences with medicine, or know someone who has.

Often there is also a degree of narcissism. 'I know best. I've investigated it. I've done my own research.'

It is very difficult to win a rational argument with people who hold these beliefs, even when the weight of evidence is against them. Their beliefs seem to be more emotional than rational. You need to engage with people about the emotional reasons for their distrust. Where did it come from?

Public health campaigns tell people the facts. That is enough to convince many, but may not convince those with this sense of mistrust. To get them to trust, they have to get the message from those who they trust. Generally we more easily and quickly trust people who look and sound like us – same gender, same age, similar appearance.

CHECKLIST

- Worrying about our health makes sense. Hypochondria is anxiety that fixates on our health and exaggerates possible risks and consequences.
- Chronic anxiety about our health can lead to headaches, feeling run down and a less-effective immune system, which those with hypochondria can misinterpret as symptoms of cancer or a mystery virus.
- To treat health anxiety:
  - Recognise it might be a problem.
  - Use anxiety reduction strategies such as:
    - Challenging anxious thoughts
    - Distracting yourself from anxious thoughts
    - Resisting seeking reassurance from the internet or by continually visiting the doctor
    - Using relaxation strategies
    - Improving your physical health
    - Accepting that not every minor ache or pain signifies disaster
    - Finding a GP who understands your heath anxiety and how to treat it.
- Just because someone has health anxiety does not mean they are not really sick. Have a trusted person you can check in with: 'If you had this symptom, would you go to the doctor?'

18

Dealing with a Crisis

Never let a serious crisis go to waste. And what I mean by that, it's an opportunity to do things you think you could not do before.

Rahm Emanuel

The power we discover inside ourselves as we survive a life-threatening experience can be utilised equally well outside of crisis, too.

Michele Rosenthal

Not many of us get through life without a crisis. As one particularly dour scholar remarked, 'Life is hard, and then you die.'

Crises are big events that rock and unsettle us. Often these events come out of nowhere, and are suddenly the dominant factor in our life.

How do we deal with big crises that change our world?

Types of Crisis

We think of crises as unpredictable, and many, such as bushfires and illness, are. Others, in retrospect, are more foreseeable. We didn't know we were going to get sacked today, but we knew the business was struggling, and people were being made redundant. We didn't know our partner was going to tell us the relationship was over today, but we knew it had been in trouble for some time.

A crisis will hurt. You will feel bad. It will leave you psychologically and physically vulnerable. There are no superheroes here. Something you care about, something you value, is gone. It matters. Don't try to pretend it doesn't.

There are reasonably predictable stages many of us may go through when a crisis happens. These are often described as 'the stages of grief'. Denial. Anger. Bargaining. Depression. Acceptance. But this is no simple step-by-step process, and it doesn't always progress easily or inevitably to acceptance.

Initial Denial

When we get a huge setback – you set sacked, find out you have cancer, or your partner tells you they are leaving – often, one part of our mind is just taking it in and working out what we need to do: 'Should I finish up tomorrow?' 'When is my first chemotherapy?', 'Do you want to take your favorite mug?' We can even present a calm, efficient face to the world.

This isn't outright denial. We understand that we have lost our job. It is prioritising what needs to be done immediately, while pushing the deeper emotional shockwaves into the background, and that is important and useful. Falling apart is not going to help. We need to carry on. Booking our first chemotherapy session is important. We have to keep functioning, and keep eating, sleeping and moving.

Suspending the real significance of an event in the short term so we are not physiologically and psychologically overwhelmed is useful. It allows some time to pass between the event, and the full realisation of the loss or the change. Without it, we might be overwhelmed, and just stop.

Long-term denial, however, can be harmful.

Grieving Death

If someone close to us dies, it is normal to feel grief. It is normal sadness. We are not solitary beings. We attach to others, often strongly, and from those attachments, we get some of our best and most satisfying experiences. If a key person in our life dies, we should be sad. Normal humans move into an abnormal state – grief – in which there are stages and a normal, and quite prolonged, time for recovery.

Grief is normal psychologically, but physiologically it is abnormal. It is associated with disruption of our stress hormones, such as cortisol, and our nervous system. When grieving, our immune system does not perform as well as it should, and is less effective at protecting us against viruses and cancer because, it seems, it is being suppressed by overactive adrenaline and cortisol production caused by chronic stress. This is similar to others experiencing chronic stress as a result of prolonged unemployment, a relationship break-up or financial problems. The end result can be more physical health problems, including infections and heart disease leading to, for example, older men dying at a higher-than-usual rate in the year following their wife's death.

Early in the grieving process our body clock can be disturbed (see Chapter 3, 'The Body Clock'), which affects our sleep, energy and appetite, causing us to feel exhausted, run down and lacking any real enjoyment in life.

So, physiologically, we are vulnerable, and often that vulnerability is increased because we don't take care of our self. Feelings of loss and despondency might sap our motivation to exercise, sleep and eat properly. Alcohol and other drugs might become more tempting. It is important to keep exercising, being active, eating well, engaging socially and maintaining a regular daily routine.

On top of that, our thoughts and memories keep telling us how terrible the crisis is. 'How can I survive without her?'

If we stayed in that state, it would be very bad, but it is normal to recover slowly over time. After someone close to us dies, recovery might initially be impossible to imagine, but for most people it happens.

The scale of grief varies. Some have periods where they are sad about the absence of the person but it does not disrupt their whole life. For others, grief is debilitating. There is constant distress and sadness, disrupted sleep, loss of appetite and energy and an inability to do anything productive.

Sometimes grief begins before death. If someone close to us is dying of cancer, we adapt to it, and sometimes go through the stages of grief while the person is still alive. We start to adjust. When they die it is sad, but not unexpected. When people get dementia, they change and sometimes people say that they have grieved for the loss of that person long before they actually die.

Almost everyone will experience grief during their life, often several times. It runs a particular course, and then we start to recover.

Other Types of Crisis

A job can be an important part of our identity and sense of self-worth. When we are told we are no longer wanted by our employer, it hurts. We miss the purposeful activity, we miss the people, we miss the money.

We often feel strongly attached to our homes. There is an emotional investment, and important memories. They can feel like a fundamental part of our sense of self. If we lose our home, we miss it.

Similarly, a partner telling us we are no longer wanted can deeply wound our sense of self-worth. Even if the relationship had been deteriorating for a while, we might be flooded with memories from the good times, and feelings of regret and loss. 'What could I have done differently?'

Our health is something we often take for granted. When confronted with a possibly fatal diagnosis, terror is common. 'I'm not ready to die.' The uncertainty ('Will the chemotherapy work?') compounds the fear. Regrets, self-pity, recriminations and more fear are all common.

Dealing with a Crisis

Two of the most important factors in dealing with a crisis are our psychological health prior to the crisis, and the level of social support we receive after it.

Psychological Health Prior to the Crisis

When someone who has good relationships, good mental health and is secure financially experiences a crisis, it won't be easy, but they are well set up to deal with it. However, if someone is already not functioning well, has other problems, has an already existing mental health issue, and doesn't have strong supportive relationships, their road is likely to be tougher.

A person might see their spouse leaving as a sudden, unexpected crisis. Their spouse, however, might see it differently. She might have seen her husband gradually become more depressed and withdrawn over the last years. There may have been financial, job, alcohol or other problems and issues that preceded the break-up. While he sees his wife leaving as a sudden seismic shock, it is actually more like the straw that breaks the camel's back, an acute problem that comes on top of other, pre-existing problems.

It is good to always be aware of the state of our mental health (like we are with our physical health). If we know we are already struggling when a crisis hits, it is a warning that we might need even more support than usual.

Social Support

When we experience a crisis, we need other people. When we fall down, they help us to get back up. They take care of us as we deal with the crisis. Often, when people get a major physical illness like cancer, people swarm to help. They drop off curries, take care of the kids, text and call.

People often say, 'I'm getting so much help. People really value me. It's awful being sick, but the support is overwhelming. I wish I didn't have to get cancer for people to be like this.'

It is interesting who reaches out to help in a crisis and who doesn't. Sometimes it is surprising. Someone makes a real effort who you did not expect to. Others you expected to help, don't.

When we know someone is going through a crisis, there is often a part of us that wants to reach out, and another part that is nervous, even scared, and wants to withdraw. Sometimes the first part wins, and we lean in and give support. Many find that helping someone they care about get through a tough time is extremely rewarding and enriching. Sometimes the scared part of us wins, and we lean out, stay away and at some point in the future, deeply regret our inaction.

It can be a big thing to ring someone and say, 'How are you coping with the fact you might be, you know, dying?' Text messages and emails can be good places to start: 'How are you coping? Call me if you feel like it.'

With marital separations, sometimes friends take sides. 'Whose side are you on?' Often the best answer is, 'I'm not on any side. I'm just here to help.'

Without social support after a crisis, there is a greater chance that we won't recover as quickly, and will move from normal grief into prolonged psychological distress that may require professional help.

Social Investment

When a crisis happens (and at some point it probably will), having support networks help us get through it. So it makes sense to invest in those social relationships and networks now, before you need them, so they are there when you do. Once the crisis comes (and who knows when it will come), if you are not socially connected, it is difficult to suddenly become so.

People might have thought about their superannuation and retirement planning, but have they thought about what their strategy is if something really bad happens? Investing in social capital means we will have supportive networks when we need them.

Purposeful Action

Sometimes, when a crisis hits, you can do something. If you are diagnosed with cancer, you can get treatment. If your friend has cancer, you can visit and drop off an apple pie. If you lose your job, you can start looking for another job. If your home burns down, you can, hopefully, get the insurance money and work out what to do with it.

Purposeful activity helps. When a crisis happens, we can feel overwhelmed and helpless. The sooner we engage in purposeful activity, the better.

It is less straightforward when a relationship ends. What can you actively do? You could start dating, but maybe you don't feel ready yet. Can a renewed effort to get in touch with friends you may have ignored or lost touch with over the years help? What about involving yourself in hobbies and activities, especially those that have a social element?

When someone dies, what can we do? There is purposeful activity in the form of a funeral and rituals. They help us cope with the reality of it, and connect us with others.

Western funerals can often be emotionally restrained. Stiff upper lip and all that. Much better to let it all out. A lot of crying, and then a lot of celebrating the person's life. Don't shake hands. Hug. A lot of coping with crises is about touching, hugging, consoling in a physical way. Physiologically, lowering arousal or distress is often better done in physical, not verbal, ways. Hugging, holding, crying.

When you lose a job, there is less ritual. Perhaps a somewhat awkward lunch or send-off. Handshakes, not hugs. Looking for a new job can create a sense of purpose – so can doing some of the things you enjoy but did not have time for when you were working.

Retirement can be a crisis for some. You feel you have lost all your purposeful activity. 'What do I do all day?' 'I've lost most of my social connections.' We need to find some other purpose, and have things to do – volunteering, gardening, bowls, golf, yoga, cooking class, studying psychology. Preferably social things.

Bushfires or floods can disrupt a whole community. How quickly can it be put back together, and lost homes and other buildings be rebuilt? Or does everyone move away and it's lost? How quickly can you re-establish school and community events? If people can quickly move toward purposeful action, the chance of longer-term psychological problems is much reduced.

Counselling after a Crisis

Do sessions with a counsellor benefit those who have experienced a crisis? Not necessarily. In the 1970s and 1980s compulsory debriefing was strongly recommended after major disasters – plane crashes, bushfires, floods, car accidents, robberies, personal assaults. The thinking was that getting people to talk about the crisis as quickly as possible was good, and would help.

Actually, it often made things worse. People felt like they were being told that they had a problem. In addition, the formal counselling process interfered with the normative process of friends and family providing support. The counsellors were getting in the way of the people you would normally talk to, who you trusted. Most people want to cry first on the shoulder of somebody they already know, who they know cares about them, and who may even share some of the same experiences and losses.

It can also depend on circumstances. If someone close to you dies, there might be a big network of extended family and friends to support each other, whereas if you are retrenched, you might be more on your own, and additional psychological support may become more relevant.

Recovery

As discussed, when you lose something important, it is normal to feel sad, and to grieve the loss. It is also normal to recover over time. But how much time? When should you expect to start feeling better? Usually, after around three months from the date the relationship ended, the job was lost, the house burned down, or the friend died, people are starting to feel better. For much more significant losses, like the death of a spouse or child, grieving periods typically last much longer.

If, after three months (for less significant losses), you aren't starting to feel better, you still feel distressed a lot, you are having trouble sleeping, you haven't started to engage in more activities and you do not want to go out and see others, that is no longer normal. Unless you do something, this state may persist and cause you harm. It might be time to recognise that the distress and sadness is not going away on its own, that you are stuck, and you need some professional help from a counsellor, psychologist or grief counsellor to help you make a plan to get better. If you feel helpless, seek help, because helpless is often followed by hopeless.

Some people who have pre-existing mental health problems or other issues might fall into a state of particularly deep despair after a crisis. If the whole world has become very difficult, or you've got a substance abuse problem, or you are feeling suicidal one month after the crisis, don't wait three months. Seek help.

Don't Say 'Should'

Sometimes we think, 'Look, everyone gets sacked at some point in their life. It's a normal thing and I should be able to deal with it.'

When it comes to how you feel, there is no 'should'. You feel how you feel. Every person is different, every situation is different. There is no particular or prescribed way you 'should' feel. All that matters is how you *do* feel. In fact, beating yourself up about how you should feel is often an indicator that it is time to seek professional help.

People get down on themselves by not only being depressed about losing their job, but also depressed about the fact that they don't think they are coping. Many of us have this image of ourselves as being very resilient and able to cope with setbacks and bounce back easily. When this view of ourselves is challenged by how hard it can be in reality, it can become a vicious cycle, as we become our own worst critic. Rather than emphasising resilience and 'being tough', we could put much greater weight on the virtue of being sensitive to loss, or change. Having strong feelings shows that we really care about ourselves and the welfare of others.

It can be hard to take that first step to get help. Many of us aren't very good at it. But we should do it.

Therapy can help us recognise and break that vicious cycle of self-criticism through cognitive strategies and purposeful activity, and help us realise that we need to be more active and engaged. Once we start doing things, we feel more confident and capable, and start to believe in ourselves again.

Long-term Effects of Crises

If you have lost something important to you – a person, a job, a home – the loss is genuine, distressing and sad. Are you supposed to eventually forget about it? Will the loss be with you for the rest of your life? Will the feelings of sadness last as long as you live?

Part of normal grief is accepting the loss, sadness and grief. While we are not okay with the loss, we do what we can to deal with it, and accept that nonetheless our life continues with that loss and sadness and hurt.

In a strange way, the longer our life expectancy, and the more comfortable our lives, the less we expect bad things to happen. If we had a much shorter life expectancy, as we did for most of human history (as well as increased vulnerability to predators, illness, starvation, plagues, wars and natural disasters), lots of people would be dying young and we would be forced to accept that that was just how life was. If we were able to get through a year without some sort of crisis, we would count ourselves lucky.

Now, with our healthcare, Uber Eats and iPhones, we almost expect nothing to go wrong, and usually it doesn't. Sometimes, however, something does.

Have we modern humans become soft? Ian doesn't think so. Our physiology and emotionality is the same as humans in past generations. In traditional societies, loss still mattered. There were still a lot of grieving practices. Loss happened a lot, but it still needed to be dealt with, as it does now. And it can be.

CHECKLIST

- Most of us will experience at least one major crisis in life.
- Often our first reaction is to push the emotional impact back and take care of the things we need to first.
- Grieving is psychologically normal, but it makes us physiologically vulnerable.
- Two factors that influence how well we respond to a crisis are:
  • Our psychological health prior to it, and,
  • The level of social support we get.
- Recovery takes time.
- Don't tell yourself how you 'should' be feeling. There is no 'should'.
- If, after three months, recovery is not underway, you may need professional help.

PART 3

IMPROVING OUR MENTAL HEALTH

19

Hope and Despair

The difference between hope and despair is a different way of telling stories from the same facts.

Alain de Botton

If you knew that hope and despair were paths to the same destination, which would you choose?

Robert Breault

Two people look at the same glass of water. One sees it as half full, the other as half empty. Why? One has a hopeful, optimistic outlook, while the other is pessimistic. Which of the two is more realistic? Which is more useful? Which is more likely to lead to better mental health?

Is despair a sign of poor mental health, or a realistic reaction to tough times? Or both? Can despair sometimes be useful?

Hope is seen as this bright, shiny jewel that will help us through tough times, but is it just dreamy escapism, a way of avoiding reality?

Lots of challenging, stressful stuff happens in life: illness, trauma, death of loved ones, relationships that end, losing jobs, injury, etc. There is some evidence that those who are pessimistic often make more realistic judgments about their own capabilities, the state of their relationships, and the state of their world.

However, it may surprise you to know that most of us have an in-built cognitive bias toward hope and optimism. We see a glass that is half full, think disaster is unlikely and that eventually things will get better. In those who are mentally healthy, lots of psychological experiments have supported this observation. Given the many difficulties we all face in life, this in-built tendency to look on the bright side probably has advantages, at least from an evolutionary perspective. It leads us to have more energy and motivation for action, rather than a retreat into despair and inaction.

That Poor, Despairing Dog

In the 1970s American psychologist Martin Seligman and colleagues started experimenting with dogs in contained cages and electric shocks. Fortunately, people don't do these types of experiments anymore. When the dog got the shock, it jumped out of the cage. When it landed, it got another shock, so it jumped back in the cage, where it got shocked again. The dog kept jumping in and out of the cage, trying to avoid being shocked. After a while, the poor dog lay down and did nothing, even when it got more electric shocks. It stopped reacting, because no action enabled it to avoid the shocks. It just lay there in a state Seligman called 'learned helplessness'.

That is despair, the desire to just stop, because whatever you do, it hurts. When we are in despair, we are incapable of taking the next productive action. We are helpless, which then puts our survival at greater risk.

Ian has seen people rocking back and forth, non-responsive to the world. He calls it agitated depression. You shut down, and cut yourself off from the world. Even when help arrives, you cannot recognise it, or respond to the opportunity. This state is dangerous for humans in terms of self-destructive behaviours. Sometimes people just can't see a way out.

Avoiding Despair

Sometimes we are confronted by problems and situations that can make despair tempting. We think that nothing can be done to improve things. COVID may have led some to feel like that. Suddenly, there was an overwhelming plague, a shutdown of many of our national and international systems and a real physical threat.

If you could say to the dog, 'I want you to be hopeful that these shocks will stop,' the dog might reply, 'No way. All the evidence suggests that whatever I do, I'm going to get a shock. There's nothing productive I can do, so I'm going to lie down and give up.'

How do people who are in prison, or other situations where there is no easy way out, avoid despair? Many cope by asking 'What can I do each day to stay sane, and tolerate this situation? There are many things I can't do, but what *can* I do that will give me at least a small feeling of achievement or satisfaction?' They shut down unrealistic expectations ('I want to be free') and substitute realistic ones ('I want to do a hundred sit-ups').

Many of us face less dramatic but still very challenging situations every day – a difficult workplace, financial stress or strenuous carer responsibilities. The same principle for coping better applies. A clear focus on what can be done rather than being preoccupied with what cannot be achieved.

The Upside of Distress

Sometimes distress can be useful. When James started doing stand-up comedy, whenever a show went well, he wouldn't analyse it.

However, when it went badly, and the audience didn't laugh, he would become quite distressed, but that led him to analyse what he had done, chuck out the bad jokes and expand the good ones. Distress led to a desire to improve.

Failure and criticism helps us learn. Ian tells young researchers, 'Ninety per cent of what we do will fail. Otherwise it's not genuine research. So, we're going to be wrong a lot of the time.'

It's important not to let the pain of failure overwhelm us. If we wallow in our negative thoughts and emotions, we can become inactive. A bit of wallowing is hard to avoid but at some point we have to switch to productive action and ask, 'What can I learn from that bad outcome? How can I avoid it happening again?'

Managing Despair

How do you control and reduce feelings of despair if you are prone to them, so that they don't turn into a long-term mental health issue? Try to recognise when you start to dip, when you are not bouncing back, when pessimism starts to make sense and become your dominant worldview. Take an action, even short-term, to change the scene, change the setting and cause a change in outlook. Even if that is a temporary change – a weekend away, a short holiday, a day off work or going out with friends – it may be enough to halt a more serious downward spiral.

People often think the cause of a depression is one event – losing a job or a relationship – but often we are already struggling. We all get stressed. We all feel low. What matters is how deep it is and how long it goes for. If, after a few weeks, you don't start to come out of it, that is when it becomes something that may require treatment.

Hope

On the other side of despair is hope. Hope is not fantasy. It's not unrealistic. It's not believing somebody will swoop down from the clouds and fix everything, or that a magical treatment will make COVID disappear. It's not thinking, 'When I win the lottery, I'll pay off my debts and everything will be great.'

Hope needs to be based in the possibility of realistic action when the opportunity presents itself.

Taking Actions that Build Hope

A part of treating depression and despair is to find productive actions that change your mental state.

If you change your behaviour first, then you will think and feel differently. An example is picking up that poor, despairing dog and moving him. The researchers did this. They had to move him several times, to *show* the dog circumstances had changed and he wouldn't get shocked again.

If you're in despair, you need to be shown positive action. For example, if you feel depressed and pessimistic about COVID, and then whenever you feel a bit better about it you get depressed and pessimistic about climate change, what should you do?

The cognitive, or thought-based, approach suggests we should first change the pessimistic or negative thought. Then the emotion follows, and then the action. The thought 'I'll never get another job' can be replaced by 'I've always worked, I've got skills, I will be employed again'. Then the emotion follows the thought and we change from anxious to calmer. The action that follows is applying for jobs.

Ian is more of a behaviourist, from the *do* differently school. Act differently, and then you will think and feel differently. If you have the thought, 'I'm so alone. No-one wants to spend time with me', then instead of sitting at home alone, *behave* differently. Go somewhere you will know people, like the coffee shop or the beach. Text a friend and suggest a catch-up. You see friends, they give you some positive feedback ('It's great to see you again'), and that starts to replace the negative thoughts you have been having on your own, and you feel better about yourself.

Not getting stuck on, or overwhelmed by, big issues like global conflicts or climate change is important. You don't have to abandon the issue, but try not to spend every day discussing what we *can't* possibly do as individuals to change the situation, because that's disempowering and depressing, and also reinforces a pessimistic mindset.

Don't focus on what you can't do. Focus on what you can do. For climate change, you can join an action group, lobby the government, protest. You can put solar panels on your roof, see if you can afford an electric car, and recycle. These are productive activities that recognise and address the problem. Knowing that you are doing what you can is often an effective antidote to pessimism and despair.

We should all try to see things a little more optimistically than perhaps they actually are, because it's good for our mental health. To do that we do need to 'accentuate the positive'. Making a real or mental list of the really positive aspects of your job, your close relationships, the place you live, your health and your financial situation can help cultivate an optimistic mindset. Adding comparisons in which you are clearly better off compared with many others helps to alter your perspective. Throw away the negative comparisons and the lists of things that are not so great about your life or circumstances.

If you can recognise that you are developing a pessimistic bias, thought-based strategies can help. When we have a pessimistic outlook, we are more likely to get stuck on the bad things, and use them to confirm our pessimistic view. If the bus is on time one day and late the next, we forget the time it was prompt, remember when it was late, and use that to confirm our pessimistic view that 'things never go smoothly'.

Assuming something bad will happen tomorrow is bad for our mental health and wellbeing. If you are prone to pessimistic thinking and particularly catastrophising, then you can consciously try to note the evidence that good things actually do happen quite regularly.

For example, with climate change, technological developments are already helping to reduce emissions. There has been a huge movement away from fossil fuels. Renewable energy solutions are already widely adopted across the globe. Whether action is happening fast enough is a matter of debate, but it is not as simple as saying, 'There's only one outcome, and it's bad.' That is not a balanced assessment of the situation.

Some people put particular emphasis on cultivating gratitude. As a way of keeping things in perspective, it has real merit. In the past, many people had specific rituals to reinforce the idea – like saying grace before dinner. We have social ceremonies and holidays, such as Anzac Day, that recognise the sacrifices of previous generations.

Perhaps even more beneficial on a daily basis is actually saying thanks to those in your life who you value and who help you to cope with life's adversities. Extending this beyond your immediate family to include work colleagues, friends and social acquaintances is worth the effort. We are quick to criticise but slow to thank.

Death is something that is easy to be pessimistic about. It is interesting that most religions, and other shared cultural beliefs, suggest something profound continues beyond this life. Our mental health benefits from believing that our individual life is not purposeless and that collectively we are engaged in something that extends beyond death. At the very least, we can all cultivate a bit of awe at how mysterious and amazing life is, rather than continually getting frustrated and despondent at traffic jams, empty Vegemite jars and all the bad stuff the daily news focuses on.

We often think truth is everything, but sometimes it's beneficial to spin your truth toward the optimistic outcome to improve your own mental health and wellbeing.

CHECKLIST

- Most of us have an in-built optimistic bias. We can cultivate that by noticing, and being grateful for, good things that happen.
- Despair is when we just give up. To avoid it, don't focus on what you can't do. Focus on what you can do, even if it seems small.
- Distress feels bad, but it can spur us to recognise a problem and take action to address it. Negative emotions can prompt deeper reflection and be powerful motivators to change.
- If you feel that you are starting to fall into despair, focus on doing things that you enjoy. Change the scene, get away, try to have fun, and challenge pessimistic thoughts with evidence of good things that happen.
- Hope should not be unrealistic. For it to be meaningful, it needs to be backed by realistic action.
- If you are in despair about a particular issue, what specific actions can you take to push things in the direction you want them to go? Taking action is much better for our mental health than retreating from the world, even when that action isn't that effective.

20

Anger

Holding on to anger is like grasping a hot coal with the intent of throwing it at someone else; you are the one who gets burned.

Buddha

He who angers you conquers you.

Elizabeth Kenny

Anger, probably the most commonly regretted of emotions, comes upon us suddenly. Something frustrates us, the anger rises and before we know it, we have lashed out at a family member, work colleague or even a stranger. Then we spend the next five hours thinking, 'Why did I do that?'

While anger has its uses, it can also make problems worse, and damage both our relationships and our reputation. Even if we promise ourselves that next time we will control our anger, and not let it overwhelm us, often in the heat of the moment, once again we lose the plot.

Why do we get angry? Can we learn to control our anger and even channel it into something useful?

Why Do We Get Angry?

Anger, like most emotions is largely involuntary. It is a fast, powerful, built-in emotional response to a threat or frustration and can cause us to lose control, and even be violent.

It is important to separate out the emotion 'angry' from any consequent behaviour, like lashing out, speaking aggressively or inflicting pain or distress on others. Simply saying that we should never feel angry isn't going to work. Feelings happen. We get sad, we get happy, we get frustrated, we get angry. What we do in response to those feelings is a different question.

For example, if you are being attacked, anger might be very helpful. When a sabre-toothed tiger approaches, cowering under a tree is unlikely to save your life. Getting angry helps you fight back. Anger empowers us, fuels us with aggression, and can be the difference between life and death. It is often motivated by our desire to protect others, particularly those we are close to.

In the modern world there are fewer sabre-toothed tigers. Unless we are being mugged, bullied, attacked or slandered, most interpersonal situations are better handled with delicacy and nuance, and with socially appropriate behaviours rather than all-out aggression. Taking anger out on those we are close to is almost always a mistake that ends up making things worse, not better.

Anger is often preceded by frustration, which causes emotional distress. When frustrated, we often look for someone, or something, to blame – our partner, the kids, the boss, the person driving the car we collided with, the internet provider who can't fix our router, the council that didn't fix the pothole on the road. Frustration can also arise from feeling powerless as a result of poverty, illness, a difficult home or work environment, troubled personal or intimate relationships, or a feeling that we are not in control of our life. Once we find someone or something to blame, we get angry at them.

Underlying frustration can combust into anger by some sort of provocation: a car nearly knocking us off our bicycle, the teenager leaving the kitchen light on again, waiting on hold for half an hour to speak to Medicare.

When we feel angry, we want to express it in some way, because that seems to demonstrate that we have control of our lives, and that we are not powerless.

Is anger the flip side of fear? Does it cover over our own lack of potency to bring about change? Clearly, we don't like feeling afraid and powerless. It feels better to get angry at someone or something than to passively accept circumstances we dislike. It feels more powerful and far less frightening.

There is a lot of complex literature in psychology (much of it Freudian) that suggests depression is simply 'anger turned inwards'. For many who work professionally with people with depression, like Ian, that is a bit too glib. Depression (see Chapter 10) is a much more complex psychological and physiological experience than that. However, as a concept, it does put the proposition that depression and anger – despite their very different characteristics – might (from an emotional perspective) be thought of as two different sides of the one coin. So, it highlights the need for us all to think, 'If I'm angry all the time, perhaps it means that I'm miserable.' It might be time to get professional help.

How Should We Deal with Anger?

Because anger is hardwired, it can be hard to control. The cables (nerve cell connections) for anger are set deep in our emotional brain. They are fast to light up, linked to action, not thought, and are slow to cool. All mammals have that circuitry, despite our capacity for love, affection, care and warmth. We do have other brain circuits to override those immediate emotions and help us to choose the most appropriate behavioural responses, but they are slower, and take some time and conscious effort to engage.

So, it's just not as simple as telling yourself to calm down or never be angry.

Many of us don't ever get past the emotional reaction of anger. 'Why is this happening to me? Whose fault is it? Who can I blame? Who can I get angry at?'

We have a range of emotions for good reasons. Evolution has decided to leave them in. Anger helps protect us, so we shouldn't beat ourselves up for getting angry. It's part of being human.

When people criticise us, it's challenging. Instinctively we react against it. If someone we live with, and even love, complains that we slurp our tea, a considered, rational response might be, 'I get that you find it irritating, but it's just how I drink. I'll try and change.' Instead, instinctively we can react by feeling threatened, blow the criticism out of proportion ('You obviously think I'm an irritating waste of space') and get angry ('I work hard to earn money to buy this tea. I'll drink it how I damn well like.')

If you are angry and upset because you believe someone has insulted or threatened you, and you react by insulting or threatening them back, then it is anger versus anger, and things can quickly escalate. Before you know it you are both furious, and neither of you understands what happened or how to fix it.

When we have an emotional reaction, it is almost invariably more useful not to act impulsively, but instead to try to follow it with a thoughtful response. The emotional part, anger, comes first. The challenge for us is to then get rational and work out what the best things is to do next.

The key question to ask is, 'How can I channel my anger in a constructive, not destructive, way?'

Channeling Anger in Productive Ways

Sometimes Ian gets angry at the lack of mental health funding. He expresses that, hopefully not by screaming at his staff, his family or ministers, but by lobbying hard for increased funding, and not being afraid to let his passion show. If people tell him that he seems a bit angry, he replies that he is, because it is an important issue. The anger creates the drive to work for change. Showing passion can be a lot more useful than writing a polite letter that gets no response.

If we identify what we are angry about, whether it be inaction on climate change, school funding or the lack of gluten-free options at the local cafe, then we can channel our anger to try and bring about change. It's being assertive and emotive, without being aggressive. Importantly, even if we don't succeed, we will usually still feel better. Psychologically we feel empowered by action, especially when we act in groups or on behalf of those who cannot do it themselves.

Telling people they shouldn't get angry doesn't help. What can help is to channel rage into productive activities, so we can develop a passion for life, a passion for change, and are able to act productively to make things better or to protect what we value.

Sometimes, however, there is nowhere productive to channel anger. A friend of James's was recently diagnosed with a fatal illness as a result of growing up in a house with asbestos insulation. The friend was initially and understandably angry, but he quickly moved through the angry phase, because there was nothing he could do. His exposure had occurred fifty years earlier, and his illness was incurable. Anger wasn't going to help. He needed to let it go, and try to enjoy the time he had left.

However, because anger is hardwired, it is not easy to let go of. Lots of people blurting out 'let it go' (apologies to *Frozen*) is often really trite. It takes real proactive steps. Bottling anger up or pretending it isn't there won't help. That emotion, that energy, has to go into another activity – even if the activity will not change the outcome.

There are good examples around. Often when people are first diagnosed with cancer, or some other serious or life-threatening illness, their first real emotion (after denial) is anger. 'Why me? I don't deserve this.' But, with time, effort and support, people often turn to focus their efforts on their close personal relationships, supporting others in the same predicament or advocating for better health care.

When we are angry, doing pleasurable activities helps. Those things that really make you feel a whole lot better. Physical activity, sex, work, relationships or yoga. Things that put real pleasure in our life. Do them with someone you love or care about. Time spent with others is a lot better than anger stored alone.

Notice that alcohol, drugs and binge-eating – although commonly described as pleasurable activities – are not on this list. If you want to make a bad situation worse, then combine anger with one of them. The more we indulge, the sooner we move from a short period of temporary relief of the distress to feeling even worse.

Controlling Anger

Anger and other emotions are in-built, but to function in complex human societies, we have to learn to moderate them and act in ways that are personally and socially productive. That means we have to control our anger. You can't punch everyone or, in fact, anyone, you disagree with.

The difficulty with controlling anger is that we can go from zero to a hundred in seconds, and before we know it, we have said or done something we will regret. We might promise ourselves we will learn from the experience, but then next time exactly the same thing happens.

Do You Get Angry a Lot?

The first step to controlling anger is to identify if you are a volatile person who becomes angry easily. If you tend to be on edge and get annoyed a lot, if you speak harshly with people you live with, and lash out at people at work, it is very likely that it might be more you than them.

Is There an Underlying Frustration?

Anger doesn't come out of nowhere. It often stems from some underlying or chronic frustration. If you are already frustrated or distressed, you will probably get angry more easily. If there is underlying frustration, if you feel trapped and ineffective in the world, it can, and perhaps should, manifest as distress. However, for some, especially men, their frustration is channelled into anger, because at least when you are angry, you feel powerful.

If you do feel frustrated, the next step is to work out why. Is there one cause, or several? Have you been frustrated for a long time, or is it recent? The cause might be financial stress, a troubled relationship, a difficult work environment, lack of opportunities you think you deserve, or something else. It might be deeply embedded in an unhappy workplace, a failing relationship, or several of the above.

When frustration becomes anger, it focuses on someone or something to blame. That might be other people ('it's my boss's fault'), organisations ('it's the Family Court's fault'), the government, internet companies or even society in general. The thought process is, 'I've been treated unfairly, so I'm justified in getting angry.'

Dealing with Frustration

How do you turn the temperature down? For example, if a couple with children split up and one parent feels the other parent is deliberately denying them access, frustration can rise quickly and turn to anger at the their former partner. What can be done?

Firstly, a specific focus on resolving the issue. Families that separate need to find ways of negotiating and reaching agreement, despite the grief and the hurt and the distress. The more it is drawn out and fought about, the more damaging it can be. People going through this require a lot of help and encouragement to resolve the issues, not fight.

Secondly, many people get depressed in this sort of situation, but people around them often don't realise. They think the person has become difficult, aggressive, withdrawn and angry. However, if the person gets alone in a room with a therapist, they often break down in tears. Most people in this situation are a mess: totally miserable about the break-up of the family, the loss of everything that's important to them, and having 'unfair' restrictions on when they can see their kids. There's a deep sense of loss and of failing at life. Their distress is coming out as anger, often exacerbated by alcohol or drug use.

Often we do not recognise our own distress and need help to deal with our underlying emotional state. We need to be encouraged to deal with the causes, the grief and loss. Getting drunk and punching people, or fighting over the kids in the Family Court for years, isn't going to help. It's better to cry. The sooner we cry, the sooner we can move on and reduce our anger.

Regular exercise can also help reduce feelings of frustration and anger. Run, swim, go to the gym, stretch or walk. Don't forget peripheral exercise as you move through the day, like walking upstairs rather than getting the lift, and walking to the train station rather than getting the bus. It all helps.

Should You Let Your Anger Out?

Is it helpful to go into a room alone and shout and punch the sofa? Should you lance the wound and let your anger out? In a word, no. It doesn't work. It might actually make things worse.

Instead, recognise the emotion, recognise the distress behind the anger, and find another productive way to deal with that. Working for change, despite the distress, is the only real way out.

If someone promises that they will do something for you and then lets you down, and you feel hurt and angry, is it better to express that to them, or bottle it up, try to forget it and move on?

Bottling up anger can be bad, particularly for those who do not feel confident expressing frustration. They say that everything is 'fine' or 'good', while inside they are boiling. Trying to avoid further rejection or hurt is an understandable response, but it may be counterproductive.

Those of us who are naturally more timid may need to really learn to be more assertive (not aggressive). You can feel great when you learn to say, 'I am annoyed with you because you keep making me promises that you do not keep.' Instead of just walking away, you stand your ground and calmly state your case: 'I'm sad because you didn't take any account of the impact of your actions on me.'

That's the role of language – to take those strong feelings, and describe them in words, so that others understand our concerns and take them seriously. To communicate effectively, you can't just blow up and yell or storm off and slam doors. It takes practice to recognise our negative emotions, compose ourselves and respond in a calm and productive way to those who have caused you to get upset or angry.

Learn to recognise when your temperature is rising and you are in danger of losing your temper. As soon as it starts to happen, take a break. Leave the room, go for a walk, cool down. The earlier you notice the signs or impending anger, the easier it is to walk away. The longer the argument goes for, the harder it is.

Getting Angry at Your Kids

When a child does something they shouldn't, like punching their friend, biting their cousin, being cruel to pets or sneaking chocolate from the cupboard, should parents let the child see that they are angry?

Some children do lash out, or do thoughtless or dangerous things more than others. Some kids with developmental or other behavioural difficulties get yelled at a lot. It rarely works. Adults need to help children moderate their behaviour, and teach them it's not okay to bite, scratch, yell or thump someone else, even if they did cheat at Monopoly.

Just saying, 'That's unacceptable. Stop it,' often won't be enough. Sometimes it's just token. It sounds like the parent has said it a thousand times before, and it has had no effect on the unwanted behaviour. It is like telling people who are anxious to 'just stop worrying'. It might actually make it worse! It's negative re-inforcement (which is not the same as punishment). It's not just an ineffective response, it's one that actually makes it more likely that the unwanted behaviour will become more common.

So, it's better to:
- Validate how the child feels: 'We all feel angry at times but it's not okay to act on anger in a way that hurts someone else.'
- Give them something practical to do instead. 'Next time you feel that way, get up, walk away and start another activity that you enjoy instead.'

It is important for parents to express their anger at certain times, but in an appropriate and effective way. If you want a three-year-old to understand that you really do not want them to bite their sister again, saying, 'Please don't do that again,' in a nice, quiet voice won't work. The child has to see the seriousness on your face and hear it in your voice. It's okay to express your emotion, as long as you remain in control. If there's too much shouting, kids just hear noise, not the message.

Pick your battles. If you get angry every day about every little thing, kids stop listening. Save up the (appropriate) anger for things that really matter, and then explain why it mattered.

Many parents feel that teenagers don't listen, but if you say something very clearly and show them by your tone of voice and facial expression that it is serious, they might not *look* like they are listening, but they probably get the message. Try and make eye contact, slow down, speak very directly and let them hear in your tone that the message you are giving them is important. That works better than lashing out in an aggressive, harmful way.

If you're speaking in a serious manner about something important to a teenager, and they turn their back and walk away, it is very easy to get angry. 'How dare you walk away from me when I'm talking!'

However, the question to ask is, 'Will that help, or make things worse?' Usually it will make things worse because your anger will lead to the teenager becoming angry, and things will go downhill from there. Silence and detachment can be powerful allies. They can demonstrate how deeply hurt you are. So, sometimes it is better to take the loss, swallow your pride and try again another day.

Some kids are more sensitive, and will get upset by being spoken to harshly. When they get shouted at, the only message they get is, 'You think I'm bad' or 'I'm about to get hurt' (physically or emotionally). They don't even listen to the words. They just register they are being shouted at, and that it feels bad.

This happens with adults too. If someone angrily strides toward us shouting, we would probably stop listening and start running. We don't listen to what they are trying to communicate. Delivering a message angrily can actually ensure that that message is never received, because the person's response to anger is to withdraw quickly to a safer place. Anger is not an engaging emotion. It is an emotion of conflict, not one that leads to productive engagement.

CHECKLIST

- Anger is a powerful emotion that is useful when we need to protect ourselves and others.
- Anger often develops when there is underlying frustration.
- Try to channel anger into productive action.
- If there is underlying frustration over something, try to resolve that issue.
- Make a plan for what to do if you feel yourself getting angry.
- If you feel anger rising, get out of there and calm down before conflict escalates.
- Yelling at children rarely works.
- Letting children see you are angry in an appropriate way, with tone of voice, eye contact and facial expression, is much more effective.

21

Religion, Spirituality and Mental Health

*To me, religion is an agreement between a group of people about
what God is. Spirituality is a one-on-one relationship.*

Steve Earle

What is the difference between religion and spirituality? How do
they affect our mental health and wellbeing? Both are about trying
to find purpose and meaningful connection in life. Religion is an
organised community-based system, with specific beliefs and practices, while spirituality can be a more individual attempt to find a
connection to something more meaningful than the day-to-day
challenges of earning money and paying the bills.

Religion

Throughout history, humans have engaged in all sorts of communal
practices centred around a belief in something more powerful than
themselves. Typically, religions combine beliefs (for example, that
there is a God) with practices (attending church on Sundays), rules

(do not steal) and a shared moral and social code (do unto others as you would have them do unto you).

Virtually all religious traditions have a culture of reciprocity. It is not just about what you get from them. There is an expectation you will give as well.

What effect does being a member of a religion have on mental health? You will be connected and united with others in a common purpose, share a common set of values and beliefs, be encouraged to maintain a moral code, and believe that life is purposeful and meaningful. These all have a positive effect on our mental health.

On the other hand, if you belong to a religion, there are things you are expected to do, like attend services and actively follow the rules and moral code. That can impact on a person's sense of personal autonomy, which is also important for good mental health. If a religion prohibits certain activities, like sex before marriage, or same-gender relationships, then members who want to have sex before marriage or a same-gender relationship can feel internal conflict, distress and guilt, which are bad for our mental health. Some religions have also emphasised the imperfect nature of humans, reinforcing feelings of guilt, self-loathing and shame, which are clearly bad for your overall wellbeing.

In Australia, while the number of people who identify as religious has been steadily declining, about half of us identify as being a member of a religion.

Spirituality

Spirituality is concerned with the concept of the human spirit or soul, emphasising personal and shared feelings that transcend individual and everyday material and physical things. Like religion, it is about trying to find a connection to something bigger than today's traffic jams, property prices and skinny lattes. Unlike religion, it can be a solitary practice. Meditation is an example. While there can be meditation classes and groups, the act itself is a solitary one where people examine their own inner landscape.

Anyone who believes they have some (impossible to prove or disprove) connection to the universe could be said to be spiritual, but surely it requires more than looking out at the ocean or the stars or your family every now and again and going, 'Wow!' Spirituality is about connecting, across generations and beyond the local perspective, to larger concerns such as the welfare of our wider community and the sustainability of the natural world we inhabit.

It is clear that a strong spiritual sense is associated with very good mental health and wellbeing. Those who feel connected in this way experience less anxiety, are less suspicious of others and more open to forming relationships with those who are different to themselves. Temperamentally, these people appear more empathic than many others. If people think and feel beyond their own immediate needs, it helps them to keep today's transitory difficulties within a broader, more universal context.

Ian, being a behaviourist, believes that for spirituality to be meaningful, you can't just talk about it. Simply saying, 'I'm a spiritual person' doesn't mean much. There needs to be some *doing*. Some form of practice. For example, meditating each morning, taking five minutes each evening to think about what you are grateful for, volunteering for an appropriate social or welfare organisation, joining a community choir, or taking physical or emotional care of those in need.

Yoga can have physical and mental benefits, but is it a spiritual practice? Perhaps the answer depends on whether you treat it simply as stretching and exercise that benefits your body, or you are more connected to the philosophy, the group practice, the focus on calm and serenity and use it to connect yourself with the moment and your place in the universe.

Some people are incredibly nice, kind and are always doing things for others. Are they, somehow, more spiritually advanced than the rest of us? Is helping others a spiritual practice? Or have they just learned that when they do good for others, they feel good within themselves, and so have made the rational decision to do good works to maintain and improve their own mental health? As is often the case with humans, our motives are probably mixed. We help others because it is good for them, *and* because it gives us a warm inner glow.

Religion's Struggle for Relevance and Mental Health

One of the biggest mental health challenges we face today is that most of us belong to fewer social groups than people in the past, and our bonds with the groups we do belong to are often weaker than in the past. (See Chapter 5, 'The Importance of Social Connection'.)

Historically, one of the most common and important groups were religions. They brought people together. Being part of a religious group enabled us to meet others, mix socially, be involved in purposeful community activities, from fetes to helping the vulnerable, and obtain support when we experienced tough times.

People used to check at church services to see who wasn't there, and visit those who didn't turn up. Today, it is not uncommon for someone to die in their home, and for no-one to find them for weeks.

Many join religions at times when they are experiencing difficulties in their lives, and the religious group and its practices support and help them. Some find comfort in the structure, the organised practices and rituals, or the concept of submitting to a higher power or purpose. For many, it is simply the unconditional acceptance by a supportive and uncritical social group.

A sense of belonging to a group, or groups, is essential to almost everyone's mental health, and religions have played an important role in collective mental health. Now that their popularity is declining, when those who are not religious hit tough times, they have one less obvious place to turn. The decline in those actively participating in religious activity leaves a big gap. What fills it? Social media? Online communities? For many it is the workplace, a cause such as protecting the environment or some less structured social group.

Geraldine Doogue, longtime ABC commentator on matters religious and spiritual, says that, 'When joining a religion, or any group for that matter, we have to accept that not everything will be on our terms. You have to sacrifice some autonomy.' Autonomy is important to mental health, but if you want to be socially connected, you have to compromise. It's a bit like joining a political party or movement. There will be things that challenge you, and things you disagree with. It runs against our modern preoccupation with convenience and immediate satisfaction.

Today, we have more options for spending our free time than ever before. Many, especially the young, do not even consider belonging to a religion. In the past, if you lost your job, or your marriage ended, or you developed an addiction, or became depressed or anxious, religions were there to offer experienced support. For centuries, they looked after those going through tough times. One of the mental health arguments in favour of belonging to a religion is that, while it may not be as easy as belonging to a streaming service, if you fall into a hole, it will be there to support you.

In the Western world some religions, notably Christianity, have struggled to be seen as relevant in the twenty-first century. Some argue they have become fossilised in the way they express their traditions. For example, the Catholic Church's conservative attitudes to contraception, same-sex marriage, and the role of women have seen many label it as out of touch and irrelevant.

In addition, when people think of the Catholic Church, despite their values and ethics and the large amount of community work they do helping the vulnerable, generally, the first thing they think about isn't something good.

The challenge for religious institutions is to become relevant and functional for today's world so they can continue to provide that sense of belonging, shared values and social connection that are important to mental health.

The mental health benefits of being religious (being connected and united with others in a common purpose, being encouraged to maintain a moral code, and believing that life is purposeful and meaningful) are also available elsewhere through meaningful work, volunteering and membership of social, community, sporting and cause-related groups.

Geraldine Doogue is optimistic. 'Good, thriving traditions are bold and durable enough to be spurred by change to reconsider their traditions. I think that is underway, in a long, slow agonising way. In my particular part of the tradition, Catholic Christianity, it's trying to do this.'

CHECKLIST

- For those belonging to a religion, the shared community and values, the belief that life is purposeful, and being encouraged to maintain a moral code can all be good for mental health.

- However, religion can also reduce our autonomy, and if it prohibits behaviour like same-relationships or sex before marriage, it can lead to internal conflict and feelings of guilt, shame and distress.
- Spirituality is about trying to find a connection with something bigger than oneself and the week's chores. Unlike religion, it can be solitary, but there should be some 'doing'. A strong spiritual sense is associated with good mental health.
- A sense of belonging is important to good mental health, and religions often help members who are experiencing tough times. However, religious membership is declining. What will fill the gap?

22

Forgiveness

*Resentment is like drinking poison and then hoping it will
kill your enemies . . .
Forgiveness liberates the soul, it removes fear. That's why
it's such a powerful weapon.*

Nelson Mandela

When someone does you wrong or treats you badly, do you hold
a grudge? Should we forgive those who have wronged us? If you
want to forgive someone, how do you actually do it?

What Is Forgiveness?

Forgiveness is more than a pragmatic compromise. It is an emotional
resolution, where you try to let go of your feelings of resentment. It
can involve letting the other person know you forgive them, or you
can forgive on your own, without the other person ever knowing.

Forgiving can allow us to let go of anger and bitterness, and be
happier. It can reinforce and strengthen the relationship between

the forgiver and the forgiven. Letting someone know that you forgive them is a generous act. If you have done something you regret, and those offended forgive you, it is liberating.

However, it is more complicated than simply thinking 'Okay, I forgive him.' It is an emotional process that involves trying to understand why the other person acted as they did, and examining and moving on from our feelings of anger and resentment.

Should We Forgive?

Is forgiving someone better for our mental health than nurturing a grudge? Could forgiveness be one of those things that, like exercise, we might not *want* to do, but we know is good for us?

There are some great forgivers in the world. Nelson Mandela somehow forgave all the things done to him and his people during apartheid. Rosie Batty, 2015 Australian of the Year, was on the radio the day after her son was killed by her ex-husband, and immediately appeared to understand and forgive. For many of us, being able to do this in such an awful circumstance is almost beyond comprehension. Those who are able to genuinely forgive appear to be more mature, and in a healthy mental state.

Holding Grudges

Sometimes we can almost enjoy thinking about those who have done us wrong. We think about how bad they were, and how good we are, and it can be strangely satisfying. We see ourselves as the noble victim and them as the evil perpetrator. However, holding onto grudges can become corrosive. We can get stuck focusing on the same unpleasant event – losing a job, a betrayal by a friend, a falling-out at work – over and over, and almost nurture our bitterness, anger and resentment. Every time we think about it, we start to get upset again. All of this is bad for our overall mental health. The persistent distress takes its toll on our stress-arousal systems, and tends to become self-perpetuating and distract us from other activities that may be more positive and satisfying.

This failure to forgive and move on can also be bad for our physical health. If we keep getting angry and emotionally wound up about past events, our blood pressure can rise, and there might be an excess of adrenaline in our system that, over time, wears us down and affects our sleep and mood.

The other thing that can happen is a gradual shift in our perception of the events that led to the grudge. At the time, we might have felt that getting sacked was unfair but understood some of the reasons why it happened and the pressure the boss was under, and have known that deep down, they weren't a bad person. Holding onto a grudge can lead us to gradually change our perception and even memory, and develop a narrative that is more extreme and self-serving. The boss changes from being someone in a difficult position into an evil ogre, while we see ourselves as a wronged, faultless hero.

Forgiving others allows us to move on, but it isn't easy.

How Do You Forgive?

Forgiveness in Families

Family members, particularly those we live with, are relatively easy to forgive, partly because we get so much practice. We all stuff up frequently in minor ways. 'Sorry, I forgot to get milk.' 'Sorry, I didn't put the bins out.' 'Sorry, I lost our life savings on cryptocurrency.' We let each other down and argue every day, and then quickly move on. Families that stay living together (and not all do) have to get good at forgiveness, because it would be too hard to function if everyone was carrying around a laundry list of resentments.

Families are better at forgiveness for several reasons. Firstly, you can hate your boss, but you can't hate your son for very long, even when he backs your car into a pole. We are deeply invested in our relationships with our immediate kin. They really matter to both our identity and our mental health. There is too much on the line to hold grudges, so we have a strong incentive to do whatever it takes to fix things. We forgive and move on, knowing that soon it will be our turn to stuff up, and they will forgive us.

Secondly, it is pragmatic to forgive those we live with. If your partner lets you down and does something that really hurts you, is it going to cause you to leave the relationship? If not, then you have to fix things. It's no fun living with someone you are angry or irritated at. We want to live in a relaxed, friendly environment, and to achieve that we have to forgive. Our proximity to each other is a strong motivator to try and sort things out.

The third reason families are better at forgiveness is assortative mating. We tend to partner with those who are similar to us emotionally. The children we produce carry our genes, so they are also likely to be similar emotionally. People who are alike are more inclined to understand each other, even when they offend and irritate each other. You might not like that your partner made a joke at your expense at a party, but you understand where it came from because you sometimes do it too. 'It hurt, but she didn't *mean* to hurt me. Like me, she just likes making jokes, and sometimes they go too far.'

You might have the weird experience of your kids doing similar things to you. Your daughter stays out to 3 am without letting you know where she is. You don't like it, but you used to do that too, so you kind of understand. That understanding is an important step on the way to forgiveness.

The Rest of Us

Even if we know that forgiveness is good for us, most of us struggle to do it. If, for the sake of your own mental health, you want to forgive but it isn't happening naturally, how do you do it? Is there a process?

Forgiveness happens gradually, and might be something you have to think about a fair bit.

The first step is trying to understand why the other person acted as they did. Can you put yourself in their shoes, see the world through their eyes and understand their motivations? If something hurts us, it is tempting to assume malicious intent, but often it wasn't meant that way. Someone might say something careless that stings us far more than they anticipated. A boss might sack us because she is under pressure from her own boss to cut costs. A friend might cut off contact with you, not because they are trying to hurt you, but because they are going through their own difficult issues.

Often, over time, we create a simple narrative. 'They hurt me, so they are a bad person.' Once we look at things from their point of view, we usually find it is more complicated. Coming to understand why the other person acted as they did does not mean you endorse or agree with it. It just means that you may come to understand, at least in part, their reasons. Reasons are not excuses. It is similar to the legal concept of mitigation. The person is guilty, but there are mitigating factors, and the sentence imposed reflects both the crime and those mitigating factors.

Part of this process is trying to understand how the other person is different to you. It is not just putting *yourself* in their shoes. It is trying to understand their actions, given how they are *different* to you. You might be upset that a friend did not stick up for you in a work meeting or friend group when you were being unjustly criticised, and know that if the positions were reversed, you would have supported them. But perhaps your friend is more shy and less confident that you, and would have found it much more difficult. Mustering that empathy to try to understand the other person is an important step toward forgiveness.

When Rosie Batty discussed the actions of her ex-husband in killing her child, she didn't simply characterise him as evil. She was able to try to understand the tortured mental state he had been in, and the other systemic failings that had resulted in the terrible outcome. She demonstrated remarkable empathy for the situation and the person in it.

Timing

Deciding when to go down the path of forgiveness is a critical step. Often the hurt caused by the actions of others is significant and the impact ongoing. The resulting anger or distress may not dissipate quickly. If people are pushed to forgive too early or too soon after the events, there is unlikely to be a good outcome. Don't rush into forgiveness before you are ready, particularly when the events have been significant. For those who have been traumatised, abused or assaulted, forgiveness can be a long way off. If you start to go through the process there is a danger that it may reopen some deep wounds and cause emotional pain. If you get the sense that you are not ready to forgive, so be it. Sometimes leaving past pain in the background is better than bringing it all up again.

Often it is necessary to let time pass before even embarking on the journey, until the acute distress and hurt begin to settle. Before going down this path, it may be worth considering:
- How often, and how deeply, are you feeling anger and resentment over what happened?
- Is feeling that anger and resentment unpleasant?
- Do you want to move on and reduce, or even eliminate, it?

- Are you prepared to try and understand what happened from the other person's point of view?
- Are you open to feeling empathy for the other person?

How to Have the Conversation

At some point you might decide that you want to talk to the other person about the incident or incidents, or tell them that you forgive them. These are tricky conversations. Rather than starting with all the fire and brimstone that might have been running around your head – 'For the last five years I've been thinking about how much I hate you' – something a little gentler might be better to start with. 'I was really upset about what happened five years ago and it still sits badly with me.' Then stop talking and see what they say. Sometimes these things are better written than spoken. Set it out in a calm and concise manner, without ranting and raving, which might rekindle the original distress. And make sure that after you write the letter, email or even text message, you don't send it immediately. Come back to it the next day and read it again.

The other person might try and explain their actions, and even concede some fault. 'I didn't handle it well. I wish I'd done things differently, and I've felt bad about it.' Suddenly, the villain is humanised. Most people want peace, not to accentuate the conflict more. They might try and defuse the situation.

As there are two sides to most conflicts, there is the real possibility that they too were hurt by the interactions, and they may not yet be as forgiving or ready to move on as you. So, be aware that there are dangers in engaging with the other party and there is a risk of rekindling the whole damaging process.

Remember that forgiveness is more about you moving on, than extracting a particular reaction from the other person. If they apologise, great. But they might not. They might think the whole incident was trivial, or that their actions were entirely justified.

If you do not get the reaction you think you deserve, try not to let that derail your forgiveness. Forgiveness should not be contingent upon the other person reacting in the 'right' way. You forgive for yourself, so you can move on. If you are only telling someone you forgive them because you want to hear them apologise, you probably aren't ready to forgive yet.

When forgiving someone, for many it is easier to speak to them, so there is a feedback loop and perhaps an apology, but you can forgive someone on your own. Role plays and visualisations work. You can imagine that the person is there sitting next to you, or talk to a picture of them, or even to a piece of paper with their name written on it. Tell them what you want to say and that you are ready to forgive them. What would they say to you? Have an imaginary conversation with them. You can get upset, even cry.

A middle ground between apologising to the person and doing it on your own is to go through the process with a therapist. In the safety of therapy, the therapist can ask, 'What would you say to the person if they were here?' A lot of therapists use roleplay. 'Imagine I am the person who hurt you. What do you want to say?'

Apologising

The flip side of forgiving someone is to seek out a person who you feel you have wronged and apologise to them. It takes courage to do this, because you do not know how they will react. They might be grateful for the apology, or they might still be angry about what you did and give you a frosty reception. That is up to them. All you can do is apologise.

The Legal System

Our British-derived legal system is adversarial. When a dispute becomes a legal proceeding, to participants it can appear to be a battle, often one that takes years to conclude, and is both finan-cially and emotionally costly. The system is not really designed to promote a common understanding, let alone forgiveness.

Drawn-out legal proceedings can be terrible for our mental health. The outcome is uncertain and there can be long delays. Both these factors can create anxiety and chronic stress. Many become preoccupied by their case and find it hard to get on with their lives until it is resolved.

Purely from a mental health perspective, if at all possible, court proceedings should be avoided. Can the dispute be resolved? Can the case be settled? People say, 'But what about justice? They should pay for what they did. My position should be validated.' These are understandable feelings, but we have to be pragmatic. Is fighting for justice more important than our mental health? If you are in a dispute with a former business partner over money, or with a sibling over your mother's will, is the stress really worth it? Is it more important than us leading as good a life as we can?

If there is a way of ending a dispute, give it strong consideration, because the evidence suggests that the longer a court case goes on, the more our mental health can suffer. This is the case *even if we eventually win*. Winning the case does not fix everything.

An alternative might be mediation, which can occur in several courts, including the Family Court. In mediation, the parties get in the same room and, with the help of a skilled mediator, they state their positions and then try to resolve the matter and find a compromise they can all live with. Mediation has repeatedly been shown to have much better mental and physical health outcomes, because it shortens the process, people gain some validation from stating their position and, because the outcome must be agreed to by all parties, there is no 'loser'.

Additionally, as mentioned, we have a tendency to demonise those we are in dispute with. If we get in the same room with them and hear their point of view in the less formal environment of mediation, we might think, 'I don't like what they did, but I kind of get why they acted like that. I don't totally understand them, but they're not as bad as that image I had running round my head. They're not a monster. They're just a person like me.'

CHECKLIST

- Forgiveness is an emotional process that can allow us to let go of anger and bitterness.
- While holding grudges can feel strangely satisfying, it is not good for our mental health.
- Family members forgive each other all the time, both because they love each other and because they don't want dinner to be tense.
- To forgive, try to understand why the other person acted as they did. Are they really an evil monster, or can you understand why they acted that way?
- If you forgive someone, don't expect them to react in a particular way. You forgive for you. How they react is up to them.
- If you talk to someone about what happened, don't rage in anger. Tell them how it made you feel, then let them speak.
- Drawn-out legal proceedings can be terrible for mental health. Is settlement or mediation an option so that you can move on?

23

What Is Love?

In real love, you want the other person's good. In romantic love,
you want the other person.

Margaret C. Anderson

Love does not dominate; it cultivates.

Johann Wolfgang von Goethe

What is love? What are the different types of love? Is obsessive infatuation really love? The great religions tell us to love everyone, but how do you love that guy at work who never rinses his coffee cup?

The Chemistry of Love

Many people say their most intimate relationships are based on 'chemistry'. If there is no chemistry, they say it is unlikely a relationship will start. Even if it does, it won't last. This concept actually has a strong basis in reality. Mammals have a built-in chemical system that underpin the development of strong attachments between intimate partners, parents and their offspring, and other key relationships.

The central chemical is oxytocin, often referred to as the 'love drug'. It is released in the brain by a whole series of important interpersonal behaviours – physical contact, eye contact, cuddling, massage and sex. Women's brains release oxytocin in the middle of their menstrual cycle, when they are most fertile, which increases the likelihood they will feel attracted to others.

Oxytocin is critical to childbirth, underpinning contractions of the uterus and early mother-child interactions. When a mother breastfeeds her baby she releases oxytocin, which causes breast milk to flow and reinforces the mother's attachment to the baby. The baby also releases oxytocin. Mum thinks, 'My kid is the best.' The kid thinks, 'That's the world's best mum.'

These interactions are not limited to humans. Domestic dogs and their human companions each release oxytocin when they engage in shared experiences. As a result, both dogs and humans form very strong attachments to each other.

'I'm in Love' – Infatuation

Infatuation is an altered mental state. Those first heady weeks of being in love can be a mix of elation, joy, anxiety, paranoia ('Why hasn't she called me back?') and obsessional, repetitive thoughts focusing on one thing (your loved one) to the exclusion of all others (family, friends, chores). 'She is *soo* much better than everyone else, *so* unique, *so* special.'

It is an intense, disorientating, narrowly focused feeling. We feel awash with emotions, not very rational, and have a distorted view of the other person as perfect. We give up seeing friends, dinner with parents and Tuesday-night tennis without a second thought, to spend more time with this incredible person.

The strong evolutionary purpose of infatuation is that it leads to sex and reproduction. However, infatuation is temporary. Physiologically, oxytocin release drives the initial bonding, but its impact wears off as we share more and more experiences. As it does, our distorted perfect view of the other person changes to something more realistic. Interestingly, those relationships that can maintain oxytocin release through a lot of physical contact and sexual activity tend to last longer.

As infatuation wears off, the relationship changes into something less intense and more realistic. Those powerful experiences during the initial infatuation stage become an important part of the history of that relationship and may even create a cognitive and emotional template for what happens later. However, many relationships do not survive once the love potion of infatuation wears off. To continue, the relationship must grow and mature.

Some argue that the initial strong feeling of being in love is a necessary factor to a long-term relationship, even if it is not sufficient to maintain it. If you have never been in love with the person, if they are 'just a friend', then is the 'chemistry' for a long-term relationship really there?

People do sometimes fall for someone they have been friends with for years, but there may well have been more intense feelings previously. Social relationships are complicated and those we spend more time with and engage more with are likely to become more important to us.

Love in Long-term Relationships

How can that early feeling of being 'in love' turn into a more realistic love that lasts?

From an evolutionary point of view, infatuation was about bonding with another person, having sex and creating more humans. Human children need parents longer than any other species, so there is also a reason for those relationships to continue beyond the infatuation period.

We are more likely to be attracted to, and form relationships with, those who are similar to us emotionally, and who have a similar temperament and sensitivity. We like people who think like us and who react emotionally in a similar way to us.

As infatuation wears off, if we continue to share experiences with the other person – travelling, going out to dinner, watching TV, supermarket shopping – we might realise that we really do enjoy doing things with them. The relationship may not be as passionately exciting as in those first few weeks or months, but there is a continuing sense of its emotional specialness. It is more pleasurable to travel with this person. It is more pleasurable to do the washing up with them. It is more pleasurable to bring up kids with them. All of these experiences can add up to love.

Ongoing physical closeness is important. It is pretty easy to spot relationships where that closeness persists, and those where it does not. When it is gone, it could mean there is a big problem in the relationship. On the other hand, with kids, jobs, shopping and putting out the bins, couples can go through periods where physical intimacy falls down their priority list. With a bit of reprioritising, that can be addressed.

Is Love Selfless?

There is one chocolate left, you really want it and your daughter hasn't seen it, so she'll never know if you scoff it. Nonetheless, you give it to her. One of the few situations where we act in a genuinely selfless way is when we do things for those we love, against our own self-interest.

Parents say they would go to any length to protect their kids, and some do. They run into fires to grab them. In other species, mothers go to incredible lengths to protect their young. After emperor penguins lay an egg, they walk up to 80 kilometres to get fish, then return and regurgitate the food for their chicks. Octopus mothers spend so much time and energy looking after their eggs that they don't have time to hunt, and then they waste away. Crab spider mothers go even further and allow their babies to eat them.

This behaviour is not learned. The desire to protect those we love appears to be built-in, selfless, non-thoughtful and automatic.

However, it may be that the infatuation, 'in love' stage is less selfless, and more similar to the other things we enjoy, like eating ice-cream. It makes us feel good, so we want more of it.

When Lovers Fight

Why can love turn controlling, possessive, ugly and sometimes even violent? Are love and hate two sides of the same coin?

When passions are high, people can get irrational and emotional, and flip quickly from 'I love her and she's the most amazing person in the world,' to 'She's ruined my life and I hate her.'

Arguments between romantic partners can combust quickly. Often we set unrealistically high standards for romantic partners. Just because they forgot to pick up the peanut butter you asked them to get, it doesn't mean that they hate you. Just because they find a grammatical error in an early draft of this book, it doesn't mean they think you are an incompetent idiot.

We trust our partners, and with trust comes vulnerability. If someone on the bus says something nasty about you, it would be unpleasant, but wouldn't hurt that much. But if someone to whom you have trusted with your most precious gift, your love, tells you that you're a useless waste of space, your whole sense of self-worth is challenged. It hurts. It feels like a betrayal. 'It was hard to open up and be vulnerable, but I did it, and now you've thrown it back in my face.'

When we trust others, and share our hopes, fears, weaknesses, secrets and the things we are embarrassed and ashamed about, we assume they won't use them to hurt us. However, when arguments escalate, not only do romantic partners know our secrets, the intimacy and closeness of the relationship means that they also know exactly how to cause us the most hurt.

When someone that you love rejects you, it really hurts. However, that doesn't mean they *meant* to hurt you. If they decide to end the relationship, it might just be because they have come to the painful realisation that they don't actually love you anymore, or they don't want to live with you anymore, or they don't want to be in a relationship anymore, not because they deliberately want to cause you pain.

Those who, because of a combination of their genetics and their environmental development, are more possessive, controlling and rigid in everyday life, may display those same characteristics in their relationships, and that can be problematic. It is not love that causes possessiveness. It happens when someone who has a propensity to be possessive gets in a relationship, and their possessiveness finds a focus there.

Many situations that end up with anger, aggression and even violence are not pre-planned, or thought out. They happen quickly and spontaneously as strong emotions swirl. Some couples who have been together a while get better at noticing the early signs of disagreement or conflict, and at developing strategies to avoid inflaming the situation. Instead of arguing, they go to separate rooms, or one goes out for a walk. They let some time pass until they both have calmed down. Maybe they are cold to each other for a day or two, until they both realise that they want to fix things up, and negotiate a truce or even exchange apologies.

Others are unable or unwilling to do this and get into patterns of behaviour that escalate the conflict, which can be unpleasant and sometimes even dangerous.

Sexual Experimentation

Why are some happy to either be single or with one partner, while others have a pattern of unfaithfulness and affairs? Is it simply about wanting sex? Or are those who keep looking for new sexual partners constantly trying to validate their attractiveness and self-esteem?

There is strong genetic evidence that the interest in sexual experimentation persists in humans because it drives the spread of our DNA via reproduction. Monogamous relationships have an upside in terms of social stability and protecting small children, but from an evolutionary perspective, the downside is that reproduction is limited. When our average lifespan was shorter, and many died in childhood, having lots of children was important, because only some of them would live to reach sexual maturity and be able to themselves reproduce.

As we live longer and longer lives, the pressure on long-term relationships increases. Hence, in the modern world, break-ups in long-term intimate relationships have become more common at all stages of life. Reasons that people constantly pursue new sexual encounters outside their one exclusive intimate relationship include:
- Seeking greater validation from new relationships
- Trying to rediscover that heady infatuation phase
- Ongoing sexual attraction to new partners
- Seeking greater novelty
- It is, in some ways, now easier to find someone than ever before via dating apps.

Some people are not well suited to the conventional monogamous arrangements that now surround the rearing of young children in Western societies. However, many do manage to stay focused on their child's welfare, no matter what else is going on.

First Love and Learning to Love

You might have seen a thousand romantic relationships onscreen, but when you experience one for the first time it can be intense, exciting, joyous, unsettling, strange and even scary. At school and beyond, we are encouraged to be logical. 'Use your brain.' 'Work it out.' Then, when first love happens, powerful, unfamiliar emotions and urges buffet you from here to there. One moment you're elated, the next you can't get in contact and you're paranoid. 'Maybe they don't like me anymore.'

Not many of us can expect to be good at romantic relationships from the start. We will all get things wrong, but from those mistakes, we learn. Sometimes it is useful to go through the painful process of thinking about why certain relationships didn't work out and the mistakes we made, and working out what we could do differently next time. Many of us make the same errors more than once, but hopefully over time there is a progression and we get the hang of it a little bit.

Intimacy is rewarding, but it can be difficult. It is a period of great vulnerability where we can get deeply hurt. In a loving relationship, there is a lot of growing up to do. Learning how relationships work usually occurs through a series of them, before the one that may lead to child rearing.

Our early relationships, especially with our parents, are important in forming patterns for our later intimacy. If, as a child, you had close, loving and functional relationships with parents, siblings, and others, then you have the template for how good intimate relationships can work, and are better placed to form them later on.

If you haven't had those experiences as a child and instead have been uncared for, abused or had traumatic experiences, it can be harder to form intimate relationships in adult life, because you lack the experiences on which to base healthy relationships. For those who have had difficult experiences when young, where their trust might have been betrayed, it is hard to change their relationship template just by thinking about it. You need to actually experience a trusting, supportive relationship.

Therapy can help. (See Chapter 25, 'How Therapy Works'.) When a therapist is nice, considerate and sensitive, the client feels safe. If the client can form a trusting relationship with the therapist, it can provide a new template for what a secure relationship can be. From that experience the client can come to believe that close relationships with others who are supportive and caring are possible, and can take that experience into the outside world.

Schools are increasingly educating students in personal development as part of the curriculum. Parents, aunts, uncles and other adults also have a role to play. It is a lot trickier talking about sex and relationships with a teenager than it is discussing Maths, History or what they want to do when they grow up, but if you can get over the initial embarrassment, it can be useful for teens to learn more about how relationships work from those they know and trust. Adults don't have to have all the answers. Simply sharing that intimate relationships can be wonderful, but also tricky, difficult and disorientating can be useful.

Loving Everyone – the Mental Health Benefits of Love

The great religions urge us to love everyone, even those we dislike. 'Love your enemy.' Is cultivating an attitude of love good for our mental health? Religion, at its best, used to encourage us to be loving and selfless, and that acted as a counterbalance to the self-interest and selfish impulses that drive many of our choices. Today, however, less people identify as religious, and religions are less influential.

For us as a species, increasing the amount of love makes sense. The more love there is, the less likely we are to engage in aggression, violence and war. Selfless love prompts us to act for the collective good, rather than advancing our own selfish needs and wants.

However, the survival instinct is strong and it can prompt us to act selfishly. It is hard to resist that last piece of chocolate, even when you know your daughter wants it.

People who live in long-term loving relationships with intimate partners, and/or families, have longer and more mentally healthy lives than those who live alone. We are social animals who benefit from being tied to small and caring groups. If you really want to thrive and survive, you need to foster those relationships. It may be surprising to some, but the evidence suggests this is even more important for adult men than women. Men, left on their own, have poor mental health and often die early.

Those who are able to overcome their desire to be angry and aggressive toward those who threaten them or do them harm, generally have better mental health than those who do not. Loving those who we do not particularly like is not easy to do, but it is good for us. We have the ability to be loving and the results of doing so are usually much more constructive than those that come from anger and aggression.

As you travel to work in the morning, you can remind yourself that, while there are people there who you don't particularly like and who you have difficult relationships with, you are going to consciously try to be nice to them and see things from their point of view. It isn't easy, but when we try to put ourselves in their shoes, we often realise that things are a bit more complicated than 'I am good. They are bad.'

We can also exercise our selfless, loving side through actions like volunteering and helping others.

CHECKLIST

- Infatuation is an altered mental state, and at some point it will wear off.
- The challenge for a relationship is finding what will sustain it. Do we enjoy spending time with the other person?
- One of the few occasions when people act selflessly is to help those they love.
- Arguments between romantic partners can combust quickly. When we trust another person, we are vulnerable. If things turn bad, we can feel betrayed and rejected.
- Those who are predisposed to be possessive can focus that trait on their relationship.
- Very few of us are good at love in our first relationship. Hopefully, we learn and improve.
- Cultivating an attitude of love towards everyone, even those we dislike, is good for us individually and good for us collectively.

24

How We Change

When we are no longer able to change a situation – we are challenged to change ourselves.

Viktor E. Frankl

If you do not change direction, you may end up where you are heading.

Lao Tzu

Sometimes we identify a way in which we are not perfect. We snap at someone at work, and then wish we were more patient, or we realise we are not good at standing up for ourselves, even when we know we are right. Perhaps we get anxious about tiny things that don't really matter, or need everything to be perfectly tidy before we can relax, or think we are too quick to anger, too sensitive to criticism, or too shy.

How do we change?

If we realise that we are overweight, we can change our diet and do more exercise. When it comes to our character, however, are some traits hardwired? And are we stuck with our short temper, or can we change? Can we rewire our brain to make it work better?

We can, but it is more complicated than simply saying to our self, 'You always regret getting angry, so don't do it anymore.'

There are different strategies. Sometimes we might have to try a few before we find one that works. Usually it is a matter of modifying and controlling our characteristics, rather than completely eliminating them.

Does the 'Why?' Matter?

If you discover you have a brain tumour and your doctor starts telling you about its causes, you might think, 'I don't care. How do we fix it?' If we want to change something about ourselves, how deeply do we need to delve into its causes? Do we need to know *why* we are shy before we can work out how to become less shy?

Some, of a Freudian bent, are eager to investigate causes. 'Let's work out how you became like this. Tell me about your mother.' However, the thing you want to change may have nothing to do with your mother, or even your upbringing. It might be a trait you have genetically inherited. (See Chapter 1, 'What Runs in Families'.)

Other therapists might say, 'Don't worry about where your impatience came from. Let's just work out how to control it.'

If you are hypersensitive to noise, it can be useful to ask, 'Is my sensitivity to noise consistent with me wanting to be generally in control of my environment? I like to drive the car, rather than be a passenger. I like little things to be right. It seems I'm generally sensitive to my environment, and want to control it, and noise is one aspect of that. So maybe to address my sensitivity to noise, I need to address my whole need to control my environment.'

Genetically we do have different sensitivities to our environment. Young children startle and react differently to noise. If there is a loud party down the road, some adults freak out, while others hardly notice. Everyone has the same pathways – sound comes in through the ears, is filtered and brought into consciousness – but those pathways don't function the same way for everyone.

How We Change

What Doesn't Work

'I'll Just change. No Problem.'

If you are sensitive to your environment, you probably like to control the amount of noise you hear and always hold the remote control. Changing to becoming more accepting of what happens around you is not easy.

If you want to become less sensitive to noise, you find yourself simultaneously wanting to react to noise (because that is what you have always done) and wanting *not* to react to it (because that is how you want to change). You are fighting against your very nature.

As you force yourself to hand the remote control to your partner, you tell yourself, 'I can do this. It's no big deal,' but nonetheless you become distressed. You might feel physiological arousal: faster heartbeat, quick, shallow breathing, sweating. As that increases, simply telling yourself to stay calm usually does not work. We have to do more than talk. We have to find ways of turning down our physiological arousal.

We can lie in bed telling ourselves to be more patient and not lose our temper, but then the next day, something provocative happens and before we know it, we have reacted in the same old way. The problem is that we are having rational discussions with ourselves about a process that is largely emotional. To change, we have to engage with the underlying emotionality and physiology.

Avoidance

Avoidance can be a tempting strategy. If you want to stop getting angry, you can try to avoid anything that might make you angry. 'I often get angry with my boss, so I'll avoid him by quitting my job.' 'I'm never going to argue with my wife because I won't get married. I'll be happier on my own.'

For many of us, especially those with an anxious or sensitive temperament, avoidance is a tempting quick fix that removes us from the things we find distressing and upsetting. However, it doesn't help us to rewire our brain. It just reinforces the character traits we wish we could change.

It also, often, doesn't work, because the same underlying cause occurs again in a different situation. If noise irritates us, we move to the country. Mission accomplished. No more noise.

Then we hear a cow moo.

The more we avoid, the more we want to avoid more. 'I moved to the country but the cows kept mooing, so now I'm moving somewhere even more remote and further away from everyone I know.' When we have problems, it is better to learn the skills to cope with them. Sometimes that means learning how to change.

What Works – Exposure

Exposure involves deliberately putting yourself in the way of the thing that causes you discomfort. It sounds like a terrible idea, but brain cells and circuitry can and do rewire through the experience of doing things differently.

To change, we expose ourselves gradually, slowly and repeatedly to the thing that makes us anxious, uncomfortable or angry, whether it be noise, spiders, snakes or the propensity to get angry when talking to a boss we dislike. While we do it, we try to turn down our level of arousal by slowing our breathing and relaxing in the face of something that we usually find distressing.

Gradually our level of arousal decreases until we can experience the noise, spider or boss with much less discomfort.

That is rewiring. It's hard.

Repeated exposure also helps lower our overall arousal set point. If our set point is high, then exposure to something unpleasant easily upsets us. We can lower our arousal set point through strategies such as meditation, mindfulness, progressive muscle relaxation and exercise, so that we are less prone to get anxious or angry over minor things.

STEP 1:

Before you expose yourself to the real stressful situation, do it in your imagination. If you find talking to your boss stressful and it makes you irritated and angry, then lie in bed and imagine walking into the boss's office. See his face. Hear his voice. You will probably then feel your pulse, breathing and heartbeat quicken.

Go through the stressful scenario in your mind as realistically and in as much detail as you can, while simultaneously doing your preferred relaxation strategy – progressive muscle relaxation, where muscle groups are tensed and then relaxed; slow, deep breathing; mindfulness; yoga; etc.

The aim is to keep repeating this stressful situation in our imagination until our arousal and discomfort level starts to decrease.

If you find that even imagining the stressful situation is peaking your arousal to an unpleasant degree, start with a low-stakes imagined scenario. Imagine talking to your boss about something unrelated to work, like the weather. If it is external noise causing you discomfort, imagine hearing noise inside your home, but it's not loud, and it's Mozart, not Metallica. When you can do that and keep your pulse rate down, move to imagining a conversation with your boss about work, or imagining intrusive noise that is Black Sabbath rather than Bach.

You can even read text messages from your boss or listen to their voicemails at home as you try to relax; more and more exposure until your body and mind get used to it. You can't get rid of the boss, but you can change your response.

If you have noisy neighbours, you can record the noise and then lie in bed listening to it until your arousal comes down. After a time on high alert, your body will get bored of it. You will feel uncomfortable, then slightly less uncomfortable, then even less uncomfortable. Your physiology, which has been put on high alert, will eventually decide that, actually, this isn't a crisis at all, and it will get bored. The noise gradually becomes background noise. Maybe you can even fall asleep to it.

The world is full of all sorts of noises, but we can learn to change our reaction to them. When we are suddenly exposed to very loud sounds, the brain has a built-in modulatory system that actually turns down the volume. Over time, we habituate to noise. An example is people who live under a flight path or next to a train line. We visit and think, 'How could they live with this?' Perhaps they thought that too when they first moved in. However, over time, they adapted to the adverse stimuli. After a few weeks living there, they automatically pause their conversation for the train or plane to pass, and then continue, and they're not upset by it.

The brain's internal regulatory systems react to this exposure, especially if the noise is predictable, like a train every fifteen minutes.

STEP 2:
Once you have lowered your physical arousal to imagined scenarios, it is time for the real thing. Go and have a chat to your boss,

but start with a low-stakes topic, like the weather, or what they did on the weekend. Letting the other person talk about themselves helps calm them down too. Have a casual, short chat about something that doesn't matter, while focusing on slow deep breathing, and staying calm.

If that goes well, and it might take a few attempts before you feel your arousal lowering, then next time talk about work, but again, something non-controversial. Keep it brief and leave the room. The brain goes, 'Oh, not every interaction with that person actually results in disaster,' and that starts the process of change.

Next time you step it up a little and discuss something that is still low stakes but where you might disagree. You can almost deliberately go to the point where you can feel the boss is pushing your buttons, yet you keep breathing, relaxing and telling yourself to be polite. This is triggering: deliberately exposing ourselves to a situation we know has previously led to anger, distress or anxiety and having a low-level interaction that does not end up in a fight or bad outcome. Maybe your pulse rate will go up, maybe there will still be arousal but you are monitoring yourself, telling yourself to breathe and stay calm, and you get through it. You can track progress with a pulse-rate monitor. Some can display your pulse rate, just like they show the time.

Eventually you will get into the habit of relaxing and breathing, and do it almost automatically, so that by the time you get to something that really sets you off, you will be able to keep your arousal low.

Some need to learn to be more assertive, without becoming too aggressive or distressed. Having difficult conversations or dealing with people who are insensitive to your needs is hard. The best way to learn to be more assertive is, again, through a series of gradual steps. Start with non-controversial topics, then move to the more confronting issues that are on your mind, while focusing on maintaining control. Eventually, you learn to say what you need to in a direct but not aggressive way.

Cognitive Strategies

There are various cognitive (thought-based) strategies that help us change. Not all work for everyone, so we need to find the ones that work for us. If we try a few problem-solving strategies and alternative ways of thinking, we can find the ones that help us. When a strategy leads to decreased arousal, we know we have found something that works.

What If?

When Ian is running late and wants to reduce his anxiety, he uses 'What if?' 'What if I'm late? What is the worst that will happen? Is it really a disaster?' Usually, the consequences aren't that bad. 'If I miss the plane, there'll be another one an hour later I can probably get.' 'If I'm late for the meeting will everyone be upset with me? No, I'm usually punctual and they'll understand that sometimes life is busy.'

That helps get his pulse rate down, and keep those smaller things in perspective.

Be Aware of Your Physiology

When approaching a situation where you can have problems – a conversation with the boss, or arriving home to find your housemates have left the house untidy – check in with your physiology and level of arousal. Do you feel agitated? Nervous? Is your pulse quickening? How's your breathing?

Your physiology acts as an early-warning system. If you are getting agitated, try to control your physical symptoms. Deepen your breathing, slow down, speak slowly, ease the tension in your shoulders, go for a walk.

Reconceptualise the Problem

If we are having a conversation with a boss, neighbour, friend or colleague who pushes our buttons, we can sometimes create the preconditions for failure before we even start. We build the encounter up into a big, terrible thing, and play out all the ways the boss could be unpleasant until they almost seem like reality.

Can you reconceptualise the upcoming conversation? Instead of telling yourself a disaster is approaching, you can tell yourself that you have an opportunity to have your point of view heard.

James uses this strategy when public speaking. If he feels nervous, he tries to relabel it as excitement. Nervousness and excitement are quite similar, except one feels bad and the other feels good. Both involve arousal and adrenaline. James tells himself. 'I've got this great opportunity. I'm going to make the most of it. I'm not nervous. I'm excited.'

Empathy

If you are irritated by your boss, or by the people in the apartment next door playing loud music, can looking at the situation from their point of view help? 'The boss must be a under a lot of pressure.' 'Isn't it great they're having a good time?'

You are trying to cognitively reconstruct your take on the situation. It will only work if at the same time you can lower your arousal.

Recognise Risky Situations

Being aware you're entering a risk zone is important. If you find you get irritated by and often lose your temper with a particular person, leaving it until you *start* losing your temper is too late.

So, *before* you walk into your boss's office, or as soon as things start to get stressful at home, be aware you are at risk, start slow, deep breathing and use your cognitive strategies.

Changing Our Children

Parents try many strategies to teach children what to do and what not do. Slowly, hopefully, they work out what works – for each child – to bring about positive change. There is a lot of trial and error. The first time a parent gets angry with their child, they might think, 'I lost my temper, so that will really show him that drawing on the wall is wrong. I'm pretty sure he won't be doing that again.' If, the next day, the child draws on the wall again, the parent might start to realise that getting angry wasn't as effective as they thought, and realise they need to try another strategy.

Parents need to try different strategies for kids with different sensitivities. Some kids can get in trouble all the time and it has no effect, whereas if you give a very sensitive kid a small amount of criticism or punishment, they may never do it again. It takes a long time for kids to grow up, so there are lots of opportunities to try different strategies at different ages. Finding those that work best can take time, patience and a willingness to experiment, but eventually you will find what works and what doesn't.

More Complex Cases

Graded exposure processes do not work for everybody. Some might not respond because they have been subject to very traumatic experiences in the past. Major mental health problems like bipolar disorder, a psychotic disorder or OCD might get in the way and need more specialised treatment. So, sometimes a more specialised assessment may be required to set down a pathway that is most likely to lead to real change.

Conclusion

We can change but it is not easy, and it cannot be done just by telling ourselves that, 'I am going to stop getting angry.' We need to engage with our emotionality and physiology too.

Think of change as a renovation rather than a rebuild, a re-arrangement within your overarching architectural structure. But it is a serious home renovation, and may require some structural realignment. We can't stop unpleasant things happening, but we can change our reaction to them. If we go through the hard, and sometimes uncomfortable, work of doing this (often through graded exposure) then, sometimes, good things happen. We might actually improve our relationship with the boss, and realise that the problem wasn't so much that they are a monster, but more us bringing a high level of arousal into every encounter. Learning to stay calmer in discussions might also improve our relationships with our partner and children.

CHECKLIST

- We can rewire our brain, but just saying, 'I'll stop getting angry,' is unlikely to work.
- Avoiding things that make us anxious is tempting, but it doesn't help us change.
- Gradually exposing ourselves to things that make us anxious can change our reaction to them and lower our anxiety.
- We can change our level of anxiety through cognitive strategies, like asking, 'What if?', and through relaxation and showing empathy.
- When bringing up children and trying to change their behaviour, different strategies work with different kids.

25

How Therapy Works

Courage doesn't happen when you have all the answers. It happens when you are ready to face the questions you have been avoiding your whole life.

Shannon L. Alder

Many people try to address mental distress and improve their mental health through therapy. They talk to a counsellor, psychologist, psychiatrist or other mental health professional about what is going on in their life, how their past might influence their current behaviour, and how they might be able to change.

How does therapy work? What is the methodology? Is it really all about your mother?

When Should You Have Therapy?

Sometimes, we recognise that things are not going well. We might hit a personal crisis, develop depression, anxiety or burnout, or see the damage that a repeated pattern of behaviour has done. It might be when we have a drug, alcohol or gambling problem, after our marriage has ended, we have lost our job, or our child has stopped talking to us.

Eventually, we get to a point and think, 'Why is this happening again? I need to stop, reflect and change.'

Much evidence suggests the most effective way to treat many mental illnesses and mental health issues is a combination of medication and therapy. Some studies have even found people can start to feel better as soon as they decide to have therapy, *before* they meet the therapist, perhaps because the mere fact of recognising that you have a problem and starting to take active steps to address it, gives you hope that better days are ahead.

How Does Therapy Work?

In much medical practice, the patient is passive. You turn up with an inflamed appendix or a broken leg, lie still and they fix you. In therapy, the client has an active role. A therapist cannot fix you by themselves. Their aim is to help you discover insights about yourself, suggest strategies that may help you to change, but it is up to you to put those strategies into action. We can change, but it can be a complicated process.

Therapy is a partnership, based around the formation of a trusting relationship between therapist and client, where sensitive issues are explored in a safe environment. The therapist encourages open disclosure by the client of events, ideas and emotions, and together they examine patterns of unhelpful behaviour and their causes.

Good therapists focus both on making the relationship work within therapy, and on helping clients to improve their relationships and life outside it. The goal is not to live life in the therapist's room. Therapy should be a stepping stone to a better life.

Insights
Central to any therapy should be a systematic analysis of the client's behaviour. Is there a repeated pattern that causes problems?

Does the client continually get angry, anxious or depressed? Are they unable to form and maintain close, trusting relationships?

Once a pattern of behaviour is identified, such as the client losing their temper or getting anxious, they can then describe the surrounding circumstances. In what situations do you lose your temper? When do you get anxious? Why can't you let your guard down and trust others? From that examination, perhaps a useful explanation can be found. Does the problem have its roots in childhood events and interpersonal relationships, including with parents? Did things happen years ago that have led to a repeated pattern of unhelpful behaviours?

Trying to genuinely open up and accurately describe current circumstances while also examining our past can be difficult, even painful. We often feel shame and guilt about our actions and past events, and when we get close to something that could be significant and painful we often stop, or get defensive. Almost automatically, we tend to reframe current difficulties or past events in a way that shows ourselves in a more favourable light. In therapy, we need to try to lower our defences and be honest and genuine.

Good therapists sense when we are shying away from painful reflections or traumatic memories and say, 'Tell me some more about that.' If the client feels safe, and the therapist keeps prompting them, maybe raising an eyebrow when they feel the client is being evasive or underplaying painful events ('It was actually fine. No big deal'), progress can be made and insights arrived at.

The therapist should not always be on your side. They are there to care for you and provide support, but they should not agree with everything you say in the way an uncritical friend might. A friend might say 'Yes, your family was terrible. Yes, your husband's a bastard. Yes, your boss is a bully. Yes, it's all their fault.' There might be some truth in all that, but often there is fault on both sides.

You can't change your boss, only yourself, and being told you are totally in the right is not going to help you to do that. A therapist should not simply be a cheerleader for your perspective. They should be engaged and interested, be able to provide insights others can't, and to tell you the critical things that you need to know.

One of Dr Phil's TV guests was explaining why he felt justified in being angry with someone, and Dr Phil asked, 'And how's that working out for you?' It is a powerful question because it shifts our perspective, and makes us think, 'Even if I'm justified in feeling angry, is it making me happy? If not, why am I doing it?'

How clients reach conclusions is important. If the therapist *tells* a client they have a hair trigger temper, the client might get defensive, go into denial or (obviously, and kind of ironically) get angry. It can be more effective for the therapist to nudge the client to reach the conclusion themselves. 'Do you see any pattern emerging in these three events?' Long pause, then, 'Oh my goodness. I get angry too much. How can I stop doing it?'

Therapists are not mind-readers. They usually cannot instantly tell you what all your issues are, but over time they can help you understand more about yourself. The aim is for the client to develop insight into how their emotions and thoughts come together to influence their behaviour. If that is occurring in a way that is sometimes problematic, then the question becomes, 'How can I change?'

Treatment

Once an insight is arrived at, then what? Being diagnosed with a broken arm does not fix your arm, but gaining an insight into your motivations and behaviours can in itself help you to change. If you have an insight that you worry too much about little things, then next time it happens you might think, 'This is less about the event I am worrying about, and more about my tendency to get over-anxious about something tiny.'

However, an insight in itself will often not be enough. In addition, a therapist should be able to help you learn skills and strategies to help you deal with anxiety, depression, burnout, losing your temper and more. There is more about these strategies in our chapters 'Anxiety', 'Depression', 'Burnout', 'Anger' and 'How We Change'.

Trust

An issue for many who have had abusive and traumatic experiences is that they find it hard to trust others. In therapy, patients spend time with the therapist in a safe place and gradually build up a trusting relationship. For those whose trust has previously been betrayed, developing this relationship with someone who behaves professionally and ethically can help them re-establish trusting relationships with others. Once they form this trusting relationship and gain insight, they should move on from forming a trusting relationship with their therapist, to establishing relationships in the outside world in a way they may not have been able to do before.

How Important Is Your Past?

Some forms of therapy place great emphasis on unravelling the underlying social or developmental causes of our present problems. What was it that happened in the past, perhaps when you were a young child, that caused your present difficulties with anxiety or anger? If you have trouble asserting yourself, or in trusting people and forming close relationships, how did that tendency originate?

Freudian-derived therapies, in particular, delve into your childhood experiences, your relationships with your parents and other significant people, and how those relationships have influenced you. At the other end of the spectrum, Cognitive Behavioural Therapy (CBT) focuses more on the here and now, and how you can deal with the problem. For example, when you have anxious thoughts, what can you do to reduce your distress and worry?

Finding root causes is complex. Did our relationship with our parents cause us to become anxious? Does anxiety run in our family? Were we born with an anxious temperament, and our parents responded to that in a way that created more anxiety? Blaming parents – 'My parents failed me, and that's why I have problems today' – might be simplistic. Even if there is some truth in it, that sort of blaming can be disempowering.

Clients and therapists also have to be wary of an examination of the past leading to the conclusion that 'I've been so wrecked and damaged that I'm stuck. I can never change.' Together the therapist and client must try to avoid that sort of hopelessness. Change is hard, but not impossible.

Having said that, understanding what happened to us and how it influences our behaviour today can be very powerful. It gives us an explanatory model. However, once we have that model, simply retelling our story again and again might not help us to get out of the hole we are in. The next question should be, 'What can I do about it? How can those insights help me to live a better life?'

Compared to Freudian-derived therapies, CBT is more solution-based, and asks questions such as:
- What are the problems?
- What are the unhelpful thoughts that you have?
- What are the distressing feelings that you have?
- What are the repeated behaviours?
- What are the triggers for those unhelpful behaviours?
- What skills can you learn to change unhelpful patterns of behaviour, and combat unhelpful thoughts and distressing feelings?
- Can strategies such as mindfulness and meditation help to break the link between experiencing a distressing emotion, and physical symptoms such as elevated heartbeat and shallow breathing?

Both approaches have real strengths. Freudian-derived therapies can help you understand how anxiety might have been baked into you when you were young, while CBT gives you strategies to respond when it happens. It is useful to know the root causes of your anger, or your unwillingness to trust, but we also need to understand what to do to address them now.

The goal of therapy is to walk away with two things: insight and action. The insight might be 'I worry too much about small things. That makes me stressed, and then I lose my temper easily.' Those insights enable you to recognise when it is happening. 'I'm worrying about small things again. I'm at risk of losing my temper.'

Action is what you do about it. The action to combat anxiety might be to divert your mind elsewhere, or do some exercise or some slow, deep breathing. If you are about to lose your temper, the action might be to break off the interaction, go outside and go for a walk.

Therapy in a Crisis

Many are prompted to seek treatment by a crisis – depression, anxiety or another mental health issue. This is not always the best time for the therapist to start a potentially painful investigation into the client's past. What they need is relief via strategies to help them in the short term. 'If you anxiously freaking out at 3 am, do these three things.' 'If you feel terribly depressed, do this.'

When a client starts to feel a bit better, that might be the best time to go into a deeper analysis of what's going on. (See Chapter 18, 'Dealing with a Crisis'.)

Types of Therapy

Some of the different types of therapy are:
- Freudian-derived psychotherapies
- Cognitive Behavioural Therapy

- Dialectical Behaviour Therapy – where the emphasis is on learning skills to cope with overwhelming episodes of emotional distress. It can be done individually or in groups.
- Behavioural therapy, where the focus is on *acting* differently via sleep, exercise, socialising, engaging with others, stopping repetitive behaviours, diet and more.
- Marital therapy or couples counselling. People are often reluctant to go, thinking they are going to get blamed, but often they find that the therapist is actually quite neutral. 'There's fault on both sides.' Participants might arrive at insights like, 'Actually it's not all his/her fault. There are things I keep doing that contribute to our problems.'
- Group therapy. These can be useful for some issues, such as social anxiety, as the very act of participating helps to address the main problem. The shared experiences of others, and seeing both the functional and dysfunctional ways that others try to cope, can be incredibly helpful.
- Virtual therapies. Online treatments now exist that allow people to ask common questions about anxiety, depression, dysfunctional thoughts and other unhelpful behaviours, and access responses drawn from thousands of actual interactions between therapists and their clients, and a large body of research and evidence about what responses work best for different problems and different people. You can ask, 'What strategies can I use to reduce my overwhelming sense of doom?' 'What are the best things to do when I start to panic?' 'Is it best to just pull out of those situations that cause me the most anxiety?' 'I'm so tired and fatigued. Is it best to just stay in bed and wait for my energy to come back?' The responses closely mimic responses you could expect from a highly trained professional.

They can also include virtual reality experiences, where the client can practise their responses to really challenging situations. Interestingly, people will often tell virtual, artificial intelligence-based programs all sorts of things that they are reluctant to disclose in face-to-face encounters, including obsessional thoughts, abnormal eating, suicidal ideas and sexual thoughts. Research indicates that many online treatments are as effective as the face-to-face equivalent.

Many therapists combine features of several of the above.

Finding the Right Therapist

If you feel you want or need therapy, ask around for recommendations. Many people have had therapy, and we are more open about it than in the past. You may want someone who is the same (or different) gender, or someone with a similar cultural or religious background.

Before a surgeon operates on you, it is normal to ask what they are going to do and how it will help you, and for the surgeon to tell you. However, many feel reluctant to ask a therapist the same questions. At your first session, ask:

- What sort of therapy do you do?
- How does it work? What is your method?
- Is your method well suited to addressing my specific problem?
- What am I going to learn?
- How is this process going to help me improve my life?

Not every therapist is right for every client. The most important thing is being able to form a trusting connection with them, and if it does not feel like this is happening, don't be afraid to try someone else.

How Do You Know It's Over?

By the end of therapy you should have gained insights, and have learned strategies and skills aimed at both prevention and cure.

Exercise, meditation, mindfulness, good sleep and diet are prevention strategies you can use all the time to lower your risk of becoming unwell. It can be tempting to think, 'I feel good now. I don't need to do all this anymore,' but perhaps you are feeling well *because* of the work you are doing taking care of yourself. Continuing to do that work is an important part of staying well.

If you do become unwell, you should be armed with thought-based and other behavioural and skill-based strategies to help you deal with it.

When therapy works well, we should gain an ability to analyse and understand our own temperament, our behaviour and the unhelpful patterns we keep repeating, recognise our faults, and acquire skills and strategies to act differently in circumstances where we have previously made mistakes. It should not take twenty years and, except in extreme circumstances, should not require the reconstruction of our whole life. While therapy is not cheap, Medicare provides significant rebates for twenty sessions.

Ian has encountered many young people who have had very traumatic, dysfunctional backgrounds, and were headed into bad places but, by engaging in supportive therapy, have gone on to have good lives, and have maintained relationships and been good parents. Their problems have not necessarily vanished but they have learned how to manage them and take care of themselves.

The basis of therapy is that we can rewire. The brain has the capacity to change (see Chapter 24, 'How We Change'), and therapy can help us to do it.

CHECKLIST

- Therapy is a partnership between a client and a therapist in a trusting, safe environment where the therapist encourages disclosure of past events, and patterns of unhelpful behaviour are examined.
- Therapy aims to arrive at insights about the client's life and patterns of behaviour.
- A therapist is more than an uncritical cheerleader for your point of view.
- Clients should learn strategies to deal with issues and problems that will help them to improve their life.
- It is important at the start to ask the therapist what their method is and how it is going to help you.

26

The Seven Secrets to Happiness

Happiness is not something ready-made. It comes from your own actions.

The Dalai Lama

You are in charge of your own happiness; you don't need to wait for other people's permission to be happy.

Roy T. Bennett

Whoever is happy will make others happy.

Anne Frank

What is the secret to happiness? According to Irish psychiatrist and author Dr Anthony Clare, there are seven of them, and they were outlined in a 2013 book by British broadcaster and writer Gyles Brandreth called, not surprisingly, *The Seven Secrets To Happiness*.

It seems sensible to end with a chapter on the things that we can do to become happier, and Ian was keen to use Anthony Clare's list. In the 1980s, Clare was one of the first psychiatrists to talk about mental health in the media in a way that was comprehensible to everyone, and to give advice on the things we could all do to become a bit happier.

One of the key points in many of his seven secrets is enjoying the journey. There is no destination, apart from death, so whatever you are aiming at, make sure you make your quality of life along the way as good as it can be. Life is not about building a great résumé and trying to get a particular level of success, status and wealth. Or at least, it's not *all* about that. Life is also about how much we enjoy each day, each hour, each minute.

Having worthwhile goals and pursuing them is important (and in fact forms the basis of the first of Clare's points), but try not to get preoccupied with continually asking if you are a success or a failure. And don't compare yourself to others. It won't make you happy, whichever way the comparison goes.

Clare based his list on his experiences as a psychiatrist for many years, his experience as a person for even more years, and on research. Subsequent research has generally added to the evidence supporting his seven points.

Here are Dr Anthony Clare's seven secrets to happiness, with our commentary.

1. Cultivate a Passion

Find something that you enjoy doing. Something that will delight you, sustain you and distract you from life's troubles. Something that gives you pleasure when times are tough. Something that is challenging, that you haven't conquered, that requires skill. Striving to improve gives you a sense of purpose. It engages you and requires long-term commitment. Your commitment to it makes you feel good. You keep pursuing it, keep trying to get better, and that gives you satisfaction. It feels worthwhile, even if no-one else knows about it.

It might be a solitary hobby like surfing, woodwork, writing, painting, playing music, yoga or other exercise. It might be group-based: being part of a sporting team, involved with a community club, campaigning for social change, being on the school board, coaching a team or doing voluntary work. It might, if you're lucky, be your work.

It might be that you have a deep investment in your family or other social relationships, and you become the person that keeps those social relationships going. You are the hub of the wheel, you organise activities, outings and holidays. It might be taking care of family members, friends or elderly residents of your street or apartment block. Cooking can be a passion that can be both a solitary activity, and a part of caring for those you live with and others. During COVID lockdowns, many discovered a passion for baking.

Finding such a passion might take a while, so keep trying new things until you discover it. Once you find that thing you are drawn to, pursue it. That doesn't necessarily mean saying, 'I love painting. I'm quitting my job as a banker.' Some make money from their passions. Many don't. If you discover that your passion is painting, a better option, at least at first, might be to ensure you spend some time each day painting, before or after work. If at some stage you can sell some paintings, great, but that is not the primary reason you do it. The main question should be, 'How can I keep doing this regularly, so it keeps enriching my life?' Not, 'How can I make money from this?'

Some people think that being pragmatic and responsible means postponing doing the things they really enjoy until they are financially secure. 'I've got a family to support and a mortgage to pay. I'll paint when the kids leave home.' These are, of course, important concerns, but don't put off your own happiness! Whatever your passion is, find a way to get some of it into your life now, because it is good for your mental health, and that is good for both you and those you live with.

2. Be Part of Something Bigger than Yourself

Anthony Clare says, 'Be a leaf on a tree.' Be part of a group. As well as an individual identity, have a collective identity. There is strong evidence that being socially connected is good for our mental health (see chapter on Social Connection). When people are socially connected, they feel better about themselves and have better mental health. They do things for the group, for the greater good, rather than always following their own self-interest. However, in the modern Western world, we have got busier, and are generally less socially connected than humans have previously been.

A good question to ask is, 'What groups am I a part of?'

It could be a friend group, a sporting club or team, a community group, a church group, a book club, an organisation you volunteer for, or being part of your street, apartment block or neighbourhood community. Many of us form strong bonds with those we work with.

What about family? The family group is of course extremely important. When we have kids, many think 'This is my priority now,' and let their other connections and relationships slide, but it is good to have other groups we belong to outside our family.

Many used to belong to strong friend groups that arose from their school, neighbourhood and post-school work and study, but as their careers and families became more important, those groups drifted apart. With a bit of effort, the closeness of those groups can quickly return. Five minutes after you meet again, the jokes from twenty years ago are back.

Another question to ask is, 'What do I contribute to the groups I belong to?' Do you act beyond your own self-interest to help the group? Do you spend time rostering the lifeguards for the weekend, or baking a cake for your book club?

Belonging to social groups is good for your happiness, so foster your groups. If you don't have any, they are not so hard to find and join.

Don't be all leaf, no tree.

3. Break the Mirror

'Break the mirror' means stop thinking about yourself. Have done with narcissism and self-regard.

To put it colloquially, no-one likes someone who's up themselves, who's always telling you how great they are.

Some people seem to almost get lost in a mirror-like conversation with themselves about how wonderful they are, and become preoccupied with their own identity. They keep talking about themselves and never ask you anything about your life. 'Enough of me talking about myself. What do *you* think about me?'

If you have few interests beyond yourself and are overly self-obsessed (and let's face it, most of us are *a bit* self-obsessed) your world becomes small. When people get preoccupied with thinking about themselves, they can get lost in their own head, and distort what is going on. They are talking only to themselves, without getting any perspective from others. Don't get captured by your Instagram account. Being egocentric is not going to make you happy, no matter how hard you smile in your posted pics.

For those who have this tendency, the best antidote is to get into lots of conversations with others, and not to talk about yourself. Ask people questions instead. That is how we learn. Taking a break from social media might help too.

This is not to say that we should not be introspective. Being thoughtful and reflective is important and useful. It is good to think about what we have said and done, both the good and the bad, so we can work out what we can do better next time.

4. Don't Resist Change

It's not just you. Everyone is scared of change.

Change can be exciting and fun. It can also be difficult and painful. When change happens, we often think more about the scary uncertainty than the exciting possibilities.

Whether we like it or not, change is going to happen. On a macro level, the pace of change now is faster than it has ever been before, and it is only likely to increase.

Change can occur because of large events like COVID, natural disasters, technological change and economic downturns. In addition, things happen to us individually. We lose our job, we get sick, our relationship ends, people we care about die. That sounds a bit depressing, but positive change happens too. We meet someone new and fall in love, we have a child, we get a great new job.

If we live long enough we will all have to deal with lots of change. Rather than hoping things stay the same, it makes sense to accept that change will come, and get ready for it. The question is not 'Will things change?' We know that they will. The question is, 'When change comes, how will I cope?'

Change can be uncomfortable and unsettling, especially when it first happens, but it can also be a time of learning and growth. A new adventure. Big changes do challenge us, but often we cope well and end up doing positive things that we would never have done otherwise. People say, 'If I hadn't have got sacked I would never have set up my own business.' 'If I didn't get cancer I'd still be working seventy hours a week and hardly seeing my kids.'

Remote work is a great example of an unwanted change leading to positive results. We had the technology for many to work from home for years before COVID, but lots of bosses were suspicious of remote work and denied requests from workers. COVID forced them to quickly change their attitude, everyone realised it could be effective, and now remote work is a normal and accepted part of office work that allows many to spend more time with their families and less on the bus.

If you are one of the many who instinctively resist and get scared of change, what can you do to make yourself more open and receptive to it? How can you change your attitude to change?

Don't Cling to the Past

When change happens, try to accept it, rather than wishing things were back the way they were. Thinking, 'I wish I hadn't lost my job,' or 'I wish COVID hadn't come,' doesn't help. In fact, it holds us back from coming to terms with the opportunities that are now available.

Focus on Opportunities

Try and remind yourself that change represents opportunity as well as threat. Ask yourself if you are focusing too much on your fears of what might go wrong, and not enough on the opportunities for your current situation to be improved.

'Safety First' Isn't That Safe

Those of us with more obsessional, rigid, risk-averse, safety-first, 'Let's protect what we've got'-type personalities can struggle with change. If you feel uncomfortable whenever someone rearranges the sofa cushions, losing your job or experiencing lockdown is probably going to create some stress.

If you have those tendencies, be aware that you have a natural bias against embracing change. When you start to worry about change, remind yourself that you tend to focus on possible bad outcomes, and try to consciously focus on the positive opportunities.

The irony is that the 'Don't take risks and protect what you've got' mindset *seems* safer, but actually it is quite dangerous, because when change happens, you won't be good at reacting to it.

So, for those who are 'safety first, second and third' here are some strategies:
- Introduce small changes to your daily routine. Travel to work at different times and in different ways. Take the bus, the train or walk. Mix it up.
- Take a holiday somewhere you've never been before.
- Try a new experience. Book into some events or challenges you've never tried before – hiking in the bush, overnight adventures, mountain-bike riding or snorkelling, preferably with people or groups you've never met.
- Take a week or two off work and do something really new and different that you've always wanted to do – an art or singing course, or a yoga retreat.

5. Audit Your Happiness

Work out how much of each day you spend doing things that make you happy, and how much time you spend doing things that make you unhappy.

Once you know how much time you spend doing things you like and dislike, can you tinker with your timetable to get a bit more happiness into your life? Can you increase the time you spend doing things that make you happy? Can you reduce the time you spend doing things you hate? Attending meetings, perhaps. Can you delegate the parts of your job you hate?

If you find that you are not spending much, or even any, time doing things that make you happy, put something you enjoy in your diary. Whatever makes you happy, start doing more of it. Walk through a park. Meet a friend for a drink. Bike ride. Go to a yoga class. Watch a movie with your family. Play the piano. If you can't play the piano, learn. People are always postponing pleasurable activities. Don't! Commit to them, because they are good for your mental health.

Keep looking for ways to reduce the time you spend doing things that make you miserable.

Some people quite like commuting. They get on a train, read a book or listen to a podcast, no-one tells them what to do, they have no responsibilities and they enjoy it.

Others hate it. If you hate commuting, and in an audit find that you spend ninety minutes a day commuting, that is nearly ten per cent of your waking time. What can you do about it? Can you reduce your commuting time by:

- Working a day or more from home?
- Living closer to work?
- Working closer to where you live?

Can you make commuting more pleasurable by:

- Swapping a commute you dislike (e.g. driving) for one you prefer (e.g. catching the train and using the time to work, watch movies or write a novel)?
- Getting on the train or bus at a later stop, and getting off at an earlier one, so you walk more of the way? This might make your commute a bit longer, but the exercise and fresh air may make it much more pleasant.

6. Live in the Moment

We spend a lot of our time in the past and the future. We think about what happened. We wonder what might happen. In the 1980s, before mindfulness got popular in the West, Anthony Clare said that to be happy we should live in the present.

If your focus is on what is happening right now, you will enjoy more of the simple pleasures of life. If instead of gulping down your lunch as you worry about whether your boss likes you, you focus on every bite of your sandwich, you can savour that delightful combination of bread, cheese and Vegemite. By focusing on the present, you change the experience from absently refuelling to something pleasurable.

As you walk back inside your building, if you are thinking about what will happen in that meeting this afternoon, rather than actively noticing everything around you, you might miss something funny or interesting. A man squirts tomato sauce that misses his pie and splats his shirt. A woman says goodbye to her companion and then as soon as his back is turned, sticks her tongue out at him. A bird squawks at his mum. She tries to ignore him, then gives up and finds him a worm. Little things that make us smile, or be curious, that we can share with others.

Living in the present doesn't mean that you have to spend twenty minutes a day meditating. It just means that every now and again, you bring yourself into the present. A good way of doing it is simply to regularly ask yourself: 'What can I see? What can I hear?' Notice what you're seeing. Notice what you're hearing. Challenge yourself to notice one interesting thing as you ride on the bus, and another as you walk down the street.

Some are so preoccupied with what will happen next, they rarely enjoy the present. Those walking though art galleries with a video camera glued to their eye come to mind. At parties, some look over the shoulder of the person they are speaking to, trying to spot who they can speak to next, and so miss out on fully experiencing the conversation they are in.

The past is over. The future is uncertain. All we have is now.

7. Act Happy

Happiness from the Outside In

Act as if you are happy. Choose to be optimistic. Put a smile on your dial, even if it hurts.

If you act happy, it will, to an extent, become self-fulfilling. It won't necessarily solve all your problems, or instantly change your mood from miserable to ecstatic, but acting happy will make you happier than you would otherwise be.

If you smile – or even laugh – you actually feel the things associated with smiling and laughing. It is an outward action that signals to your mind and body that you are enjoying yourself.

Our normal method of addressing unhappiness is from the inside out. We work out what thoughts, feelings and behaviours are making us unhappy, and try to address them. Acting happy works the opposite way, from the outside in. By manifesting the signs of happiness, we try to influence positively our thoughts and feelings.

It is similar to when we feel tired. If we can muster the energy to act energetic and go for a walk or run, afterwards we have more energy. It's counterintuitive, but it works.

The Story We Tell Ourselves

We can get stuck in our own unhappiness and create our own narrative around it. 'I'm unhappy because I lost my job, and I'm no good at meeting people and I'm not a famous filmmaker like I wanted to be when I was a kid.' The narrative focuses on adverse events and our perceived failures, and ignores our successes and favourable events.

The same events can be looked at in different ways. 'Every one of my six relationships failed,' can be reframed as 'I have been lucky enough to have been loved by six wonderful people.' 'I'm a loser because my novel didn't get published,' can be reframed as 'I started writing a story, I kept going even when it got hard and I finished it. I'm proud of that achievement.'

Narrative therapists identify the negative stories clients tell themselves and help them to change it to something more positive. When people are focusing only on bad things, they challenge them to mix in more of the good things they are ignoring.

We all turn past events into stories. If you told someone about your childhood, you would share some details, omit others, and weave it into some sort of a narrative. We are continually filtering in some bits of information and filtering out others. When we are happy, we tell ourselves how great our life is and leave out the bad bits. When we are unhappy, we do the opposite. Both are, to a degree, distortions of reality.

Those who are depressed can get so used to being unhappy that they treat it as their normal state, and latch onto every bit of evidence that backs up their view that life is terrible. 'It's raining. We're out of milk. No-one has texted me today to see if I'm okay.' They ignore any evidence that suggests things aren't that bad: actually, the rain is light and about to stop, they can walk to the shop to get more milk, and yesterday three people texted them.

So, 'Acting Happy' can also mean changing the negative story you have been telling yourself. If you have been telling yourself a negative story,

- Be aware that you have probably been filtering in only the bad news and filtering out the good news.
- Try to take notice of more of the good things.
- Try to change the story you tell yourself to a more positive and optimistic one. 'I feel terrible. I might not get better. One day I'll die,' can become, 'I'm alive. The sun is shining. This is a tough period, but things will improve.'

Social Inclusion

The third aspect of 'Act Happy' is that if you can make yourself look and act happy, people are more likely to engage with you. If you smile, they smile back. If you laugh, they join in. If you are gloomy, people want to get away and it can lead to social exclusion. 'Don't get caught with that negative guy.'

The Ones Anthony Clare Missed

Anthony Clare's seven secrets of happiness are comprehensive, but we each wanted to add another one that has been important to our own happiness.

James

Take care of your physical health. Exercise, eat well and get good sleep. The body and mind are related. If you take care of your body, you feel good and have more energy and that can positively influence your mood and mental health.

Ian

The quality of our most intimate relationships are very important to our happiness. If we come home to someone we are happy to see, and who is happy to see us, it is very good for our mental health and happiness. Conversely, if we dread coming home because there is tension and conflict, it is bad for our mental health.

For about ninety or ninety-five per cent of us it is harder to be happy if we are alone and do not have a close, intimate relationship. Around five or ten per cent of us seem perfectly happy alone, but for most of us, the happiest state is to be in an intimate relationship that is working well.

CHECKLIST

To be happy:
- Cultivate a passion
- Be part of something bigger than yourself
- Break the mirror – don't be egotistical
- Don't resist change
- Live in the moment
- Audit your happiness
- Act happy.

And:
- Take care of your physical health
- Get in a good intimate relationship.

Recommended Reading

Ian has compiled this list of books and websites that readers may find to be of additional interest. There is a clear focus on common mental health problems and how to recognise them, sharing personal experiences and what sorts of treatments are of greatest value. Additionally, there are many reputable government-sponsored and academic websites on mental disorders, how the brain works and the optimal social setting for emotional and cognitive development.

We have a range of other very good organisational websites for mental health information in Australia, such as those operated by Beyond Blue; Orygen Youth Health; headspace, the national youth mental health foundation, and the Black Dog Institute. We also have many very good online resources, training or treatment programs. We are particularly keen (for adults) about THIS WAY UP, originally initiated by Professor Gavin Andrews and his Clinical Research Unit for Anxiety and Depression (CRUfAD), and MindSpot, operated out of Macquarie University and directed by Professor Nick Titov. For children and younger audiences, where the emphasis is much more on anxiety disorders and school management, the work led by Professor Ron Rapee at Macquarie University has led to many books, online tools and programs under the Cool Kids banner.

Preferred websites

- Brain and Mind Centre, University of Sydney: https://www.sydney.edu.au/brain-mind/
- The National Institute for Health and Care Excellence (NICE) in the UK: https://www.nice.org.uk/guidance/conditions-and-diseases/mental-health-and-behavioural-conditions

- The National Institute of Mental Health in the US: https://www.nimh.nih.gov/health/publications
- Beyond Blue, the national depression initiative: https://beyondblue.org.au/
- Orygen Youth Health: https://oyh.org.au/
- headspace, the national youth mental health foundation: https://headspace.org.au
- Black dog Institute: https://www.blackdoginstitute.org.au/
- THIS WAY UP: https://thiswayup.org.au
- MindSpot: https://www.mindspot.org.au
- Cool Kids: https://coolkids.org.au

For further help in accessing care and information about mental health services in Australia, go to https://www.headtohealth.gov.au/

Books and Journal Articles

A great deal of emphasis in this book is not simply on the brain as a 'neurological' machine (controlling movement, speech, sight, hearing, etc.) but rather on the development of the 'social brain' and our resultant emotional and cognitive processes. It's more about how the social brain grows (under genetic and environmental influences) and how it operates.

So, really interesting reads include works by Larry Young, an eminent scientist in the field, who is particularly well known for his work on the influence of oxytocin ('the love chemical) on animal and human behaviour. Another important writer in this explanation of brain functions and linked emotions is Joseph LeDoux. For a more prolonged critique of much of modern cognitive neuroscience, try the work by Max Bennett and Peter Hacker.

Dan Blazer is one of the most thoughtful psychiatrists Ian has ever worked with. Much of his work has been devoted to how we understand the impact of social circumstances on mental health, how we reconcile the social risk factors that are at work more broadly and the need to provide more effective psychological and medical treatments to those individuals affected.

For one of the most accessible books on how important circadian rhythms (body clocks) are to our health, try the very engaging and leading European researcher in the field, Till Roenneberg. For another, try the recent releases by Oxford neuroscientist Russell Foster. And if you are keen to hear things directly from a world leader in the field, go to this TED talk by legendary US biologist Joe Takahashi: https://www.youtube.com/watch?v=ocqn3wYTCRM.

Much of this book strongly promotes the physiological (body changes) and neurological (brain), and not just psychological features that characterise common anxiety and depressive disorders. Much of my own research career has been tied up with these issues, and for those who may wish to look in more detail at these approaches, I'd suggest various works from Gordon Parker and colleagues, who established specialist services now overseen by the Black Dog Institute in Australia.

One of the most impactful books in the public discourse about depression in recent decades was Dr Peter Kramer's *Listening to Prozac*. Written with the deep insights gained from time spent in long-term psychotherapeutic settings treating clients with chronic depression, it challenged many psychologically orientated thinkers to reconsider their own negative perceptions of the role of antidepressant medicines. *Ordinary Depression* is a must-read for those who are serious about the roles of medicines in treating depressive disorders.

On the history of psychiatry and the coming of the modern age of medicines, the Canadian Historian Ed Shorter is the stand-out writer. I have greatly enjoyed his books, most notably his *A History of Psychiatry*. Tom Insel was previously the Director of the National Institute of Mental Health in the US. His recent book, *Healing*, deals with the gaps between basic neurosciences research and the more urgent need to deliver better mental health care.

Much of this work emphasises the importance of early intervention for common anxiety, depressive and psychotic disorders. It rests on the key observation that most adult-type disorders commence during the teenage years – the period of life where we should focus much of our therapeutic effort. Our previous Australian of the Year, Professor Pat McGorry, and his Melbourne team have led the world in these efforts, and it has been a great pleasure to co-edit a book with Pat on 'clinical staging' – a tool we use to emphasise intervening before any disorder becomes overwhelming.

A broader international perspective on youth mental health can be accessed in the excellent volume co-edited by Peter Uhlhaas and Stephen Wood. Our own perspective on how to best manage the common mental disorders that arise in adolescence and early adult years is best summarised in our 2019 supplement to the *Medical Journal of Australia*.

- Young, Larry. *The Chemistry Between Us: Love, Sex and the Science of Attraction*, Penguin Group, USA, 2012.
- LeDoux, Joseph E. *Anxious: Using the Brain to Understand and Treat Fear and Anxiety*, Penguin Books, 2015.
- LeDoux, Joseph E. *The Emotional Brain*, Simon and Schuster, New York, 2004.
- Bennett, Maxwell R. & Hacker, P.M. S. *Philosophical Foundations of Neuroscience*, Wiley-Blackwall, 2003.
- Rapee, Ron. *Helping Your Anxious Kids*, New Harbinger Publications, USA, 2008.
- Blazer, Dan G. *The Age of Melancholy*, Routledge, 2005.
- Roenneberg, Till. *Internal Time: Chronotypes, Social Jet Lag and Why You're So Tired?*, Harvard University Press, 2017.
- Foster, Russell. *Life Time: The New Science of the Body Clock*, and How It Can Revolutionize Your Sleep and Health, Penguin Books, 2022.
- Crouse, J.J.; Carpenter, J.S.; Song, Y.J.C.; Hockey, S.J; Naismith, S.L.; Grunstein, R.R.; Hickie, I.B. (2021). 'Circadian rhythm sleep–wake disturbances and depression in young people: Implications for prevention and early intervention', *The Lancet Psychiatry*, 8(9), 813–823.
- Carpenter, Joanne S.; Crouse, Jacob J.; Scott, Elizabeth M.; Naismith, Sharon L.; Wilson, Chloe; Scott, Jan; Merikangas, Kathleen R.; Hickie, Ian B. (2021). 'Circadian depression: A mood disorder phenotype', *Neuroscience & Biobehavioral Reviews*, Volume 126, 79–101.
- Parker, G. and Hadzi-Pavlovic, Duscan. 'Melancholia: A disorder of movement and mood', Cambridge University Press, 1996.
- Kramer, Peter D. *Listening to Prozac*, Penguin Books, 1997.

- Kramer, Peter D. *Ordinarily Well: The Case for Antidepressants*, Farrar, Straus and Giroux, 2017.
- Van Der Kolk, Bessel. *The Body Keeps the Score*, Penguin Publishing Group, 2015.
- Morton, Rick. *One Hundred Years of Dirt*, Melbourne University Press, 2018.
- Morton, Rick. *My Year of Living Vulnerably*, HarperCollins Publishers, 2021.
- Shorter, Edward. *A History of Psychiatry: From the Era of the Asylum to the Age of Prozac*, Wiley, 1998.
- Shorter, Edward. *Before Prozac : The Troubled History of Mood Disorders in Psychiatry*, Oxford University Press Inc, 2008.
- Insel, Thomas. *Healing: Our Path from Mental Illness to Mental Health*, Penquin Press, 2022.
- Cole, Neil. *Colonel Surrey's Insanity*, Beagles' Den, 2010.
- Cole, Neil. *Stability in Mind: Living with Bi-polar Disorder*, New Holland Publishers, 2012.
- Cole, Neil. *Alive at Williamstown Pier*, Esson Press, 1999.
- Cowan, Graeme. *Back from the Brink: Australians Tell Their Stories of Overcoming Depression*, Bird in Hand Media, Australia, 2007.
- Wigney, Tess; Parker, Gordon; Eyers, Kerrie. *Journeys with the Black Dog: Inspirational Stories of Bringing Depression to Heel*, Allen & Unwin, 2016.
- McGorry, Patrick and Hickie, Ian. *Clinical Staging in Psychiatry: Making Diagnosis Work for Research and Treatment*, Cambridge University Press, 2019.
- Uhlaas, Peter J. and Wood, Stephen J. *Youth Mental Health: A Paradigm for Prevention and Early Intervention*, MIT Press Academic, 2020.
- Hickie, I.B.; Scott, E.M.; Cross, S.P.; Iorfino, F.; Davenport, T.A.; Guastella, A.J.' Naismith, S.L.; Carpenter, J.S.; Rohleder, C.; Crouse, J.J.; Hermens, D.F.; Koethe, D.; Markus, Leweke F.; Tickell, A.M.; Sawrikar, V.; Scott, J. 'Right care, first time: a highly personalised and measurement-based care model to manage youth mental health', *Med J Aust*, 2019, Vol 211, Suppl 9:S3-S46.

Acknowledgements

When we decided to do the *Minding Your Mind* podcast, we felt reasonably confident about the talking bit. We both know how to talk about stuff. Everything else about podcasts, however, was a mystery. How did we turn our conversation into something people could tap on their phone and listen to? We still don't know, but luckily we found Rod Morri of Sydney Podcast Studios who does. We go to his studio; he twiddles some knobs, adjusts some levels and pushes some buttons; then he tells us to start talking. Forty minutes later we shut up, and then Rod does more stuff that somehow makes it a podcast. Magic. Thanks, Rod. Without you, we would be talking to no-one.

Thanks to everyone who has listened to the podcast, and especially to those who have got in touch and suggested topics.

Thanks to everyone at Penguin Random House. Our publisher Brandon VanOver has been continually enthusiastic, which really helps when you are sitting all alone trying to write, and provided wonderful and insightful feedback that has made the book much better. Everyone else at PRH has done a fantastic job.

JAMES

Thanks to Ian. I always enjoy working with you, and after all these years I am still yet to see you operate at anything less than 99.9 per cent energy.

Thanks to friends, family, people I've sat next to at dinner, and even a particular taxi driver in Adelaide, who have been open enough to have conversations with me about their mental health, or who have listened to me talk about mine. It's a bit scary at first. You feel much more vulnerable saying, 'I've been feeling a bit down,' than you do saying, 'I've got a sore knee,' but one of the great things about talking about your mental health is that, just by doing it, you can actually feel better. That doesn't work with your physical health. Telling someone about your sore knee doesn't fix your knee. But talking about your worries, your stress, or about feeling burned out or depressed can actually help you feel better. Sometimes the person you are talking to might share a strategy or a piece of advice that helped them when they felt bad; sometimes they might ask you a question that pushes you toward some sort of insight; sometimes they might just listen and give you a pat on the shoulder. It all helps.

Thanks to friends for being early adopters of the podcast and for their kind and helpful feedback.

Thanks to Graham O'Loghlin – Dad to me. You're a legend.

Thanks always to my wonderful family: Lucy, Bibi, Nina and Lily. Ian is huge on the importance of social connection and close relationships for good mental health, and I am very lucky to come home to four people who always make me feel good.

IAN

Thanks to James. It takes two to tango!

Thanks to the many professional colleagues whose ideas, technical expertise, engaging discourse and commitment to mental health and wellbeing have so influenced me and the ideas expressed in this book and the podcast. Any technical errors are mine alone.

Thanks to the many people I have encountered professionally in my clinical role as a psychiatrist – those with a whole variety of mental health problems, difficult life situations and a capacity to endure an endlessly frustrating (and disorganised) health care system. My greatest education has come from the direct experiences of those who have dealt personally with the challenges described here. It has been a privilege to share the journey with many. I am particularly indebted to those who have also stepped into the public domain to share those experiences directly.

The really useful feedback on the podcast has come from some unexpected quarters. My favourite critics are the twins, Kate and Daniel. It's great when one's own adult children are so insightful and enthusiastic! Those many people who've stopped me in the street, at the local coffee shop, or over a quiet drink to argue the toss (or just suggest new topics) have inspired me to stick at it.

The podcast was only made possible through the generous support of philanthropic organisations (most notably Future General Global) and families who are committed to improving public knowledge of, and action for, better mental health. Without their support, there would be no podcast and no complementary book.

All this stuff does interfere with other aspects of my professional and family life. So, many thanks to my close colleagues at the Brain and Mind Centre, University of Sydney, for their tolerance, and to Liz and the kids for their willingness to endure the disruptions (some might say chaos) that surrounds my daily life.